WHERE ARE WE NOW?

The State of Christian Political Reflection

Edited by

William A. Harper
Theodore R. Malloch

UNIVERSITY
PRESS OF
AMERICA

To Colin and Ian

and

a Future Generation of

Christian students of Politics

ACKNOWLEDGEMENTS

Our appreciation is expressed to many pub-
lishers for their permission to use the publications cited below. As well we are thankful
to Judith Richmond for her typing of this
manuscript.

Vanguard Magazine, Toronto, Canada
    Mark O. Hatfield, "Judgment and Repentance",
    1972.
    Bernard Zylstra, "Do Christians Have A
    Political Future?", 1972.
    Theodore Plantinga, "The Jewish Problem as
    a Challenge for Christians", 1973.

The Guide, Toronto, Canada
    Bernard Zylstra, "The Individual Gospel",
    1972.

Reformed Presbyterian Publishing Co., Phila-
delphia, Pa.
    Herman Dooyeweerd, In The Twilight of
    Western Thought, 1960.
    Hendrik Van Riessen, Society of the Future,
    1957.

International Reformed Bulletin, London, England
    Philip Edgcumbe Hughes, "Biblical Guidelines
    for Christian Involvement in Society",
    1979.
    Jan Dengerink, "The Universal Reality of
    God's Kingdom", 1977.
    _____, "The Christian and Modern
    Democracy", 1964.
    Bernard Zylstra, "The Bible, Justice, and
    the State", 1972.

Eerdmans Publishing Co., Grand Rapids, MI
    Arthur Gish, The New Left and Christian
    Radicalism, 1970.

Christian Scholars Review, Grand Rapids, MI
Nicholas Wolterstorff, "Contemporary Christian View of the State: Some Major Issues", 1974

The Reformed Journal, Grand Rapids, MI
Theodore Malloch, "Promethean Faith", 1978.

Jubilee Enterprises Ltd., Indiana, Pa.
James Skillen, Christian Politics: False Hope or Biblical Demand, 1973.
Rockne McCarthy, Christian Politics: False Hope or Biblical Demand, 1973.

Wedge Publishing Foundation, Toronto, Canada
Bob Goudzwaard, Aid for the Overdeveloped West, 1975.
John van der Hoeven, Karl Marx: The Roots of His Thought, 1976.

The Christian Patriot, Pittsburgh, Pa.
Stanley Carlson, "Jostlers, Jugglers, and Justice or Is This Anyway to Run a Government?", 1975.

Van Gorcum Ltd., Assen, N.L.
S. U. Zuidema, Communication and Confrontation, 1972.

Inside Magazine, Boston, MA.
William A. Harper, "Launching A New Ship", 1976.

Inter-Varsity Press, Downers Grove, Ill.
Rene Padilla, Is Revolution Change?, 1972.

Where Are We Now? The State of Christian Political Reflection

FOREWARD

Where are Christians with respect to political
matters? What is the state of Christian political reflection? For many years Harry Blamires,
in his book The Christian Mind, summed up the
bleak situation with these words:

> Except over a very narrow field of thinking,
> chiefly touching on questions of personal
> conduct, we Christians in the modern world
> accept, for the purpose of mental activity,
> a frame of reference constructed by the
> secular mind. There is no Christian mind.
> There is no shared field of discourse in
> which we can move at ease as thinking
> Christians by trodden ways, and past
> established landmarks.

Fortunately, Blamires' challenge to think in
self-consciously Christian categories has been
answered by increasing numbers of persons in
many areas of life, including politics. Though
unanimity is an elusive goal, some "trodden
ways" have been established, some signposts of
the Kingdom are beginning to direct the activities of more and more people.

Until now, this growing sense of political
community has found expression in the work of
a bewildering variety of individuals, organizations, and publications, many of whom were
unknown to the larger Christian public. With this
reader, we intend to bring some of the best of
this writing together, not as final act of
triumph, but as a means of enlarging the boundaries of the Christian political community and
encouraging its further maturation. This book
is offered then as both a catalyst for Christians
who want to begin to take their faith more seriously, as well as a reference for all students
interested in religion and politics.

The editors gratefully acknowledge the timely

support of the Andreas Foundation with respect
to the preparation of the final manuscript. We
also call attention to the work of the Association for Public Justice (Box 56348, Washington,
D.C. 20011), a distinctively Christian political movement in this country. The Association's
vision of a public order normed by justice has
been a continuing source of encouragement to us,
and to an increasing number of persons who take
seriously the Lordship of Christ.

Theodore R. Malloch
and
William A. Harper
Wenham, Massachusetts
1981

I. The Foundations

The roots of a Christian understanding of politics are found in an appreciation of the grand biblical summary of reality as creation, fall into sin, and restoration in the person and work of Jesus Christ. Built on that kind of understanding, political activity has the potential to be a source of healing and reconciliation that the Apostle Paul points to so clearly in the thirteenth chapter of his letter to the Romans. He speaks of a "divine institution", "God's agent for your good"; such potential can be realized if we see politics as part of God's creation, standing in need of renewal through the power of the gospel.

In the opening selection, U.S. Senator Mark O. Hatfield reminds us that our first obligation, if we want to honor God as creator, is to recognize our sin--our shortcomings and inability to make our own way--and repent before the process of renewal can begin. It is clear to Hatfield that both sin and renewal have institutional as well as personal dimensions.

Bernard Zylstra picks up this theme in his pointed essay The Individual Gospel. He argues that the gospel is understood properly as "good news" for the entire creation, including cultural activity, and that repentance from sin must lead to a life of service in all parts of the creation. Anything short of that, reduction of the gospel to merely a cure for the soul, for example, will inevitably produce a Christianity which is irrelevant to determining the course of public affairs. At best it may serve, and Hatfield concurs with Zylstra in this, as a "civil" religion, a rationalization of the existing secular order.

Given a gospel meant for the whole creation, how are we to respond? This is the burden of Philip Edgcumbe Hughes. Not written with politics exclusively in mind, it sets out, nevertheless, those qualities which should characterize any

1

biblically inspired attempt to be a living
presence in a society. He notes that such
efforts are not optional, indeed they are the
very material of which our Christian witness
is made and ultimately, judged.

JUDGMENT AND REPENTANCE

By Mark O. Hatfield

We run the risk of misplaced allegence, if not idolatry, by failing to distinguish between the god of an American civil religion and the God who reveals Himself in the Scriptures and in Jesus Christ.

We want to believe that our nation, and its leaders, are right, just and pure. We want to put our country beyond the reach of God's judgement. Why? Because everything is so much simpler then. We want to believe, in the words printed on the back of our Great Seal, that "God hath ordained our undermakings," and not believe that God also judges them. This impulse is born out of our lives.

We want to believe we merit God's blessing. But how hard it is to admit that we stand in need of God's forgiveness.

We would rather celebrate Easter than Good Friday. But without Good Friday, there can be no Easter.

So, I have no intention of issuing a few platitudes about how our nation is the nation under God, and therefore, we as leaders must go home and say a prayer that God will ordain and bless the plans we have already made.

We must look to Biblical religion - not civil religion - for the wisdom to guide our lives, and the life of the nation. Then we discover that our prayers must begin with prayers of repentance.

We must start talking about sin again. Sin in our personal lives, and sin in the corporate life of our country. I know that's an old-fashioned term that many people think is irrelevant to this modern age. But if we really reflect upon the

3

crisis that afflicts us at the national level,
and the dilemmas in our own personal lives, then
we come face to face with the unavoidable reality
of sin.

In the words of St. John: "If we refuse to
admit that we are sinners, then we live in a world
of illusion and truth becomes a stranger to us."
(I John 1:8)

Any of us in positions of leadership find it
terribly difficult to deal with the whole concept
of sin. We may be able to handle this in our
personal lives well enough. We have some idea
about what is right and wrong in our personal
treatment of others.

But when we enter our public or professional
lives, we tend to conveniently leave our thoughts
about sin at home or in the church. For a leader,
this is all the more true. When we are given a
position of leadership, it becomes natural, almost
second nature, to avoid admitting that we may be
wrong.

Confession becomes equated with weakness. The
urge to self-vindication becomes enormous, almost
overpowering. A politician faces this temptation
in a very special way, for somehow, it has become
a political maxim never to admit that you are
wrong. I can attest to this from my personal
experience in political life. Now that may be
wise politics. But it's terrible Christianity.
In fact, it's the very opposite of Biblical faith.
Herein lies the vulnerability of leadership.

For, the more one gains power, whether in
business, economics, government, or religion,
the greater the temptation to believe that he
stands beyond the scope of transcendent judgement.
This holds true for political power at all levels.

We see this especially clearly in the office
of the Presidency. And every man who has held
that office has known the unbelievable temptation

4

of identifying the power of that office with self-righteousness.

When power becomes the end, in and of itself, power always will corrupt. Any means that sustain power become justifiable. So in the end, we can transgress upon the law, whether man's or God's, because we are accountable only to ourselves, and our ability to wield power. The roots of this temptation, however, lie not only within the hearts of those who aspire to power and vainglory, but within the attitudes in each of us here today, in our worship of political power.

There is an idolatry of the Presidency; we, as Americans, bow to the powers and prestige associated with that office in a way that can be ungodly. This makes the temptations and burdens that fall on the shoulders of any mortal who occupies that office to be almost inevitably unbearable, and corrupting.

That is why any President deserves our compassion, and needs our fervent prayers. For in certain ways he is victimized by our idolatrous expectations. He suffers burdens that no man should be expected to bear - demands of righteousness, wisdom and virtue worthy of an office of our adoration. When this aura is perpetuated, and turned to for strength and support, the results become tragic.

There is often a cultism that springs up around personalities of power. Perspective becomes lost, and reality is distorted, as the ego is constantly massaged. The plaudits, the honor, and the unswerving allegiance can create of moral vacuum. So bribes become referred to as inappropriate gifts. Crime is reduced to misguided zeal. Lies become misspoken words.

But the fault lies with us all.

Why do we want so desperately to believe in man-centered power? Why do we want to place such a total and uncritical faith in our institutions?

5

Why is it that each one of us wants to belive that God blesses America more than He blesses any other land? I believe it is because we have let the wellsprings of deep spiritual faith in our lives run dry.

Man will always have a god. In Communist countries, where the death of God is made a tenet of government belief, the leaders and their dogma are deified so they can be worshipped.

Man has an inherent instinct to worship; if God is not the source of his ultimate allegiance, he will then create his own gods. He will worship other people, or his country, or institutions, or money, or power, or fame - and all of these are different ways of worshipping himself.

As a people, we lack the firm foundations of a deep Biblical faith in God; we have allowed our spiritual resources to be mocked, explained away, ignored, forgotten or reduced to mere tradition. So we have transferred our allegiance to other gods; to materialism; to nationalism; to hedonism; to all the modern forms of idolatry that make claims on our fundamental allegiance.

If we are to forsake these gods, and also reject the platitudes of civil relijion, and turn to Biblical faith, what do we find? We discover that our actions, and all our lives stand under God's judgement and mercy. We are accountable to Him - accountable for the motives in our hearts, and accountable for the conditions in our land. So our prayers must begin with repentance; individual repentance and corporate repentance:

"If my people...shall humble themselves and pray, and seek my face, and turn from their wicked ways...then I will forgive their sins, and will heal their land." (II Chronicles 7:14)

The promise is that with this repentance, and allegiance to God, comes healing, reconciliation, and new life. We are made whole as persons, and

6

we see that the wounds of the world can also be healed.

We can see this wholeness of life demonstrated in the person of Christ. As we receive for ourselves the love that molded His life, then our entire selves can be transformed and made new. Our whole understanding of leadership, and power, and the purpose of life is then recreated. A source of ultimate allegiance beyond the ego established in our hearts. Then leadership is seen as service to others.

We discover from the Scriptures that if we are to save our lives, we must lose them; we must give ourselves away for the sake of others. We then have a standard of values that gives a basic framework of integrity for our lives, whether it be in our business or profession, or in political life in Washington. We can no longer seek power at any cost; we can no longer serve the demands of our ego; we can no longer isolate ourselves from reality, and vindicate our actions.

I am convinced that this is the only way we can guard against the vulnerability of leadership. I know of no other formula for the world's power than to give our lives over to a higher power, the power of God's love. Of course, this can seem foolish in the eyes of the world. But there are times when each of us must choose where we give our final allegiance.

The one who follows Christ belongs to two "cities." He is in the world but must not be of the world. He is a stranger, a pilgrim. He is also a citizen of a different kingdom, he has another Master, his allegiance is to a new order from which he derives his ways of thinking, feeling and judging. His heart and thought and ties are elsewhere. He therefore cannot give ultimate allegiance to the world and its way of operating. His first duty is to be faithful to the Lord. The central life commitment for a

Christian must be to the lordship of Jesus Christ. In following this life, we are gripped by a vision of the world, and a love for all mankind.

We sense the mandate for every man to be made whole; for his physical and spiritual needs to be fulfilled, and his culture to be expressed.

We see our swords being turned into ploughshares, our spears into pruning hooks. "Every Valley shall be exalted; every hill made low; the crooked made straight, and the rough places plain." (Isaiah 40:4)

We want justice "to roll down like a river," in the words of Amos, "and righteousness like an ever-flowing stream."

To the ears of conventional politics, this vision sounds almost irrational, irrelevant and totally unrealistic. But the world normally regards God's word, and his truth as nonsense. The world believes in the power of power; the one who follows the life of Crist achieves in the power of love. Because of that love, we are compelled to give ourselves for the needs of others. We involve ourselves totally in the task of healing others, and healing the world. So we find ourselves in the midst of the world, many times under conflicting demands and pressures.

Personally, I continually find it hard to know how, at any given point, to live out this calling. Frequently the way may not be clear at all. But when the difficult choice or decision is made, we must be open to wherever we may be led. And then we must rely simply on our faith rather than expect human certainty about every choice we make. But while we may not always know all the precise answers and actions, we do know that leadership is expressed through service. We cannot separate our allegiance to God from our love for our fellowmen.

In our nation, this must especially include a love for the poor, and the dispossessed. Here again it is so easy for us to neglect the reality of God's judgement on us as a people. We often tend to think that the millions of impoverished citizens in our land are merely an unfortunate fact of life. But God takes the suffering of the poor far more seriously. What for instance, was the greatest sin of the city of Sodom, which caused its destruction by God? Sexual immorality?

Listen to the words of Ezekiel, in the Old Testament: "This was the iniquity of your sister Sodom: she and her daughters had pride of wealth and good in plenty, comfort and ease, and yet she never helped the poor and wretched." Wherever wealth abounds, and the poor continue to suffer, we must confront God's judgement.

Christ opened his public ministry by rising in the synagogue and reading these words: (from Isaiah) "The spirit of the Lord is upon me because he has annointed me; he has seen to announce good news to the poor, to proclaim release for prisioners and recovery of sight for the blind; to let the broken victims go free, to proclaim the year of the Lord's favour."

He began to speak: "Today," he said, "in your very hearing this text has come true." If we are gripped by this love, then we will have an unquenchable compassion for the poor and the needy.

When we consider the crisis of these days for our nation, we can learn from our history. The thought of turning our national attention, at appropriate times, to the need for repentance should not be foreign to us.

President Abraham Lincoln had a profound sense of the sovereignty of God. He knew how the nation stood accountable to God's judgement. In the midst of the Civil War, the U.S. Senate requested President Lincoln to set aside a day for national prayer and humiliation. That might be a very appropriate action for the U.S. Senate to take today.

One April 30, 1863, three months after the Emancipation Proclamation, and three months before the battle of Gettysburg, President Lincoln composed a Proclamation for a Day of Humiliation, Fasting and Prayer.

"Whereas, it is the duty of nations, as well as of men, to owe their dependence upon the overruling power of God, to confess their sins and transgressions, in humble sorrow, yet with assured hope that genuine repentance will lead to mercy and pardon, and to recognize the sublime truth, announced in the Holy Scriptures and proven by all history, that those nations only are blessed whose God is the Lord...And, Inasmuch as we know that...We have been the recipients of the choicest bounties of Heaven. We have been preserved these many years in peace and prosperity. We have grown in numbers, wealth, and power as no other nation has ever grown. But we have forgotten God. We have forgotten the gracious hand which preserved us in peace, and multiplied and enriched and strengthened us; and we have vainly imagined, in the deceitfulness of our hearts, that all these blessings were produced by some superior wisdon and virtue of own own. Intoxicated with unbroken success, we have become too self-sufficient to feel the necessity of redeeming and preserving grace, too proud to pray to the God that made us.

"It behooves us, then, to humble ourselves before the offended Power, to confess our national sins, and to pray for clemency and forgiveness."

Rebuilding the inner strength of our nation today requires the same of us, in each of our hearts.

THE INDIVIDUAL GOSPEL

By Bernard Zylstra

PART ONE

For the purpose of this article, "the individual gospel" is sufficiently described as the view (a) which holds that man is first and foremost an individual being whose humanity lies in an identity separate from other men; and (b) which looks upon the Gospel of Christ mainly as a power for the salvation of the souls of individuals.

Will the social gospel do?

In subjecting the individual gospel to a critique it must be clear at the outset that my alternative does not lie in the social gospel, which (a) holds that man is first of all a social being whose humanity lies in his relations to his fellow-men; and (b) which looks upon the Gospel as the source of inspiration for improving and restructuring these relations. The error of the social gospel is not that it sees man constantly interacting with his fellowmen in the execution of his tasks in culture and society. We also acknowledge that. For the very notion· of mankind as a community brings us to that conclusion. However, the uniqueness of Biblical revelation on this score lies herein, that this community is founded on mankind's covenantal bond with the Creator. For this reason the first and great commandment of the Christian religion is: "You shall love the Lord your God with all your heart." The implication of this is that man is not first of all a social being; he is a religious being whose life is service of God. This service includes obedience to the second commandment: "You shall love your neighbor as yourself." Love to God demands love to neighbor. But the motivation for love to neigh-

11

bor does not lie in the first place in our
neighbor himself but in God Who reveals that
our neighbor is a fellow-creature whom we must
respect and honour in his creatureliness. The
interpersonal love requires a supra-personal
reference-point and norm. That, I take it,
is what we must learn from the first letter of
the apostle John, summed up in these words:
"If God so loved us, we also ought to love one
another." (4:11) For this reason humanitarian
concern for our neighbor is not to be equated
with love to God. That is the error of the social
gospel. Biblically based social action is not
identical with social philanthropy. The lasting
impact of any Christian social endeavour lies in
the implementation of the Biblical conception of
a genuinely open society whose members are
imagers of God and whose final point of reference
lies beyond the social-horizontal relationships
in Christ Jesus, to Whom all power belongs. A
conception of society whose final point of reference is either autonomous individual man or autonomous humanity cannot provide a lasting foundation
for an open society: its horizon is too limited.
And the absolutization of limited horizons is
idolatry: service of the creature rather than
the Creator. (Rom. 1:23-25)

Is conversion necessary?

Yes, conversion is necessary. The difficulty
with the individual gospel does not lie in its
emphasis on personal repentance from sin, conversion and regeneration and commitment to the
Lord in the joy of faith. The scriptures make
it quite clear how men, broken-hearted because
of sin and idolatry, can again become members
of the spiritual community which is the Body of
Christ. They must surrenderingly pray with
David: "Create in me a clean heart, O God....
Take not they Holy Spirit from me." (Ps. 86:11f)

But why is personal conversion so important?
Because the Kingdom of Christ can only enter
human life and society via the avenue of radi-

12

cally changed heart commitments. The heart is
the motor from which are the issues of life.
It must be regenerated, filled with the new life
of the Holy Spirit, before a person can acknowledge Christ as Saviour and Lord. Nicodemus,
a fine representative of doctrinal purity and
moral uprightness in the church, had to be told
by Christ: unless one is born anew he cannot
see the Kingdom of God. (John 3:3) Paul makes
it very explicit: "No one can say 'Jesus is
Lord' except by the Holy Spirit." (1 Cor. 12:3)

This brings into clearer focus the real
problem of the individual gospel and the aims
and strategies of its adherents. For the latter
have not sufficiently understood that conversion
from a life of sin must lead to a new life of
Kingdom service. They have not fully seen the
context of repentance since they tend to sever
the link between individual rebirth and the
totality of God's Kingdom plan for the entirety
of creation, culture and society, where the
Father wants to establish His gracious, sovereign,
and loving rule. They neglect to notice, at
least in part, that the motive for rebirth is
the coming of the Kingdom, as Christ so clearly
stated throughout His entire ministry: "Repent,
for the Kingdom of heaven is at hand." (Matt.
4:17; cf Mark 1:14)

PART TWO

CAUSES and CONSEQUENCES

Over against the Biblical motive of regeneration and conversion as a first step in a life of
sanctification, that is, a life of integral
discipleship and service to the glory of God,
the individual gospel posits the motive of the
salvation of individual souls. In the Scriptures, the soul is the life of the body in all
of its earthly activities. How are we to understand the loss of the vision of the Kingdom of
God and the reformation theme of soli deo
gloria - to God alone be the glory? When did

13

this vision and this Scriptural theme become
narrowed down to the salvation of man's soul?

John Locke and individualism

   In order to answer this question we will have
to look at some of the conceptions of a great
British philosopher, John Locke (1632-1704).
We can only highlight a few basic points.

   Locke developed a conception of society which
supplied both elements of the individual gospel
as described above. To begin with, he maintained that society is a collection of individual beings whose humanity lies in an identity
separate from other men. In defending this
position, Locke in effect opposed the Scriptural
revelation that God created mankind as a spiritual
community which is restored through the reconcil-
ing work of Christ, the Head of the Body of
believers. The foundation of society in Locke
is no longer Jesus Christ but the will of the
individual.

   The will of individual man is the key to
Locke's conception of society since only through
its expression can human needs and interests be
met. There are all kinds of human interests
and needs, but they fall into two basic categories. Man has earthy needs, since man has a
body. He has heavenly needs, since he also has
a soul.

The acquisition of soul salvation

   Man's heavenly needs concern the salvation of
the individual soul. Souls must get to heaven.
Religion and the church must meet this human
interest in salvation. A man's sould can be
saved only by the proper expression of a man's
individual will. In Locke's famous Letter concerning Toleration (1689) he writes: "The care...
of every man's soul belongs unto himself, and
is to be left unto himself...Nay, God Himself
will not save men against their wills." A person

does not become a member of the Church of Jesus
Christ by the operation of the Holy Spirit but
by the voluntary expression of his human will.
He should be able to choose any sect that suits
him best since there are "several paths that are
in the same road" to heaven. Religion in Locke
has been largely reduced to the man-centered
search for salvation. Very little is left of
the Scriptural view that religion is man's loving
service of Christ, Saviour and Lord.

The acquisition of private property

Man does not only have a soul. He also has
a body. That body, too, must be taken care of.
How can one best meet the needs and interests
of the body? It is highly significant to note
that the answer Locke gives to this question
runs parallel to the answer concerning soul
salvation. In both cases the answer lies in
an expression of the individual will. The individual person, in trying to meet the needs of
the body, must learn to shift for himself by
acquiring private property. If you've got
something you can call your own you can begin to
take care of your earthy needs.

The Bible teaches certain basic principles
about "property". Some of these are: (1) man
belongs to the Lord Who created him; (2) the
earth belongs to the Lord; and (3) man's use of
the earth is a matter of stewardship over a
possession inherited from the gracious heavenly
Father. Man's use of the earth, in agriculture,
industry, and trade, is placed in the context
of the convenant between God and man which
provides the conditions of responsibility within
which man may utlize the resources of creation
for the welfare of those who are in need: the
orphan, the widow, the alien, and the poor.
In this covenantal setting the nation of absolute
private property is absent.

Locke rejects this Biblical normative setting. In the chapter on property in the Second

15

Treatise on Government he teaches (1) that man
has a property in his own person; (2) that he
has a property in the labour of his hands; and
(3) that the fruit of the earth can only fulfill a person's needs if it belongs to him,
that is, it must be "a part of him, that another
can no longer have any right to it."

On reading these passages it is not surprising that several modern scholars have
called attention to the relation between religion and the rise of capitalism. As a matter of
fact, for many the founders of Protestantism --
Luther and especially Calvin -- are supposedly
the real originators of today's acquisitive
society. I believe that this is a gross error.
The roots of modern society cannot, I think, be
properly understood unless one makes a clear
distinction between the early reformers of the
sixteenth century and the later seventeenth-
century developments in which the spirit of an un-
Biblical individualism twisted Christian thought
and action into a direction foreign to the Gospel
itself. The Gospel does not know an unfettered
individual who can rely on individual will and
reason to shift for himself in the acquisition
of soul salvation - neo-Pelagianism and traditional Arminianism - and the acquisition of
absolute private property - capitalistic liberalism. John Locke was not a Calvinist. His
friends in England and Holland were not the
divines of the Presbyterian and Reformed Churches.
His friends were the rationalists among the
Arminians, the forerunners of the later enlightened deists and the modern liberals - in theology
and politics!

Separation of religion and politics

There is another matter on which Locke exercised an immense influence. It is the relation
between religion and politics. Having neatly
divided human interests between heavenly and
earthly because of the "separation" between
soul and body, Locke found a way of keeping

16

religion out of politics. "The church itself is a thing absolutely separate and distinct from the commonwealth. The boundaries on both sides are fixed and immovable." In this way Locke could find a foundation for the secular state of classic liberalism which exists to preserve private property. Locke is the founder of the religion of absolute private property. He is the father of laissez-faire doctrines not so much in the sense of keeping politics out of property questions (the state exists to protect property relations) but in the sense of keeping God and the Bible out of property relations.

Intolerant toleration

Having thus limited religion to matters of soul salvation, having cut the body out of Biblical religion, Locke can readily propose toleration between the various sects of Christendom: private religious opinions should not in any way affect the affairs of society. Society could be established on the basis of rational agreement between individuals pursuing the same end: property. Since most men are endowed with a spark of reason, toleration and consensus can readily be achieved. Persons not so rationally enlightened are permitted to find a basis for social morality in private religion. That kind of a basis is better than no basis at all. In other words, besides serving as the avenue of soul salvation, Christianity could also function as a civil religion, as the support of a particular political order after that order had been secularized, severed from the fountain of life in Christ Jesus.

However, Locke made it very clear that the political order had to determine the range of influence of the Christian religion; for only in that way could toleration be maintained. Here toleration becomes intolerant: if the Christian religion would come into conflict with the political system, the Christian religion had to surrender. In this way Locke formulated the

17

essential ingredients of the relation between
the social-political order and the Christian
faith that we find today in Canada and the United
States: "no opinions contrary to human society,
or to those moral rules which are necessary to
the preservation of civil cosiety, are to be
tolerated by the magistrate."

The individual gospel as civil religion

The results of the conception hastily sketched
here are these:

a. The polite totalitarianism of liberal rationalism reduced the catholic claims of the Gospel
of Christ to matters literally out-of-this-
world. The sweet reasonableness of this totalitarianism determines the decision-making process
in education, the trade unions, the political
parties, and most professional organizations.

b. American and Canadian Christians, also those
in the orthodox churches, have grown more and
more accustomed to this reduction of Christ's
Lordship over life. The wall of partition between religion and the state, established by
the enlightened deists of the eighteenth century
(Voltaire, George Washington, Thomas Jefferson,
etc.), has now become a bulward of mainline
orthodoxy itself. Behind that bulward the churches
and "sects" were allowed to pursue their programs.
What was accomplished must not be despised. But
the thrust of these accomplishments, in revivals,
in missions, in evangelism, in Sunday Schools,
was largely limited to the salvation of individual souls and the well-being of the isolated
and fragmented denominations.

c. The individual gospel, implicitly or explicitly, proceeds from the assumption that the
individual person or at least the individual
soul can somehow be lifted out of the context
of God's creation. That context is then left
to itself, neutralized, or avoided as the devil's
domain. But what do we see in recent decades?

The proponents of the individual gospel become proponents of an individualistic social order as well. And their methodology of "social action" is a methodology of "individual witness and action". This is not surprising since human life is indeed of one piece. A basic conception defended in one area of life will soon influence one's thinking in remaining areas. Careful commentators have indeed corectly concluded that it is precisely the religion of individual soul salvation that is now becoming the civil religion of the United States. Billy Graham and Richard Nixon are fast friends.

The Christian religion, without the wide horizons of Christ's redeeming Kingship over men and nations, narrowed down to man-centered soul-salvation, has become for many the moral justification for nationalism, the "American way of life," and all that it stands for in the world today.

Precisely here we must listen to Christ Himself: "My Kingdom is not of this world." (John 18: 36) Or to the Apostle John: "Little children, keep yourselves from idols." (1 John 5: 21)

BIBLICAL GUIDELINES FOR CHRISTIAN INVOLVEMENT IN SOCIETY

By Philip Edgcumbe Hughes

In the original Greek of the New Testament, the word for ferment (yeast, leaven) is zyme. We are all familiar with the term 'enzyme', which has been taken into English from the Greek language, and which means literally something that works as a ferment within - that is, within a mass larger than itself. An enzyme, we should notice, is produced by a living organism, and it promotes specific chemical reactions in the mass within which it is placed. It is in fact a catalyst, which sets the reaction in motion and not only keeps it in motion but accelerates it. The potency of the enzyme is such that it succeeds in affecting and transforming the entire mass of which it was originally but a small part. The enzyme most familiar to us in everyday life is yeast, a small quantity of which, when placed in a lump of dough, causes that dough to rise until it is ready to be baked into bread. The opportunity for a parable here of the effect of the Christian individual or the Christian community in the mass of society is almost too obvious to be missed. It was not overlooked in the teaching of our Lord.

Active involvement

'The kingdom of heaven', Jesus told his audience, 'is like leaven which a woman took and hid in three measures of meal, till it was all leavened' (Matt. 13:33; Luke 13:21). The three measures of meal represent the world, the totality of human society. The leaven represents the Christian presence in the world, the evangelical presence of Christ acting in and through his followers who are placed within the mass of human society. The yeast is hidden in the flour - there is so little of it that is passes unnoticed - but God has put within this unconsidered entity a power so remarkable that its environment cannot remain unaffected by its presence. So, too, the Christian presence in the world may seem so small as to be insignificant and unnoticed; but the potency implanted by God in the gospel is so tremendous that the Christian presence cannot fail to have a dynamic and transforming effect on the society by which it is surrounded. It may seem hidden, but it is potent.

Let us remember, however, that the dynamic operation of the enzyme is evidence of the presence of the living organism by which it is generated. A dead church, or an empty and hollow profession of faith, is not and never can be the same thing as the Christian presence in the world: quite the opposite, indeed, for it is what Paul meant when he warned against 'holding the form of religion but denying the power of it' (2 Tim. 3: 5). Where there is no gospel ferment, there is no kingdom of heaven secretly at work. The confession we are exhorted to hold fast (Heb. 4:14) is not merely the faith which we hear witness by lip and life. It is not merely what we believe in our heart but also what we profess publicly before men (Rom. 10:9f). A dead orthodoxy is spurious Christianity.

'Reformed' is a past participle and also a passive participle, and it was never our intention to convey the impression that we were content passively to preserve something that is of the past. That would be anything but faithful to the Reformation itself. It would certainly not be following faithfully in the steps of the Reformers.

The Reformers rediscovered the vitality of the

21

Bible as the Word of God to sinful man and, at
one and the same time, the dynamism of the gospel
of the grace of God in Christ Jesus to which its
pages bear witness. The ferment of the gospel
first worked transformingly in their own lives,
and then their own living faith set the evangelical reaction going in the mass of human
society of which they were but a tiny part.
Through them the apostolic enzyme went powerfully
to work. The Reformers were active, not passive;
they were dynamic, not static; and if there is
one thing they have to say to us it is that we
too should, in God's hands, be agents of that
ferment which emanates from the life of Christ
within us and which can dynamically permeate
the society to which we belong.

If it is objected that our Lord declared that
his disciples are not of the world (John 17:14,
16) and the conclusion is drawn that therefore
they ought not to allow themselves to be involved
in this world's society, we must insist that
not of the world is not at all the same thing as
out of the world. The world in its fallenness
is no longer native to us who are Christ's, because through the new birth God 'has delivered
us from the dominion of darkness and transferred
us to the kingdom of his beloved Son' (Col. 1:13).
In doing this, however, God has not taken us out
of this world. It is true that we now belong to
the number of those who 'wait for new heavens
and a new earth in which righteousness dwells'
(2 Pet. 3:13); but it is the same world. The
difference is between the world as fallen and
under a curse and the world as redeemed and
evermore blessed by God. The fallenness of man
communicates itself to the whole created order.
The redemption of man in Christ leads to the
redemption of the whole created order. In Christ
we witness the restoration and the fulfilment of
all God's purposes in the creation of the world.
The new creation is the old creation brought to
the glorious perfection for which it was always
destined. The final world is the original world
as God indefectibly intended it to be. That is

why Paul speaks of even the creation as 'groaning
in travail', 'waiting with eager longing' as it
were for its own rebirth, and instructs us that,
though at present 'subjected to futility', yet
it is 'subjected in hope'. Why? 'Because the
creation itself will be set free from its bondage to decay and obtain the glorious liberty of
the children of God.' (Rom. 8:19-23)

Meanwhile the ferment of the new creation is
working secretly in this world of ours. This it
cannot do if it is out of the world; only if it
is in the world. And that Christ never meant his
servants to be out of or away from the world is
perfectly plain from the very passage where he
asserts that they are not of the world:

> I do not pray that thou shouldst take
> them out of the world (the Son says
> to the Father) but that thou shouldst
> keep them from the evil one. They
> are not of the world, even as I am
> not of the world. Sanctify them in
> the truth; they word is truth. As
> thou didst send me into the world,
> so I have sent them into the world.
> And for their sake I consecrate my-
> self, that they may also be conse-
> crated in thruth. (John 17:15-19)

Clearly, then, it is not the divine will that
we should be taken out of, or should disengage
ourselves from, the world: on the contrary, we
have been sent into the world, consecrated in
the truth and empowered to overcome the assaults
of the enemy. In other words, it is through us,
and flowing from the new life that is ours in
Christ, that the ferment of the grace of God is
active in society. We ourselves are the true
heart of the eager longing of the created order
for the incomparable glory that is yet to be
revealed (Rom. 8:18).

Compassionate involvement

It is apparent, further, that our involvement

23

in society as Christians derives from, and is intended to be, a reflection of the involvement of Christ himself: 'As thou didst send me into the world, so I have sent them into the world.' (John 17:18; cf. 20: 21) The logic is inescapable. The incarnation of the Son is precisely his involvement, indeed his identification, with the world in its fallenness not to sanction it, but to redeem it. He did not share in our fallenness, because he came to gain the victory where we have suffered only defeat. But he experienced, to the full, the consequences of our fallenness: the humiliation of being born in the stable at Bethlehem; the poverty of having no place he could call his own; the anguish of rejection; the hostility of the self-righteous; the savage cruelty of brutal men; and, finally, the deep torment of alienation and of hell itself. And then the resurrection (!) demonstrating that he is indeed the Prince of life (Acts 3:15) who had power to lay down his life and power to take it again (John 10:17f) and who is the living source of the gospel ferment that, thanks to his coming into the world, is now active in the world.

What better illustration of this costly involvement could there be, than that given by the Lord himself in the parable of the Good Samaritan (Luke 10:25-37)? The question that gave rise to the parable was the brief but basic question: 'And who is my neighbour?' This in turn had suggested itself from the second of the two commandments that summarize the Decalogue, namely: 'You shall love your neighbour as yourself.' The man who asked the question was a lawyer, that is, a person schooled in the law of Moses and the numerous traditions that had accumulated around it. His approach to Jesus, even with so central an inquiry as 'Teacher, what shall I do to inherit eternal life?', may well have been motivated by the desire to stimulate an intellectual debate, providing an occasion perhaps for the display of his own competence, rather than by spiritual seriousness. The system of casuistry that had been elaborated over the

generation made room for the postulation of a
variety of qualifications in determining the
identity of one's neighbour. (We are told that
his purpose was to test Jesus our (verse 25)
and then, on receiving a direct answer which was
hardly conducive to public debate since it challenged him to obey rather than dispute the law,
that he sought to justify himself by attempting
to initiate a discussion on the identity of one's
neighbour (verse. 29.) Certainly, the omission
of Samaritans from the classification of neighbours to be loved would have been approved by
the rabbinists, for not only was it customary
for Jews to despise and have no dealing with
Samaritans (John 4:9) but the appellation 'Samaritan' was itself a term of abuse - hence the
intentionally slanderous taunt of Jesus' opponents
that he was a Samaritan and demon-possessed
(John 8:48). The purpose of Christ's parable is
to show that it is not open to us to pick and
choose who are and who are not neighbours to be
loved, and that 'Who is my neighbour?' is not at
all an academic question - indeed that there can
be no justification for turning a practical
command into a theoretical inquiry.

The traveller from Jerusalem to Jericho who
was set upon by bandits, robbed, stripped,
beaten, and left dead by the roadside was a Jew.
His desperate plight was obvious to any who might
pass that way, and the first two to do so were
both fellow Jews; accordingly, within the framework of the current sophistry, they had no excuse
on the ground of nationality for not accepting
him as a neighbour to be loved. Presumably the
line of rationalization they followed was that a
disaster of this dimension could have overtaken
only a man who was a dreadful sinner, and that
to go to his aid would mean contamination and
complicity in his guilt; and so, refusing to be
involved, they kept their distance and lost their
self-respect. The next to come along, however,
was a Samaritan who, on seeing the injured man,
might more speciously have argued: 'This man is
a member of the Jewish nation who despise Sam-

aritans and have no dealings with us. Why should I now have any dealings with him? Why should I endanger myself by going to his aid? What possible claim can he have on me and my sympathy?' But, refusing to entertain such considerations, he immediately involved himself with this Jew and his need, tending his wounds, placing him on his own mount, and bringing him to an inn where, at his own expense, he provided for his continuing care. He did not even pause to inquire whether the half-dead man was a neighbour to be loved, simply because it was himself whom he regarded as neighbour--neighbour to anyone who was near and whom he could help, whoever he might be.

This is the implication of Christ's question: 'Which of the three was neighbour...?' The lawyer's 'Who is my neighbour?' was the wrong question, for it indicated an attitude that was already aloof and unwilling to be involved. The proper attitude is that which says, 'I am neighbour, and I must show myself as neighbour to anyone whom I meet.' A neighbour is one who is nigh, and who therefore is always near at hand to help and minister to all who come his way. But the deep meaning of the parable is this: Christ himself is the true Good Samaritan, not in fiction but in action, even as he is telling the parable; he showed himself to be our neighbour, by his incarnation making himself nigh to us when in our fallenness we had no claim whatsoever upon him, and fully identifying himself with us in our desperate plight in order that by the perfection of his life and of his self-sacrifice for us in death he might restore to use the true integrity of our humanity.

The ferment of our faith operates through neighbourliness, through our being nigh at all times to minister to the spiritual and physical needs of all our fellow men without respect to race, colour, or social status. And this Christian neighbourliness of ours derives from the prior neighbourliness of Christ to us: as the Father sent him into the world, so he has sent

26

us into the world to wash the feet of others, that is, to serve them with self-denying humility. Our call is not to go our own way but to follow him. This is what he says to his disciples:

> If I, your Lord and Teacher, have washed your feet, you also ought to wash one another's feet. For I have given you an example, that you also should do as I have done to you. Truly, truly, I say to you, a servant is not greater than his master; nor is he who is sent greater than he who sent him. If you know these things, blessed are you if you do them. (John 13:14-17)

His example cannot be followed if we are unwilling to involve ourselves actively and compassionately in human society.

Neither imitation of the world...

Let us be quite clear, however, that involvement in the world does not mean imitation of the world. There are too many in the church today who entertain the vain hope that, by imitating the world, the church will succeed in establishing its relevance before the world; that the world will take notice when the church copies its frenetic fads and fancies. But why should the world be impressed with an imitation, seeing it is best at doing its own thing, and why should it not say to the church, 'Instead of imitating us, join us'? The church must of course be contemporary and comprehensible, but it must be the church, the community of the twice-born, and as such it cannot become the unregenerate world's shadow without ceasing to be itself. Imitation is totally incompatible with the catalytic activity of the evangelical ferment that secretly and dynamically is permeating and transforming the whole lump of society. It is Christ whom we are to imitate, and it is his likeness into which we are being transfigured (2 Cor. 3:18); all the more need then for the apostolic admon-

27

ition to be proclaimed anew, that 'All that is in the world, the lust of the flesh and the lust of the eyes and the pride of life, is not of the Father but is of the world', and that 'the world passes away', whereas 'he who does the will of God abides for ever.' (1 John 2:16f)

...nor withdrawal from the world

At the opposite extreme form imitation of the world is withdrawal from the world. In the history of the church this dissociation from the world has been most strikingly expressed in the monastic movement. Conscious of the evil attaching to this fallen world, many have sought to escape its contamination by isolating themselves from society, either as solitary hermits in the desert or in the company of other likeminded persons in cloistered remoteness. There have been (and still are) monastic communities whose withdrawal has been partial, in that their members have retained contact with society by educating the young or preaching to the populace or ministering to the poor and needy; but I am referring here particularly to those who, by a withdrawal that is complete, have taken themselves out of circulation. Such persons have a commendable perception of the world's depravity and at the same time of the holiness that is God's demand; but even so, their isolationism is governed by some serious misconceptions.

In the first place, their motivation is one of self-concern; they are introverted, not outward-going or giving. Naturally, it is right and proper to be concerned about one's own eternal destiny, but not exclusively so. A person's salvation in Christ should indeed be the start, but also once it is given - the end, of self-concern. These devotees of solitude have been venerated as having achieved a level of saintliness that is unattainable by the ordinary Christian engulfed in the contaminated mass of human society. But their preoccupation has been with justification rather than sanctification. Their desire has been to please God by escaping from the corruption of the world and denying themselves the pleasures and conveniences of civilized living, to atone for past sins by self-induced pain and hardship, and thus in the end to win divine acceptance. But such a programme is radically unevangelical, for insofar as it is a programme of self-justification or self-salvation it is strangely blind to the central truth of the once-for-all perfection of Christ's propitiation and the unique and total effectiveness of his blood for the cleansing of all sin. It virtually ignores the truth which belongs to the heart of the Christian gospel, namely, that our justification is in Christ alone and not at all in ourselves, and that this justification is appropriated by faith, not achieved by human effort (cf. 1 John 1:7-2; 1 Cor. 1:30; Eph. 2:8; Rom. 5:1).

Secondly, these isolationists fail to take into account the fact that though one may escape from society it is impossible to escape from oneself, and that deep within every individual there is a root of sin and defilement; indeed, that a person's defilement comes not from outside but from within himself, as Christ himself taught:

> What comes out of a man is what defiles
> a man. For from within, out of the
> heart of man, come evil thoughts, forn-
> ication, theft, murder, adultery, covet-
> ing, wickedness, deceit, licentiousness,
> envy, slander, pride, foolishness. All
> these evil things come from within, and
> they defile a man. (Mark 7:14-23)

Accordingly, to separate oneself from society is not ipso facto to separate oneself from defilement. This is a reality to which the inside history of monasticism all too frequently and sadly beats witness.

Thirdly, total withdrawal is unevangelical

because it displays an inexcusable disregard
for the dominical teaching according to which,
as we have seen, Christians are sent, as Christ
was sent, into the world, not out of it - sent,
moreover, as his ambassadors to carry the message
of the gospel to all lands and peoples (Acts
1:8; Matt. 28:19f). The person who has chosen
isolation from society is in no position to
play a part in the fermentation of society.
Nor is the Lord's commission to his disciples to
permeate the world with the gosepl really a
matter of choice, an option which may be taken
up or set aside at will. It is, rather, as Paul
well knew, a debt that we owe (Rom. 1:14); and
to pay one's debts is obligatory, not optional.
The recognition of our indebtedness should drive
us to the most serious involvement in society.
And our indebtedness is a total indebtedness.
We owe everything, in Christ, to God: the eternal
redemption of our whole being, soul and body,
through the offering of that sinless sacrifice
on the cross to pay off the debt of our guilt
by bearing our judgement. It is no thanks to
ourselves, for we have nothing that we have not
received (1 Cor. 4:7). Bought at so great a
cost, we are not our own (1 Cor. 6:19f; cf.
1 Pet. 1:18f). The realization of our utter
indebtedness to God is the cause of our inex-
haustible gratitude, and our gratitude is the
impulse of our single-minded dedication, in the
power of the Holy Spirit, to God's cause in the
world.

A debt to discharge

We owe everything to God for an infinite debt
that, in Christ and by him, has been discharged
for us; that debt has been wiped out. But there
is also a debt for us to discharge, namely, our
indebtedness to make Christ and his gospel
known to the world. Jesus Christ, as John has
reminded us, is the propitiation not for our
sins only but also for the sins of the whole
world (1 John 2:1f). The gospel does not stop
with us; it must spread from us, and we are under
obligation to make Christ known in the world.

30

Our total indebtedness has a two-way perspective. First, it goes back to the full and perfect redemption that the grace of God has provided for us; and then, and only then, it goes forward to the obligation that is upon us, as redeemed persons, to proclaim this redemption throughout the world. The first was the debt paid for us; the latter is the debt paid by us. As P.T. Forsyth has put it: 'We are brought out of a debt of guilt which we could never begin to pay, into a debt of love we can never cease to pay.' (Missions in State and Church, London 1908, p. 262.) Forsyth, who had learnt for himself the hollowness of humanitarianism that is divorced from evangelical passion, recognized that 'the weakness of much current work and preaching is that it betrays more sense of what has yet to be done than of what has been done', that there is an imbalance if 'we feel man's need more than Christ's fulness' (ibid., p. 17; cf. his Modern Preaching and the Modern Mind, London 1907, pp. 282ff). This dual indebtedness is the dynamic motivation of all witness, all evangelism, all mission, and all social and compassionate service that is genuinely Christian. Over the generations, starting with the apostles, it has inspired the missionary heroism of uncounted men and women who have joyfully left home and kindred for distant and inhospitable climes in order to bring the good news to those who have not yet hear. Dan Crawford, in characteristic style, has given us a moving illustration of this devoted and selfless discharging of the Christian debt in the days when tropical Africa was accurately known as the white man's grave.

Benjamin Cobbe (he wrote) has a holy man sent from God, if ever God sent a man to the Garenganze. Welcoming him to the country, I met him at the Lualaba crossing, a white, fragile-looking traveller, with a Pauline gleam in his eye. 'Have come to pay my debt!' said he, with a winning smile, and there you have the whole story in two words--that white fever face trying,

31

but failing, to kill that glad smile...
This holy man, if you please, had drunk
so deeply of God's wine of joy-the wine
that came to him last in life-that it kept
him going at high pressure right on to the
end. The new wine, in fact, was busily at
work breaking up his old bottle of a body,
for when these two meet in Africa then one
of the two must be lost, but that one
thing will never be the new wine - that is
hid with Christ in God. So the fragrant
saint died at his post, the 'old skin
bottle' broken in a ferment of fever.
Africa got the holy dust, and God received
him into glory. He foresaw it all - saw
certain death ahead, yet resolved to pay
his debt to the heathen.   (Thinking Black,
pp. 101f)

The ferment of the new wine may be too potent
for the old wine skin of our present physical
nature which is on its way to death; but at the
same time precisely because it is the ferment of
the recurrection life of Jesus who gave his own
physical nature to death, conquered death on
its own territory, and came back from death -
this ferment is active in preparing our human
nature to come back from death revitalized and
glorified. And, doing this in us, the ferment
of the new wine is also inescapably active in
the human society to which we belong. The more
we involve ourselves, the more its regenerating
activity is experienced. This is what Paul is
speaking about in 2 Corinthians 4: 7ff:

We have this treasure in earthen vessels,
to show that the transcendent power belongs
to God and not to us. We are afflicted in
every way, but not crushed; perplexed, but
not driven to despair; persecuted, but not
forsaken; struck down, but not destroyed;
always carrying in the body the death of
Jesus, so that the life of Jesus may also
be manifested in our bodies. For while we
live we are always being given up to death

32

for Jesus' sake, so that the life of Jesus may be manifested in our mortal flesh... knowing that he who raised the Lord Jesus will raise us also with Jesus and bring us with you into his presence...So we do not lose heart. Though our outer man is wasting away, our inner nature is being renewed every day.

The true inner history of the Christian church is the history of its Benjamin Cobbes: men and women who have said 'No' to self in order that, though no longer of the world, they might follow their Master into the world as agents of the dynamic ferment of the gospel both at home and abroad. They are unsung and for the most part unremembered, but their line stretches back to the apostles and to Christ and their names are known and recorded in heaven. Let us make sure, by God's grace, that the line is continued and that the ferment of faith is active in us and through us. Historically, evangelicals have always been intensely involved in human society, and their ministry has been a full ministry because they have sought to minister to the whole man: outwardly as they have fed the hungry, clothed the destitute, healed the sick, cared for the homeless, educated the ignorant, and opposed injustice; and also (for the issue is not one of either-or but of both-and), and primarily, inwardly as they have applied the balm of the gospel to the sick heart of man's being, so that he may enjoy citizenship of that eternal kingdom in which there will be no more injustice or pain or sorrow or hunger or brutality or death (Rev. 21:1-4). What greater service could there be than this? Ministry to the physical and material needs of mankind is good and necessary, but it is not enough--only the gospel of the grace of God in Christ Jesus penetrates with transorming power to the very heart of the human predicament.

Regrettably, there are congregations today

which have succumbed to the temptation of monastic withdrawal from the world. There may be teaching that is theoretically orthodox and worship that has the appearance of being devout, but where the ferment of faith that reaches out to the world has been put into cold-storage for safe keeping, there is no longer an effective church of Jesus Christ. Instead, there is a facade, and that facade has become a wall of separation which isolates the (so-called) faithful from the surrounding mass of humanity and its contaminating influence. Such powerless churches (which should be a contradiction in terms) degenerate into clubs for the pious, coteries of those who pride themselves on being divinely electable and respectable, aseptic culture-chambers for the breeding of pharisaic self-esteem. They are a hindrance to the dissemination of the gospel, and their members are in danger of being condemned by the Lord as wicked and slothful servants who have wrapped up the talents entrusted to them and hidden them away instead of putting them profitably into circulation (Matt. 25:14ff; Luke 19:12ff). Let us give the last word to James, whose saintliness was nothing if not practical: 'Religion that is pure and undefiled before God our Father is this: to visit orphans and widows in their affliction, and to keep oneself unstained from the world' (Jas. 1:27): That is, to be involved in society, to go forth into the world taking both spiritual and material aid to the needy, while always remembering that we are not of the world, and therefore are not to be conformed to this world (Rom. 12: 2).

II. Theoretical Orientation

Though it is the boast of most citizens of North America that their politics is not encumbered by ideological or philosophical considerations, in fact all human activity rests on some theoretical assumptions, whether they are acknowledged or not. It is the editors' judgement that there are three theoretical assumptions which must be considered by the Christian who wishes to engage in political reflection.

The first of these has to do with the existence of God's Kingdom. Writing on the topic, Jan Dengerink urges us to ". . . take seriously the universality of God's Kingdom and the absolute authority of Jesus Christ as Savior and Lord of the World." With a strong appreciation of God's kingdom as universal, embracing all people and all cultural activities, Christians are impelled to work hard at the task of uncovering the biblical norms for political life and to ponder the common responsibilities which a kingdom life implies.

Without a kingdom vision, the record is clear: culture takes on a radically devalued character for Christians. Characteristically, this is marked by a retreat into an individualistic faith which, if it takes politics seriously at all, does so on the basis of an authority other than that of the lord of life. The result is a secular society and politics which is reaping the whirlwind of denying its own creator.

The second assumption has to do with human beings, particularly their origins, nature, and purpose. Clearly what one assumes to be true-- for example are we capable of knowing what is good by our own efforts and reshaping our nature to do it?--will have an enormous impact on one's ideas for such things as the purpose of the state and the responsibilities of citizens. Herman Dooyweerd's essay "What is Man?" is an attempt to sketch out an anthropology which is faithful to the biblical understanding of reality mentioned in the first section of this book - of creation, fall into sin, and restoration in Christ. The understanding of what we are and can be which results from such an anthropology can be ignored by political theorists only at their peril, as events of the recent past will attest.

The final assumption involves the nature of society. Government and politics do not operate in a vacuum and so the relationships which one posits between social institutions as well as the nature and task of the various institutions assume an importance beyond themselves. Historically, most Christians concerned with politics have been content to adopt whatever arrangements the existing society had to offer, in the same form of either individualism or collectivism. As Hendrik Van Riessen notes at the beginning of his selection, a choice such as the principles by which a society should be structured is necessarily conditioned by one's own commitments and world view. For him, as a Christian, these principles must be derived from an examination of scripture. The theory which results will not please everyone, but it is offered here as a provocative and plausible attempt to lay out the broad outlines of a Christian theory of society.

One group of Christians most likely to take issue with Van Riessen (and probably Dengerink as well) are those in the Anabaptist or Mennonite tradition. Though split into many groups and never able to practice their ideas on a society-wide basis for any length of time, they nevertheless are custodians of an enduring vision of state and society which has excited much new interest among Christians in our own day. The selection by Arthur Gish captures the flavor of the Anabaptist vision in its long and complex struggle to live out a view of society that was true to their biblical understanding and forms a bridge to section two on the nature of the state.

36

THE UNIVERSAL REALITY OF GOD'S KINGDOM

By Jan Dengerink

Many Christians and church communions are at the present time engaged in reflection upon the subject of their place and task in the modern world. In itself, this is a reason for rejoicing. It allows us to remark that the Christian community, the people of God, does not content itself with floating along in the current of tradition. By vocation, the Christian has to adopt a critical attitude. He must try the spirits to see if they come from God (1 John 4: 1) and, in fact, it is not against flesh and blood that we have to fight, but against powers in heavenly places (Eph. 6:12).

The kingdoms of heaven and of this world are at war

We must first recall that the spiritual warfare does not go on in an abstract world. We enlist in it in the actualities of our daily life. As members of the church of all ages we confess the Incarnation of God in his only son Jesus Christ. But equally we have an experience of that other incarnation, namely of the Devil, under various forms. He manifests himself in movements, in political structures, in sciences, in the artistic life and in objects of art, in an education system; and quite simply in the disturbed relations between men and social communities, by negative and destructive thoughts, and so on.

We can even say that there is no single domain of human life untouched by Satan. The warfare between God's kingdom and that of Satan is engaged throughout life, penetrating both the depths of the human heart and all aspects of human existence. Nowhere can be found that neutral territory where we think we might discover asylum. Christ calls us to keep vigilant (Matt. 24:42;

25:13; Mark 13:35). There is no individual, no group, which enjoys shelter. In his first epistle, John writes 'If we say that we have no sin, we deceive ourselves, and the truth is not in us' (1 John 1: 8, 10); and for this reason Paul warns us, referring to the history of Israel, 'Therefore whoever thinks that he stands let him watch lest he fall' (1 Cor. 10:12).

A critical awareness, we repeat, and above all self-criticism, is essential to the Christian life. This concerns not only the individual life, but also life within the structures of the world of today. It is crucial, therefore, to know from what point of view, on what base, and by what criteria, our critique ought to be advanced.

One thing is clear enough: by definition the Christian is not conservative or progressive, traditionalist or modern, verticalist, horizon-talist, of the Right or of the Left. These are not biblical alternatives. Whoever lives out of the fulness of the Gospel recognizes the reign of God which, because of its radical and indis-soluble unity, comprehends heaven and earth and all their history in a totalitarian fashion. Every dichotomy comes from the Devil.

Of this kingdom of heaven, John the Baptist tells us 'It is near, therefore we must repent' (Matt. 3: 2). Again, of this kingdom, Jesus tells us 'All power has been given to me in heaven and on earth' (Matt. 28:18). In effect the Gospel of our Lord Jesus Christ is the Gospel of the Kingdom of God. And it is essential to remember that Jesus Christ received this power in following the way of the Cross (Phil. 2: 5-11). What the Gospel of the Kingdom signifies, is at the same time, the Gospel of the Cross.

Orientation in history

It is well known that Christian attitudes to culture and to political and social institutions

38

have varied from time to time. Tertullian (160 to 240 AD approximately), for example, strongly opposed Christianity to classical culture. According to him, Athens and Jerusalem, academy and church, had nothing in common. It is an attitude that does not surprise us very much if we remember that classical culture was still entirely impregnated with a radically pagan spirit.

Justin Martyr (100 to 165 AD approximately) took a totally different position, seeking to establish a rapport between Stoic thinking, in which he had been trained, and the Christian message. For him, there was continuity between the teaching of the Stoics on reason and universal illumination, and what was written in the first chapter of John's Gospel about the light of men; between the germs of universal knowledge, present in every man, and the light which shines in each child of God.

Basil of Caesarea (329 to 379 approximately) regarded Greek culture as a sort of preparatory step towards Christian culture, though Christians would have to approach that Greek culture in a critical and selective manner to purify it.

It was Augustine (354 to 430 AD) who developed the idea of one universal history, in the course of which is developed a warfare between the kingdom of God and the earthly kingdom of Satan. For him, the confession of God's absolute sovereignty thus became central.

The same line is taken later by John Calvin. It is quite understandable that, after the christianization of the Roman Empire, Christians had considerable difficulty in seeing clearly the right relation between Paul's teaching on the mystical body of Christ and the so called natural institutions of state and society. Augustine had shown them the line of thought to follow. For him, the idea of Christ's mystical body was not to be tied only to the inner life of the church, but had also its importance for the relation between church and state.

The overarching idea was of a universal and harmonious order of divine origin, in which was accorded a place to every creature and where every creature had its own function and value. Thus the whole of temporal and material life received its orientation towards an eternal communion with God. The christianized state and its institutions also had their place in the mystical body of Jesus Christ in the kingdom of God.

This idea of the 'Corpus Christianum' demonstrated during the Middle Ages an effective political power in western culture, though it developed in a direction that withdrew markedly from Augustine's position. By a very complicated historic process the church became a power of such magnitude that it constituted a factor of unity and possessed an authority of first rank in the whole of western culture.

This process attained its zenith in the high Middle Ages towards the twelfth century and after. It was the great century for the Roman Catholic Church. The church was considered as the incarnation of the supernatural life of grace, where the so called natural life arrived at its fulfilment. This found its expression in the bosom of the ecclesiastical organization, where the clergy, with the Pope as head, became the mediator between God and the faithful. The church, in its official organization, is the exclusive agent of divine salvation and must radiate this salvation to the whole of society.

According to such thought, the secular power of public authority, the state, was in principle only an authority delegated by the church. Consequently, western culture and ethics in the Middle Ages owed their unity and Christian character to the spiritual unifying power of the Roman Catholic Church. This unity was broken by

the Renaissance and humanism on the one side, and
the Reformation on the other.

The Reformation

The Reformation, and most particularly that
which is bound to the names of Luther and Calvin,
brought important changes in Christian thought.
For example, the authority of the state became
much more independent, vis-a-vis the ecclesiastical institution. According to the reformers,
the state had a specific independent task alongside the church, that of the maintenance of
order and public justice. As such it had a direct
responsibility to God, although one of its most
important tasks remained the protection of the
church and therefore the promotion of the true
preaching of the Gospel.

A second important point was the abolition
of the distinction in principle between the spiritual and secular aspects of life and consequently
between the clergy and the laity. Luther and
Calvin both stressed that in principle every profession results from a vocation given by God.
It is necessary, however, to add concerning Luther
that the ancient distinction of two reigns, the
reign of nature and the reign of grace, that of
the external life and that of the internal life
of a man, made itself felt again, particularly in
his manner of opposing Law to Gospel. The central question for Luther was 'How can I be saved?'
It was a reaction clear. and comprehensible enough
to the practice of the Roman Catholic Church.

For Calvin, this question was certainly no less
essential and vital. Nevertheless, the proclamation of God's universal and absolute sovereignty
was placed at the heart of his thought and life.
How are we to serve God with all our existence
and in every area of our life? This explains why,
in his Institutes of the Christian Religion, written
with the intention of systematically exposing Christian doctrine, he had included, quite naturally,
a chapter concerning civil magistrates. It is

probably the reason why the influence and effect of Calvinism in areas of politics, education and culture in general, have been much more intense than those of Lutheranism. The Reformation in France, the Netherlands, Scotland and later in the United States, was not limited to the church and to personal life, but made itself effective also in the educational system, in the sciences, in industrial development, the artistic, the political life and so on. It is a remarkable thing that so many institutions of higher education and universities in the countries mentioned were established by the Protestants.

Since the Seventeenth century, however, the Reformation has lost, in large measure, its spiritual power. The rationalism which dominated humanist circles penetrated the church as well. This explains the spiritual decline of those institutions such as the Universities of Harvard and Yale, which were protestant at their origin.

The church herself, the living church, as the body of Christ, continued rather in the manner of a submarine current, introverted and pietist. Without doubt, in the course of the eighteenth and nineteenth centuries, there were several revival movements, but they exercised little influence on cultural, political and social life, school system and universities. They were rather concentrated on the spiritual and moral life, entirely personal.

Exceptions existed, however. From time to time revival movements of a typically reformed character arose. I think chiefly of the Calvinist revival in my own country in the nineteenth century and thereafter, under the impluse and spiritual direction of Guillaume Groen van Prinsterer (1801 to 1876), Abraham Kuyper (1837 to 1921), Alexander Frederik de Savornin Lohman (1837 to 1924), Herman Bavinck (1854 to 1921) and others.

In general, we can say that evangelical Protestantism - I make no exception for reformed Protestantism - developed in an individualist manner. It fell back often on the distinction, non-biblical in origin, between the two kingdoms of secular and spiritual, of nature and grace, without attempting, as in the Roman Catholic Church of the high Middle Ages, to unite them in a global vision. While in the Roman conception the sphere of nature found its fulfilment in the sphere of grace, evangelical Protestantism often assigned parallel positions to these two spheres. In fact, it accepted a dichotomy in both individual and communal Christian life, between its spiritual and secular parts, between church and world, without establishing any interior or intrinsic relation between them.

Evangelical Protestantism often lacked a Biblical message for the world, for culture, and for the life of its separate spheres. This lack was often prejudicial to the image which the world had of the church and of Christianity, and consequently of the Gospel itself. In my opinion this partly explains the reaction of the Left within the church, with its excessive accent on political and social engagement, its inclination to radical change of social structures and so on. There are many evangelical Protestants who, despite their confession of the absolute authority of Holy Scripture, failed to take seriously the central message of the Bible concerning the universality of God's kingdom and the absolute authority of Jesus Christ as Saviour and Lord of the world.

Creation -- Man the trustee of creation

It is my belief that the cause of this dualism lies in the exiling, from our concrete and daily activities, of faith in God as Creator of heaven and earth. This is why we have some difficulty in recognizing that our daily life, in its great diversity, is fundamentally a vocation given by God. The life that we call natural, and activities of everyday in industry and politics and

43

culture etc., are regarded as inferior to the life we call spiritual.

And this failure of real faith in God as Creator of the world has consequences, too, for our understanding of the depth and scope of man's fall, as also for the depth and scope of the redeeming word of Jesus Christ. That is why it is so vitally important to concentrate our attention on what the Bible teaches us about creation. Doing so, I think we are justified in drawing the following conclusions: the reality in which we live is wholly a divine creation. There is not a single thing which has any original autonomous existence sufficient to itself. Even the reality of the Evil One is not independent of God. Satan does not escape his creaturely nature (Isa. 54:16). There is not one place in the whole universe where we can flee from God (Ps. 139, Heb. 4:12, 13). Everywhere we are called 'coram Deo' (in the sight of God), 'for in him we live, move, and have our being' (Acts 17:28).

The Scriptures teach besides that each person of the Trinity is engaged in the work of creation; and not solely God the Father, as the Apostles' Creed leaves us to understand. Genesis 1:2 relates that 'the Spirit of God moved on the waters' and the New Testament teaches us that the Son has a central role in the creation of the world. John reveals that 'all things were made by the Word and nothing which was made was made without it' (John 1:3). Christ is revealed to us as the image of an invisible God, the first born of all creation. In him everything was created, in the heavens and on earth. All was created by him and for him and all things exist in him (Col. 1:15-17). It is consequently improper to distinguish God the Father, the Creator, from God the Son, the Redeemer. The God who creates and who redeems is the same God.

It is not legitimate, therefore, to speak of two kingdoms; one in which God has power as

Creator (that is the sphere of nature, or of so called common grace), and another in which God has power as Redeemer. We are everywhere before the face of the same God, three in one, who showed himself in definitive fashion in Jesus Christ, the Word made flesh (John 1:14, Heb. 1:1, 2). This is why Christian life does not exist in two sectors. It is fundamentally one and indivisible.

The second point especially revealed in the first chapter of Genesis, and which is vitally important for the understanding of our position in the world, is that God made man in his image and after his likeness and called him to have dominion over the earth (Gen. 1:26). Man has a royal position in the world. God created him a little lower than God, crowned him with glory and magnificence, and gave him the rule over the works of his hands. He put all things under his feet (Ps. 8:6, 7). That is to say that man is not made for the earth but that the earth exists for man; though it is necessary to add immediately that man does not exist for himself, but for God. 'O Lord, our Lord, how excellent is your name in all the world' (Ps. 8:10).

Therefore man is not autonomous, nor his own legislator. He is submitted to a particular command of God: 'Increase and multiply, fill the earth, have dominion over it, over the fish of the sea, the birds of the air, and over every beast that lives on the earth' (Gen. 1:28). Nevertheless, in fulfilling this command man remains the trustee for his Lord. The earth and those who inhabit it remain the inalienable property of God (Ps. 24:1). Man has his maturity but it is a maturity 'coram Deo'. Therefore he is not free to exploit the earth for himself. He must cultivate it, keep it, for the honour of God (Gen. 2:15).

There is a fundamental difference between man's cultural and imaginative activity, and God's creative activity. God creates 'ex nihilo'

45

(out of nothing). Man, on the contrary, is
never the creator; rather he fashions given
materials. He uses such possibilities that God
has placed within the creation. Activities of
God and of man have no common denominator. Man
is created in God's image, but the image is not
identical to him who made it.

The command of God given to man in the creation has lost none of its force through the fact
of the fall. We read nowhere in Scripture that
God has revoked it. Indeed, in God's covenant
with Noah, he is confirmed rather in this command
(Gen. 9:6). Here, as everywhere, appears the
difference between God's word and the words of
man. Man's words are lost in history, at least
to the extent that he has not repeated those of
God. On the contrary, the words of God once pronounced, keep their power for all ages (1 Pet.
1:25). That is why they make themselves heard in
unbelieving hearts - though their origin is there
ignored, as is their true meaning (Rom. 1:18-23).

The fact that man's creation mandate has kept
its power is of essential importance for our
understanding of the scope and depth of Christ's
redeeming work. Upon this subject, we must
bring another matter into focus. We may not
oppose man as 'lord of creation' to the creation
itself. There is no such duality. Man, without
doubt, transcends his environment in the depth
of his consciousness, in the heart of his existence, but at the same time man is bound to the
world by all of his temporal existence. The Bible
teaches explicitly that God made man of the dust
of the earth (Gen. 2:7).

We should not, therefore, attempt to excise
man from his natural environment. Precisely
because man is intrinsically bound to creation
in its whole, the world was entrained in man's
fall. God cursed it because of man (Gen. 3:17).
Therefore the Apostle Paul speaks to us of the
vanity to which the whole creation was subjected
(its enslavement to corruption) and of the whole

creation which groans as if in labour (Rom. 8: 20-22).

We know that cause of all that. It is man who, discontent with his position as trustee of the creation of God, permitted himself to be seduced by Satan and wished, in his turn, to be God (Gen. 3:5). In place of serving he wished to rule. This was also the great temptation which Satan placed before Jesus during those forty days in the desert. But unlike the first man, he did not succumb to the diabolic temptation (Matt. 4:1-11).

Our knowledge of the radical and universal fall should help us to understand the true depth and scope of God's redeeming work in Jesus Christ.

God's redemption, radical and universal

Inasmuch as man's fall was radical and total, so also redemption in Christ is radical and total. It touches man at the heart of his existence and encompasses his whole life; that is to say, all his earthly existence. Christ, as the Son of God, took the vacant place of Adam as head of the new humanity (Rom. 5; 1 Cor. 15:21, 22). He is the first born of all the creation (Col. 1:15). His redeeming work has its individual and col- lective dimensions as much as its cosmic ones.

The Gospel asks of each of us a personal response. There is no redemption outside of individual and personal regeneration: 'Verily verily I say unto you, except a man be born again he cannot see the kingdom of God' (John 3:3). There is no collective assurance in which we automatically participate, having 'Abraham for our father' (Matt. 3:9, Luke 3:8). Each of us is called to repent and produce good fruit. 'Every tree which does not bear good fruit will be cut down and thrown into the fire' (Matt. 3: 10). 'The branch cannot bear fruit of itself if it does not remain attached to the vine. So you

too will carry none if you do not dwell in me'
(John 15:1).

Yet this image of the tree carries in itself
the idea of a collectivity, of a communion which
seems to have priority over the individual. It
is noteworthy that the promises of God are
addressed, primarily, not to individual men but
to men in community. In Genesis 3:15, God speaks
to us already of the woman and her posterity.
God establishes his covenant with Noah and with
all his posterity (Gen. 9:9). He blesses all
the families of the earth in Abraham (Gen. 12:
3, 17). It is the same for Isaac (Gen. 26) and
for Jacob (Gen. 28:18). Throughout the history
of the people of Israel the promises of God are
addressed not to individual men but to Israel
in its totality.

The New Testament teaches us that the body
of Christ comes first and that we become members
of it by our personal rebirth. As we have already seen, Christ takes the place of Adam as
the second head of the human race (Rom. 5; 1
Cor. 15:21, 22). There is also a continuity of
the people of Israel and the church of the New
Testament, the people of God under the New
Covenant. The latter is grafted on to the former
(Rom. 11:22-24). Besides, the promises of God
are not only addressed to men individually or to
human kind, but to all the creation. The covenant of God with Noah not only included Noah and
his posterity, but all living creatures who were
with him; the birds, cattle and all beasts of
the earth. Henceforward no creature should be
exterminated by the flood waters (Gen. 9:10,11).
God keeps faith with the earth because it is his
creation. He carries it in his hands even after
the Fall (Ps. 19:24; 104; 148). Just as Adam
carried with him the whole of humanity, so it
will be restored in its totality in Christ: 'Because the creation itself will be set free from
bondage to decay and obtain the glorious liberty
of the children of God' (Rom. 8:20, 21).

'Jesus Christ is the propitiation for our sins and not for ours only, but also for the sins of the whole world' (1 John 2:2; 4:14). 'In him we have redemption through his blood, forgiveness of our trespasses, according to the riches of his grace, which he lavished upon us. For he has made known to us in all wisdom and insight, the mystery of his will, according to his purpose, which he set forth in Christ as a plan for the fullness of time to unite all things in him, things in heaven and things on earth' (Eph. 1:7-10).

Only when we place it in the true biblical perspective of the world's redemption does our personal salvation have true significance and can it be understood in its fullness. This world remains God's world, despite what we have made it (Col. 1:15-23). Even though the whole world still groans, and is as it were in labour, Christ is its King. He has been given all power, in heaven and on earth. He maintains the order of creation and he is the Lord of history (Matt. 28:18; Col. 1). With him, we also are inheritors of the world (Rom. 8:17). We await those new heavens, that new earth, where righteousness dwells (2 Pet. 3:13; Rev. 21:1).

The message of the Bible is clear enough in this regard: the new earth will not arrive gradually as the result of our activities. The crucial moment will be the Lord's return at the Last Judgment. This signifies more than a purification and does not imply a universal reconciliation, but rather a separation. I refer, for example, to what Jesus said about the wise and foolish virgins, about the sheep and the goats (Matt. 25). The Apostle Peter speaks of the Day of the Lord, which will come as a theif; when the heavens will pass away with a great noise, the elements will dissolve in violent heat, and the earth with the works that it contains will be consumed (2 Pet. 3:10, 12).

Despite the radical and total character of

49

this Last Judgment, there remains continuity in the history of the world and of the human race. The Scripture teaches us that the works of those who die in the Lord will follow them (Rev. 14: 13). We might spiritualize these words and detach them completely from the reality of the creation in which we live our daily life. This attitude, however, is quite inadmissible, since the Bible tells us that the nations will walk in the light of the new Jerusalem and that the kings of the earth will carry into it their glory and their treasures (Rev. 21:24-26).

There is an intrinsic tie between God's redemption of man and that of the world, because man, as trustee of the world, is intrinsically tied to the creation. We believe in the 'resurrection of the body' and in the redemption of man in his totality. The kingdom of God is universal and the Gospel of Jesus Christ is itself the Gospel of the Kingdom, which has already come and which is to come (Matt. 3:2; 4:23; 6:33; 24:14; 28:18).

Our calling

Our task and our calling are therefore certain. If God remains faithful to his creation, we can only follow him in remaining faithful to the world - to his world, despite all - in remaining obedient to the original commandment by which he placed us within the creation.

The question remains: Is there not then a conflict with the missionary command given to the disciples to 'Go therefore, teaching all the nations, baptizing them in the name of the Father, and of the Son and of the Holy Spirit, and teaching them to keep all that I have commanded you' (Matt. 28:19)? Does not God want us, above all, to be fishers of men? (Mark 1:17). Has not this missionary command always been the central spiritual power of every missionary endeavour?

At first sight, there is no intrinsic relation

50

between these two commands. Culture is agriculture, technique, artistic accomplishment, industry or commerce, politics, education and science. Is not all that totally different from the preaching of the Gospel? We might repeat Tertullian's question: 'What has Athens in common with Jerusalem?'

Have we not, however, placed ourselves before a false dilemma? Are we not falsely opposing God as Creator to God as Redeemer, subordinating the former to the latter? In the preceding text I have said expressly that there is only one God, one in three, Creator and Redeemer; that there is an intrinsic relation between creation and re-creation. The Apostle Peter tells us that we are 'a chosen race, a royal priesthood, a holy nation, a people for God's own possession, in order that we should declare the wonderful deeds of him who called us out of darkness into his marvellous light' (1 Pet. 2:9). These marvellous deeds of God are his acts in creation, redemption, and fulfilment. In our missionary work, the Gospel is to be announced in its fulness. It is that Gospel which teaches us that Christ not only came into the world to save individuals or a Christian community, but to reconcile all things with God the Father, things which were on earth as much as things which are in heaven, establishing peace by the blood of the cross (Col. 1:20).

Then it is also a matter of the renewal of relations broken and corrupted by sin. In the first place, there are the relations between God and man, and consequently between men, between man and himself, man and his work, man and nature, and his environment in general. It is a matter of expiation, of reconciliation, of renewal of the creation in all its structures and all its aspects. That is the great task which Christ is in process of bringing to a completion. But it is also the great task for which Christ called us to his service. 'If anyone is in Christ, he is a new creature. Old things are passed away;

51

behold all things have become new. All this comes from God who has reconciled us with himself in Christ, and has entrusted to us the ministry of reconciliation...we are therefore ambassadors for Christ as if God commanded you by our mouth: we pray you, in Christ's name, to be reconciled to God' (2 Cor. 5:17-21).

This ministry of reconcilation ought not to be carried out only in words but also in deeds: it demands from us a radical and total surrender. 'You are the light of the world. A city set on a hill cannot be hid. One does not light a lamp to put it under a bushel, but one places it on a candlestick; and it illuminates all those who are in the house. Let you light therefore shine before men, so that they will see your good works, and give glory to your Father who is in heaven' (Matt 5:14-16). That is to say that we are not permitted to retire to the catacombs; for our Lord still gives us the freedom to fight in the open while it is yet day. We have to confess Christ as Saviour of the world in the fulness of life: in our families, our work (whatever it be), our politics, our teaching, our industry, our artistic life, our social works, our charitable works, and so on.

It is impossible to serve two masters: God and mammon, God and science, God and sex, God and politics, God and art, God and our family. God and economic prosperity. It is necessary that our whole life, all our thoughts, all our activities, as much as all our so called structures, be led captive to the obedience of Christ (2 Cor. 10:5), in order that God shall be all in all (1 Cor. 15:28). This is that true liberty which is to the glory of God.

WHAT IS MAN?

By Herman Dooyeweerd

The question, "What is man?" occupies a central place in contemporary European thinking. This question is certainly not new. After every period in the history of Western thought, wherein all interest was concentrated upon the knowledge of the outer world, the immense universe, man began to feel unsatisfied. In this situtation human reflection always turns again to the central riddle of man's own existence. As soon as this riddle begins to puzzle human thought, it seems as if the external world recedes from the focus of interest.

In one of his splendid dialogues, Plato pictures his master, Socrates, as a man obsessed with but one aim in his search for wisdom, namely, to know himself. As long as I have not succeeded in learning to know myself, said Socrates, I have no time for meddling with other questions that seem to me trifles when compared with this.

In contemporary thinking, however, the question, "What is man?," is no longer asked from a theoretical viewpoint merely. Much rather it has become a crucial issue for many thinkers because of the spiritual distress of Western society and the fundamental crisis of our culture. It may be that in America this crisis does not occupy the same central place in the reflection of the leading thinkers, as it does in Europe. Nevertheless, America, too, is concerned with the same problem, since it belongs to the sphere of Western civilization.

What, then, is the character of this crisis? And why does the question, "What is man?," today sound like a cry of distress?

The crisis of Western civilization is depicted as a complete decline of human personality, as the rise of the mass-man. This is imputed, by different leading thinkers, to the increasing supremacy of technology, and to the over-organization of modern society. The result, supposedly, is a process of depersonalizing of contemporary life. The modern mass-man has lost all personal traits. His pattern of behavior is prescribed by what is done in general. He shifts the responsibility for his behavior upon an impersonal society. And this society, in turn, seems to be ruled by the robot, the electronic brain, by bureacracy, fashion, organization and other impersonal powers. As a result, our contemporary society has no room for human personality, and for a real spiritual communion of person with person. Even the family and the church often can no longer guarantee a sphere of personal intercourse. Family life is, to a large degree, dislocated by increasing industrialization. The church itself is confronted with the danger of the depersonalization of congregational life, especially in the big cities.

In addition, the average, secularized man nowadays has lost any and all true interest in religion. He has fallen prey to a state of spiritual nihilism, i.e., he negates all spiritual values. He has lost all his faith, and denies any higher ideals than the satisfaction of his appetites. Even the Humanistic faith in mankind, and in the power of human reason to rule the world and to elevate man to a higher level of freedom and morality, has no longer any appeal to the mind of the present day mass-man. To him God is dead, and the two worlds wars have destroyed the Humanistic ideal of man. This modern man has lost himself, and considers himself cast into a world that is meaningless, that offers no hope for a better future.

Western civilization, which displays these terrible symptoms of spiritual decline, finds itself confronted with the totalitarian ideology of Communism. It tries to oppose the latter with the old ideas of democracy, freedom, and of inalienable human rights. But these ideas, too, have been involved in the spiritual crisis, which has sapped their very fundamentals. In earlier times, it is argued, they were rooted both in the Christian faith and in the Humanists's faith in reason. But the increasing relativism, which has affected our Western civilization, has left no room for a strong faith, since it has destroyed the belief in an absolute truth. The traditional faith, which gave man his inspiration, has to a great extent been replaced by technical methods and organization. And in general it is due to such impersonal means that the traditional Christian and the Humanistic traits of our culture are outwardly maintained.

But Western civilization cannot be saved by technical and organizational means alone. The Communistic world-power, whose ideology is still rooted in a strong faith, also has these means at its disposal and has used them very well. Besides, the atom bomb, which terminated the second world war, is no longer an American mono-poly. This terrible invention of Western tech-nology can only increase the fear of the impending ruin of our culture. The amazing technical development of Western society, which has produced the modern mass-man, will also destroy our civili-zation unless a way is found to restore human personality.

It is against this background of spiritual distress that the question: "What is man?" has become truly existential in contemporary European philosophy. It is no longer merely a question of theoretical interest. It has become, rather, a question concerning the whole existence of man in his spiritual anxiety. It is a question of to be or not to be. This also explains the power-ful influence of contemporary personalistic and and existentialistic philosophical trends upon European literature and upon the youth. Here it is no longer an abstract idealistic image of man as a rational and moral being, which is at issue. Rather, the new philosophical view of man is concerned with man in his concrete situation in the world, with his state of decay as the contemporary mass-man, and with his possibilities of rediscovering himself as a responsible personality.

This philosophy no longer considers the intellect as the real center of human nature. It has tried to penetrate rather to what it conceived to be the deepest root of human selfhood and the deepest cause of man's spiritual distress. Man is thrown into the world involuntarily. To sustain his life he is obliged to turn to the things that are at hand in his world. The struggle for existence characterizes man's life. But, in this situation of concern, man is in danger of losing himself as a free personality so that he delivers himself to the world. For the human selfhood surpasses all existing things. The human ego is free, it is not at hand as a concrete object. It is able to project its own future, and to say to its past, "I am no longer what I was yesterday. My future is still in my own hand. I can change myself. I can create my future by my own power." But when man reflects on this creative freedom of his selfhood, he is confronted with the deepest cause of his distress, namely, the anxiety and fear of death. Death is here not understood in the merely biological sense, in which it also applies to the animal, but much rather in the sense of the dark nothingness, the night without dawn, which puts an end to all human projects and makes them meaningless. This anxiety, this fear of death is usually suppressed, for such is the massman's depersonalized manner of existence. To arrive at a proper, personal existence, man should frankly, and by anticipation, confront himself with death as the nothingness which limits his freedom. He should realize that his freedom is a freedom unto death, ending in the dark nothingness. Thus this first existentialistic approach to human self-knowledge revealed a profoundly pessimistic view of man.

However, other existentialistic thinkers showed

a more hopeful possibility of rediscovering man's true personality. In accordance with the personalistic philosophy of Martin Buber, they pointed to the essential communal relation in our personal life. You and I are correlates, which presuppose each other. I cannot know myself without taking into account that my ego is related to the ego of my fellow-man. And I cannot really have a personal meeting with another ego without love. It is only by such a meeting in love that I can arrive at true self-knowledge and knowledge of my fellow-man.

In this way this philosophy, then, seemed to offer various perspectives for a more profound knowledge of man's selfhood. And there are also many theologians who are of the opinion that this existentialistic approach to the central problem of man's nature and destiny, is of a more biblical character than the traditional theological view of human nature, oriented to ancient Greek philosophy.

I fear that this theological opinion testifies to a lack of self-knowledge in its radical biblical sense. It will presently appear why I think so.

However, let us first establish that the whole preceding diagnosis of the spiritual crisis of Western civilization fails to lay bare the root of the evil. For the symptoms of the spiritual decadence of this civilization, manifesting themselves in an increasing expansion of the nihilistic mind, cannot be explained by external causes.

They are only the ultimate result of a religious process of apostasy, which started with the belief in the absolute self-sufficiency of the rational human personality and was doomed to end with the breaking down of this idol.

How, then, can we arrive at real self-knowledge? The question: "Who is man?" con-

tains a mystery that cannot be explained by
man himself.

In the last century, when the belief in the
so-called objective science was still predominant in the leading circles, it was supposed
that by continued empirical research science
would succeed in solving all the problems of
human existence. Now there is, doubtless, a
scientific way of acquiring knowledge about
human existence. There are many special sciences
which are concerned with the study of man. But
each of them considers human life only from a
particular viewpoint or aspect. Physics and
chemistry, biology, psychology, historiography,
sociology, jurisprudence, ethics, and so forth,
they all can furnish interesting information
about man. But when one asks them: "What is
man himself, in the central unity of his existence, in his selfhood?" then these sciences have
no answer. The reason is that they are bound to
the temporal order of our experience. Within
this temporal order human existence presents a
great diversity of aspects, just like the whole
temporal world, in which man finds himself
placed. Physics and chemistry inform us about
the material constellation of the human body,
and the electro-magnetic forces operating in it;
biology lays bare the functions of our organic
life; psychology gives us an insight into the
emotional life of feeling and will, and has even
penetrated to the unconscious sphere of our mind.
History informs us about the development of
human culture, linguistics about the human faculty
of expressing thoughts and feelings by means of
words and other symbolical signs; economics and
jurisprudence study the economic and juridical
aspects of human social life, and so forth. Thus
every special science studies temporal human
existence in one of its different aspects.

But all these aspects of our experience and
existence within the order of time are related
to the central unity of our consciousness, which
we call our I, our ego. I experience, and I

exist, and thus I surpasses the diversity of
aspects, which human life displays within the
temporal order. The ego is not to be determined
by any aspect of our temporal experience, since
it is the central reference point of all of
them. If man would lack this central I, he could
not have any experience at all.

Consequently, contemporary existentialistic
philosophy rightly posited that it is not possible to acquire real self-knowledge by means of
scientific research. But it pretended that its
own philosophical approach to human existence
does lead us to this self-knowledge. Science,
so it says, is restricted to the investigation
of what is given, to concrete objects at hand.
But the human ego is not a given object. It
has the freedom to create itself by contriving
its own future. Existentialistic philosophy
pretends that it is exactly directed upon the
discovery of this freedom of the human I, in
contrast to all the data at hand in the world.

But is it true that we can arrive at real
self-knowledge in this way? Can this philosophy actually penetrate to the real center and
root of our existence, as many contemporary
theologians think? I am of the opinion that
it is a vain illusion to think so.

Philosophical thought is bound to the temporal
order of human experience, just as the special
sciences are. Within this temporal order man's
existence presents itself only in a rich diversity
of aspects, but not in that radical and central
unity, which we call our I or selfhood. It is
true that our temporal existence presents itself
as an individual, bodily whole, and that its
different aspects are related to this whole,
in fact, are only aspects of it. But as a merely
temporal wholeness, our human existence does not
display that central unity which we are aware of
in our self-consciousness.

This central I, which surpasses the temporal

order, remains a veritable mystery. As soon as
we try to grasp it in a concept or definition,
it recedes as a phantom and resolves itself
into nothingness. Is it really a nothing, as
some philosophers have said?

The mystery of the human I is, that it is,
indeed, nothing in itself; that is to say, it
is nothing as long as we try to conceive it
apart from the three central relations which
alone give it meaning.

First, our human ego is related to our whole
temporal existence and to our entire experience
of the temporal world as the central reference
point of the latter. Second, it finds itself,
indeed, in an essential communal relation to
the egos of its fellowmen. Third, it points
beyond itself to its central relation to its
divine Origin in Whose image man was created.

The first relation, namely, that of the human
ego to the temporal order of the world, in which
we are placed, cannot lead us to real self-knowledge, so long as it is viewed in itself alone.
The temporal order of human life in the world,
with its diversity of aspects, can only turn
away our view from the real center of human
existence, so long as we seek to know ourselves
from it. Shall we seek our selfhood in the
spatial aspect of our temporal existence, or in
the physico-chemical aspect of the material
constellation of our body, or in the aspect of
its organic life, or in that of emotional feeling?
Or should we rather identify our ego with the
logical aspect of our thought, or with the
historical aspect of our cultural life in a
temporal society, or with the aesthetical, or the
moral aspect of our temporal existence? By so
doing we would lose sight of the real center and
radical unity of our human nature. The temporal
order of our experiential world is like a prism,
which refracts or disgerses the sun-light into
a rich diversity of colors. None of these colors
is the light itself. In the same way the central

human ego is not to be determined by any of the
different aspects of our temporal, earthly
existence.

The second relation, in which our selfhood
is to be conceived, is the communal relation of
our own ego to that of our fellow-man. This relation can no more lead us to real self-knowledge,
than can the relation of our ego to the temporal
world, as long as it is viewed in itself alone.
The reason is that the ego of our fellow-man
confronts us with the same riddle as our own
selfhood does. So long as we try to understand
the relation between you and me merely from the
temporal order of this earthly human existence,
we must posit that this relation presents the
same diversity of aspects as our own temporal
existence. Whether we conceive of it in its
moral, psychological, historico-cultural or biological aspects, we will not arrive at any knowledge of the central relationship between your
and my selfhood. By so doing we only lose sight
of its central character, which surpasses the
diversity of aspects in our temporal horizon of
existence.

The personalistic and existentialistic views
of man have tried to determine the I-thou relation as a relation of love, an inner meeting of
the human persons. But within the earthly
horizon of time even the love-relations present
a diversity of meaning and typical character.
Does one refer to the love between husband and
wife, or between parents and their children? Or
is it the love-relation between fellow-believers,
belonging to inter-related churches, that we
have in mind? Or is it perhaps the love-relation
between compatriots, who have in common the love
of their country? Or have we rather in mind the
general love of the neighbor in the moral relations of our temporal life? None of these temporal
communal relations touch at the central sphere of
our selfhood.

And when contemporary philosophy speaks of an

inner meeting of the one person with the other, we must ask, "What do you understand by this inner meeting?" A real inner meeting presupposes real self-knowledge, and can only occur in the central religious sphere of our relation with our fellow-man. The temporal love-relations, in the above mentioned typical diversity of meaning, cannot guarantee a true inner meeting. Jesus said, in the Sermon on the Mount, "If ye love them which love you, what thank have ye? for sinners also love those that love them." Jesus here apparently speaks of a love that does not concern the real center of our lives, but only the temporal relations between men in their earthly diversity. But how can we love our enemies and bless those who curse us, and pray for those who persecute us, if we do not love God in Jesus Christ?

Thus the inter-personal relation between you and me cannot lead us to real self-knowledge, as long as it is not conceived in its central sense; and in this central sense it points beyond itself to the ultimate relation between the human I and God. This latter central relation is of a religious character. No philosophical reflection can lead us to real self-knowledge, in a purely philosophical way. The words with which Calvin starts the first chapter of his text-book on the Christian religion: "The true knowledge of ourselves is dependent on the true knowledge of God," are indeed the key to answer the question: "Who is man himself?"

But if that is so, it seems that we should apply to theology for real self-knowledge, since theology seems to be especially concerned with the knowledge of God. However, this too would amount to self-deceit. For as a dogmatical science of the articles of the Christian faith, theology is no more able to lead us to real knowledge of ourselves and of God than philosophy or the special sciences which are concerned with the study of man. This central knowledge can only be the result of the Word-revelation of God operating in the heart, in the religious center of our existence by the power of the Holy Spirit. Jesus Christ never blamed the scribes and Pharisees for their lack of dogmatical theological knowledge. When Herod asked the Chief priest and scribes where Christ was to be born, he received an answer that was doubtless correct from a dogmatical theological viewpoint, since it was based upon the prophetical texts of the Old Testment.

Nevertheless, Jesus says that they did not know Him nor his Father. And how could they have had real self-knowledge without his knowledge of God in Jesus Christ?

The traditional theological view of man, which we find both in Roman Catholic and Protestant scholastic works on dogmatics, was not at all a biblical origin. According to this theological conception of human nature, man is composed of a mortal, material body and of an immaterial, rational soul. These components were conceived of as united to one substance. Nevertheless, according to this view the rational soul continues to exist as an independent substance after the separation from the body, i.e., after death. In line with this view of human nature, man was called a rational and moral being in contrast to the animal which lacks a rational soul.

This view of man was, indeed, taken from Greek philosophy, which sought the center of our human existence in reason, i.e., in the intellect. But in this entire image of man there was no room for the real, i.e., the religious center of our existence which in the Holy Scripture is called our heart, the spiritual root of all the temporal manifestations of our life. It was constructed apart from the central theme of the Word-revelation, that of creation, fall into sin, and redemption by Jesus Christ in the communion of the Holy Spirit. And it is this very core of the divine Revelation which alone reveals the true root and center of human life. It is the only key to true self-knowledge in its dependency on the true knowledge of God. It is also the only judge both of all theological and philosophical views of man. As such, this central theme of the Word-revelation cannot be dependent on theological interpretations and conceptions, which are fallible human work, bound to the temporal order of our existence and experience. Its radical sense can only be explained by the Holy Spirit, who opens our hearts, so that our belief is no longer a mere acceptance of the articles of the Christian faith, but a living belief, instrumental to the central operation of God's Word in the heart, namely, the religious center of our lives. And this operation does not occur in an individualistic way but in the ecumenical communion of the Holy Spirit who unites all the members of the true Catholic Church in its spiritual sense, irrespective of their temporal denominational divisions.

Naturally, creation, the fall into sin and the redemption through Jesus Christ as the Incarnate Word, in the communion of the Holy Spirit, are also articles of faith, which are treated in every theological dogmatics, in addition to other articles which are also, actually or supposedly, founded in the Holy Scriptures. But in their radical sense as the central theme of the Word-revelation and the key of knowledge, they are not merely articles of faith, which are only the human formulations of the confession of the Church; much rather, they are the word of God itself in its central spiritual power addressing itself to the heart, the religious core and center of our existence. In this central confrontation with the Word of God, man has nothing to give but only to listen and to receive. God does not speak to theologians, philosophers and scientists, but to sinners, lost in themselves, and made into His children through the operation of the Holy Spirit in their hearts. In this central and radical sense, God's Word, penetrating to the root of our being, has to become the central motive-power of the whole of the Christian life within the temporal order with its rich diversity of aspects, occupational spheres and tasks. As such, the central theme of creation, fall into sin and redemption, should also be the central starting-point and motive power of our theological and philosophical thought.

Is it necessary, at this point, to consider the radical meaning of this central theme of the divine Word-Revelation? Is it not rather well known to all of us since the beginning of our Christian education?

It may well be questioned whether this is really true. I am afraid that many Christians have only a theological knowledge of creation, fall into sin and redemption by Jesus Christ, and, that this central theme of the Word-Revelation has not yet become the central motive-power of their lives.

What is the radical biblical sense of the revelation of creation? As Creator, God reveals Himself as the absolute Origin of all that exists outside of Himself. There is no power in the world that is independent of Him. Even Satan is a creature and his power is taken from creation, namely, from the creation of man in the image of God. If man had not been created in God's image, Satan's suggestion that man would be like God would have had no single power over the human heart. He could only give this power an apostate direction, but his power does not originate from himself. If our heart finds itself fully in the grip of the self-revelation of God as Creator, we can no longer imagine that there would exist a safe and neutral zone which is withdrawn from God. This is the fundamental difference between the living God and the idols which originate from an absolutization of what has only a relative and dependent existence. The ancient Greeks, whose conception of human nature had such a predominant influence upon the traditional theological view of man, worshipped their Olympian gods, who were merely deified cultural powers of Greek society. These gods were represented as invisible and immortal beings endowed with a splendid beauty and a supra-human power. But these splendid gods had no power over the fate of death, to which mortals are subjected. This is why the famous Greek poet, Homer, said: "Even the immortal gods cannot help lamentable man, when the horrible fate of death strikes him down." And the same poet says that the immortal gods fight shy of every contact with the realm of death.

But hear now what Psalm one hundred and thirty-nine says about God: "Whither shall I go from thy Spirit? Or whither shall I flee from thy presence? If I ascend up into heaven, thou art there: If I make my bed in the realm of death, behold, thou art there." Here we face the living God, as Creator, whom the ancient Greeks did not know.

In an indissoluble contact with this self-revelation as Creator, God has revealed man to himself. Man was created in the image of God. Just as God is the absolute Origin of all that exists outside of Himself, so He created man as a being, in whom the entire diversity of aspects and faculties of the temporal world is concentrated within the religious center of his existence, which we call our I, and which the Holy Scripture calls our heart, in a pregnant, religious sense. As the central seat of the image of God, the human selfhood was endowed with the innate religious impulse to concentrate his whole temporal life and the whole temporal world upon the service of love to God. And since the love for God implies the love for His image in man, the whole diversity of temporal ordinances of God is related to the central, religious commandment of love, namely, "thou shalt love the Lord, thy God, with all they heart, soul and mind, and thy neighbor as thyself." This is the radical biblical sense of the creation of man in the image of God. It leaves no room for any neutral sphere in life, which could be withdrawn from the central commandment in the kingdom of God.

Since the image of God in man concerned the radix, that is, the religious center and root of our entire temporal existence, it follows that the fall into sin can only be understood in the same radical, biblical sense. The entire fall into sin can be summed up as a false illusion, which arose in the human heart, namely, that the human I has the same absolute existence as God Himself. This was the false insinuation of Satan, to which man gave ear: "Ye shall be like God." This apostasy from the living God implied the spiritual death of man, since the human I is nothing in itself and can only live from the Word of God and in the love-communion with its divine Creator. However, this original sin could not destroy the religious center of human existence with its innate religious impluse to seek for its absolute Origin. It could only lead this central impulsion in a false, apostate direction by diverting it to the temporal world with its rich diversity of aspects, which, however, have only a relative sense.

By seeking his God and himself in the temporal world, and by elevating a relative and dependent aspect of this world to the rank of the absolute, man fell a prey to idolatry. He lost the true knowledge of God and true self-knowledge. The idea that true self-knowledge may be regained by an existentialistic philosophy, apart from the divine Word-revelation, is nothing but the old vain illusion that the human I is something in itself, independent of God who has revealed Himself as the Creator.

It is only in Jesus Christ, the incarnate Word and Redeemer, that the image of God has been restored in the religious center of human nature. The redemption by Jesus Christ in its radical biblical sense, means the rebirth of our heart and must reveal itself in the whole of our temporal life. Consequently, there now can be no real self-knowledge apart from Jesus Christ. And this biblical self-knowledge implies that our whole world-and-life-view must be reformed in a Christo-centric sense; so that every dualistic view of common grace which separates the latter from its true religious root and center in Jesus Christ should be rejected in principle.

The history of dogmatic theology proves that it is possible to give an apparently orthodox theoretical explanation of the articles of faith pertaining to the threefold central theme of the Holy Scripture, without any awareness of the central and radical significance of the latter for the view of human nature and of the temporal world. In this case theological thought does not really find itself in the grip of the Word of God. The latter has not become its central basic motive, its central impelling force. Rather, it proves to be influenced by another, a non-biblical central motive, which gives to it its ultimate direction.

Such was the scholastic theme of nature and grace (introduced into Roman Catholic theology and philosophy since the 13th century) which ruled the traditional theological view of man. It led scholastic theology to divide human life into two spheres, namely, the natural and the supra-natural. Human nature was supposed to belong to the natural sphere, and was supposed to find its center in natural reason. This human reason would be able to acquire a right insight into human nature, and into all other so-called natural truths, apart from any divine Revelation, by its own natural light alone.

Of course, it was granted that this rational nature of man was created by God. But this theological acceptance of creation as revealed truth did not influence the view of human nature itself. This view was much rather ruled by the dualistic pagan religious basic motive of Greek thought, which led to a so-called dichotomistic conception of the nature of man.

68

In addition to his rational-ethical nature,
man was supposed to have been endowed with a
supra-natural gift of grace, namely, participation in the divine nature. According to Roman
Catholic doctrine this supra-natural gift of
grace was lost by the fall into sin. It is
regained by the supra-natural means of grace,
which Christ has entrusted to his Church. In
this way, the human rational nature would be
elevated to that supra-natural state of perfection
to which it was destined after the plan of creation. It was, however, granted that man cannot
arrive at this state without faith, which is
itself a gift of grace to the human intellect;
it is, therefore, only by faith that we can accept
the supra-natural truths of divine Revelation.
But the supra-natural sphere of grace presupposes
the natural sphere of human life, namely, human
nature. This nature, according to the Roman
Catholic view, was not radically corrupted by
sin; it was only wounded, since, after the plan
of creation, it was destined to be united with
the supra-natural gift of grace. As a result of
original sin, human nature lost its original
harmony. The sensuous inclinations are in
opposition to natural reason which should rule
over them. Nevertheless, man can arrive at the
acquisition of natural virtues by which the rule
of reason over the sensuous inclinations is
realized. Only the supra-natural virtues of
faith, hope and Christian love belong to the
sphere of grace.

This is the view of human nature which has
been sanctioned by the doctrine of the Roman
Catholic Church. It has completely abandoned
the radical sense of creation, fall and redemption, as they are revealed to us in the Word of
God.

The Roman Catholic view of this central theme
of Revelation was rejected by the Reformation.
But how is it to be explained that the conception
of human nature as a composite of a material body
and an immortal, rational soul was, nevertheless,

generally accepted by both scholastic Lutheran and Reformed theology. Was this conception not taken from Greek philosophy, whose pagan religious basic motive was radically opposed to that of Holy Scripture? Did this Roman dualism not fail to evaluate the biblical insight into the religious root and center of human existence? Was it, consequently, not incompatible with the biblical doctrine concerning the radical character of the fall into sin, which affected human nature in its very root?

How, then, could this un-biblical view of man be maintained? The reason is that the scholastic basic motive of nature and grace of Roman Catholicism continued to influence the theological and philosophical views of the Reformation. This motive introduced a dualism into the entire view of man and the world, which could not fail to withdraw Christian thought from the radical and integral grip of the Word of God.

It is this very dualism which testifies to its un-biblical character. It was the result of the attempt to accommodate the Greek view of nature to the biblical doctrine of grace. In fact, this scholastic motive of accommodation resulted in a radical deformation of the central theme of the Word-revelation. The scholastic view that created human nature finds its center in an autonomous human reason cannot be accommodated to the radical biblical view of creation. It implied that in the natural sphere of life man would be independent of the Word of God. This false division of human life into a natural and a supra-natural sphere became the starting-point of the process of secularization, which resulted in the crisis of Western culture, in its spiritual uprooting. In fact, it abandoned the so-called natural sphere to the rule of the apostate religious basic motive, initially to that of Greek thought, later on to that of modern Humanism.

Human reason is not an independent substance; much rather it is an instrument. The I is the

hidden player, who avails himself of it. And
the central motive that rules both human thought
and the human ego itself, is of a central religious nature.

The question: "What is man? Who is he",
cannot be answered by man himself. But it has
been answered by God's Word-revelation, which un-
covers the religious root and center of human
nature in its creation, fall into sin and redemption by Jesus Christ. Man lost true self-knowledge since he lost the true knowledge of God.
But all idols of the human selfhood, which man
in his apostasy has devised, break down when they
are confronted with the Word of God, which unmasks
their vanity and nothingness. It is this Word
alone, which by its radical grip can bring about
a real reformation of our view of man and of our
view of the temporal world; and such an inner
reformation is the very opposite of the scholastic device of accommodation.

STRUCTURAL PRINCIPLES OF SOCIETY

By Hendrik VanRiessen

The idea of an unprejudiced investigation of
facts resulting in their so-called objective
description is an instance of self-deception.
Any investigator is far more objective if he
acknowledges the nonscientific criteria he employs
in his research. The charge that by so doing his
analysis becomes onesided and dogmatic, is not
fair; no one can escape in science a starting
point beyond science, in the field of world view
and principles. So it is better that one distinctly realizes what principles are employed
in one's historical investigations. And this
is a definite gain. It explains why we regard
some facts as important or unimportant, normal
or abnormal.

It is necessary, therefore, that we first
discuss the principles by which society and its
history ought to be tested. Since our concern
is with the formation of society, only those
principles will be examined that contribute to
the more or less permanent organization of society.

Man forms various types of lasting societal
relationships. Together with others the individual lives and works in labor unions, associations, schools, the state, the church, business
concerns, the family, and so on.

The scriptural principles valid for such vital
relationships and their inter-relations are the
balance of authority and freedom, and sphere-
sovereignty.

We cannot treat these principles exhaustively;
nor do we pretend to solve such difficult questions
as those concerning the task of the government, a
subject again of central interest. It is suffi-

cient for our purpose if we can show that these principles are better guides for our social life than the current trend toward a hierarchical and collective society.

The most important advantage that can be gained for our analysis is that it will free us from the dilemma resulting from a forced option between collectivism vs. individualism; the community vs. the individual. It is wrong to think that if one is dissatisfied with individualism and with collectivism (respectively ascribing primacy to the individual and to the community) the only course open is to choose an agreeable compromise position in the middle. Another possibility is open if in addition to the over-simplified problem of the individual and the community, we also consider the problem of the relation between the individual and authority, and the problem of the relation between various socal units.

This other possibility, typified by the principles named above, is able to prevent the justification of collectivism on the basis of the defects of individualism. And since individualism has been defeated in our society, humanity is confronted with a decisive choice between a collective course and a trend which would recognize the principles of sphere-sovereignty, and of the balance of authority and freedom.

Sphere-sovereignty

Abraham Kuyper (1837-1920) founded the Free University of Amsterdam on the principle of sphere-sovereignty. After seventy years, however, many of his spiritual heirs now snicker or become incensed at the mere mention of sphere-sovereignty.

I do not have in mind those who believe this principle merely means that social units, such as the state and business, have nothing to do

with each other and are completely isolated so
that the state, for example, may not concern
itself with economic life. Such would do well
to read up a bit on the subject.

I am more concerned with the idea that sphere-
sovereignty between the state and economic life
has become meaningless in practice and can therefore be disregarded. There is much truth in the
first statement. But because in practice a
principle does not fit the historical situation,
it does not follow that such a principle can be
abolished. Practice is not normative. Many
principles have been discarded in the practical
life of the Soviet Union!

The fact that sphere-sovereignty between the
state and economic life is being disregarded
might lead to the conclusion that society is in
a process of decay, a process obviously started
in our time in the relations between these two
spheres. A wrong conclusion drawn from this
fact has its consequences for other fields; e.g.,
if the freedom of the press is curtailed, if
universities lose their independence or are
closed by the state, should the principle of
sphere-sovereignty then also be abandoned, since
in fact it no longer exists? And if not, what
is the difference from the above-mentioned case
of economic life?

Hitler comprehended sphere-sovereignty to
the extent that he knew that whoever would rule
the souls of men must first conquer their
institutions, the independent living associations
of society. One by one they had to fall under
his power, i.e., the institutions of economic
life, the press, the schools, the unions, the
family, and so on. Do not be deceived by a
difference in tempo. When institutions are
abrogated slowly and silently, we must be on
our guard all the more.

Another objection sometimes raised is that
sphere-sovereignty practically did not exist in

long past centuries, so it is not strange if
it should now disappear again. This argument
is not valid. If sphere-sovereignty is a legitimate normative principle for the historical
development of society, a proper attitude will
gradually put it into practice. A good historical development is one in which the social
units of life will gradually enjoy a more and
more differentiated and independent existence.

A preliminary orientation.

Let us examine the meaning of the above mentioned principles in greater detail. Generally
speaking, in our case sphere-sovereignty expresses the mutual independence of the social
units or lasting relationships of society. And
it expresses in particular the mutual independence of the authority inherent in units of a
different nature.

If by "sovereignty" we should mean complete
power, the choice of the term would be unfortunate. But this was not Kuyper's intention.
By "sovereignty" he understood an authority that
includes the right, the duty, and the power to
break and to avenge any resistance it encounters.
In its original absolute form this sovereignty
is identical with the Majesty of God. No particular bearer of authority on earth is the highest
power from which other forms of authority are
deduced and derived. From this state of affairs
we can deduce the most important fact about the
sphere of validity of the principle of the balance
between authority and freedom. Each sphere of
authority is limited by its own societal relationship. The relation of authority and freedom
exists within such relationships and not externally
(e.g., not between them).

Parents have authority over their children
within the family; they do not have authority
over the school. Therefore, insofar as children
are pupils they are under the authority of the
principal, their teachers, and the school board.

75

The government has authority insofar as its subjects are citizens; it does not rightly control
economic activity and enterprises; the latter
are subject to the owner, the director, the
board of trustees, and the stockholders. The
session or consistory of a church has authority
over the congregation, but not over other forms
of association, even if composed only of church
members; the exercise of authority in such other
groups rests with their independent committees.

The social relationships exist together on a
basis of equality; the one is not subordinate to
the authority and control of the other. Subjection to authority exists only within a relationship. Societal relationships properly stand
in a coordinate relation to each other, not in
a preferred or subordinate position.

The thesis defended here is of greatest weight
for our consideration of the society of the
future. The struggle against the totalitarian
formation of society can be waged with any pro-
spect of success only from this position both in
principle and in practice. But does not the
struggle against totalitarianism lie in a plea
for freedom? Certainly, it does; but this
freedom is first of all the freedom and independence of the different societal relationships
against any totalitarian relationship. The
liberty desired in practice and corresponding
to man's inner liberty (which is untouchable
from without) is guaranteed by the forms of
society, primarily by the independence of the
latter's various associations and institutions.
When this position falls, a dictator need not
fear any serious resistance from any quarter,
because the subordination of various spheres of
society is then already a fact. So eventually
totalitarianism can gradually and quietly take
over by appealing to the so-called "general welfare". Only a personal position then remains
from which the battle against the power of an
integrated totalitarian relationship must be

waged individually. Such an individual struggle
for a proper balance between authority and
freedom, in a deformed all-embracing relationship,
has nearly always proved hopeless, and today
modern technical and scientific means render
such a struggle impotent before it begins.

The success of the Netherlands' resistance to
National Socialism during the German occupation
lay in the fundamental and practical maintenance
of the sphere-sovereignty of the various societal
relationships. Individual resistance led to
deeds of great heroism and sacrifice, but the
power of the resistance did not lie in the individual.

So if adherence is given to the subordination
of societal relationships instead of to their
coordination, the resistance to be offered to
totalitarianism will be weak from the start.
This is the weakness of socialism, and to a
lesser degree of the Roman Catholic position.
The Roman Catholic position distinguishes two
spheres, the natural and the supernatural. The
first is subordinate to the second. In the sphere
of nature the state is the highest and most
perfect relationship; in the supernatural realm
of grace, the church is the highest. In the
realm of nature the state stands at the apex of
a hierarchy constituted by all other forms of
society. Of course, the principle of "subsi-
diarity" (the idea of the higher relationship as
a subsidiary for the lower) mollifies the fact
of superordination; the state permits "its parts"
to do what they can; it provides only such needs
as the other relationships can not provide. But
that does not change its preferred position of
superiority. In the Roman Catholic view of the
structure of society the state is the final
organizer and the director of the common good
in the domain of nature. The background to this
view of the structure of society is the philosophical requirement of a rational construction of
nature governed by the principle of the whole and

77

its parts. It does not, however, fit the present problem, as we shall see. At any rate in the application of this view the first fortress against totalitarianism is seriously undermined. Nevertheless, one must remember that the church must keep a watchful eye and that growth from below is here of great significance.

The socialistic standpoint with regard to the aforementioned resistance is even weaker. The hierarchical collectivization of society is undoubtedly mollified by the principle of functional decentralization, the distribution of responsibility. Such only signifies, however, that power ought to be more or less centralized, depending on the circumstances. Authority is from above. The idea of socialization comes first and the decentralization is a movement from the top to the bottom. (We will not go into the fact that socialists do not understand authority to be of divine origin. It is therefore a relative matter. Such a position is dangerous in itself. If authority has no basis it will be respected only in proportion to its power.)

The state is here the highest organ of society. There is no limit in principle to its interference in other organizations. There is no reason for the government to respect the coordinate independent authority of other forms of society, such as business enterprises and schools. A totalitarian regime can take over a socialistically constructed society by simply carrying out the process of centralization step by step. The abandonment of the independence of a number of societal relationships in favor of the state is not simply a matter of theory in socialism. In practice in the name of the community, socialists employ various collective measures to introduce a hierarchical structure into society, a hierarchy with the state at the apex.

In principle and in practice socialism paves the way for a totalitarian regime. Amidst the

well-meant pleas for liberty frequently uttered
by present day socialists, one would do well to
remember this fact. When the chips are down, the
socialist, because of his own standpoint and
because of the social transformation he has introduced, is forced into an indefensible position.

Whether or not the relationships of society
are arranged coordinately or subordinately is
a matter of practical and fundamental consequence.
To minimize this difference because of practical
considerations necessitating adjustment is to lose
sight of the fact that the course chosen is
decisive.

In defending sphere-sovereignty in principle
and in practive, Christianity ought to remember
that it is here that the decisive battle will
be fought against totalitarianism and in the
contest for a Christian society.

The writings of Kuyper himself on this subject
sometimes present difficulties. One has the
impression that they are caused by certain scholastic ideas. At times the state is considered to
be higher than his so-called society and the
family. Elsewhere the authority of parents is
derived from that of the local civil authorities,
in turn subject to state and federal authority,
so that the state is all-inclusive. Such statements are clearly in conflict with the main line
of Kuyper's thinking. The state is not above
but coordinate to other forms of society. Why?
Because every sphere ought to obey its own laws;
each after its own kind, and according to its
own created structure. This is the key to the
problem of sphere-sovereignty...And this is the
starting point of the Dooyeweerd and Vollenhoven
school of philosophy.

The authority within a given sphere is not
derived from that of another sphere, such as the
state or the church. It exists according to its
own nature and by reason of the charge from Him
who is absolutely sovereign, namely, Christ, to

whom God has given all power in heaven and on earth (Matt. 28:18; Col. 2:10; Eph. 1:21; 1 Cor. 15:27, 28).

With Kuyper we conclude that on earth there is no highest power, no unlimited, absolutely independent authority. Christ distributes authority to the office bearers in the various aspects of life. Such owe responsibility directly to Christ. Their authority exists solely within the organization with which they are concerned.

Of course, there is a difference in value between the various organizations. Nobody would think of placing a football club on the same level as a state. Such difference is due to the order established at creation. Undoubtedly the church occupies a primary position in the arrangment according to the importance of societal forms. But as far as the authorities in these social units are concerned, this arrangement is not hierarchical but coordinate. The direction of a football club does not derive its competence from the government; it is, therefore, not responsible to the latter for the internal affairs of the club.

What is striking in socialistic literature is that it does not do justice to the different nature of a number of social forms in society. It has, therefore, no adequate basis for the recognition of the independent authority of such associations, and so can only control the relations between such spheres of authority in terms of the "general welfare". The ideology of the socialist does not permit him to admit the essential significance of the fact that the various associations of society, e.g., the economic, political, and ecclesiastical, have a nature of their own.

The Bible teaches us of such diversity as was present in Biblical times. Relationships of society are clearly in evidence. At times they are explicitly mentioned, e.g., in the letters to the Ephesians, the Colossians, and to Titus. Office bearers and subjects are addressed according to the nature of the associations in which their relation subsists; parents and children, masters and servants, rulers and citizens, elders and members of the congregation. What is most apparent is that nothing suggests any subordination of the bearers of authority of the different relationships, the one to the other. The independence of the authority, directly inaugurated by Christ, and the obligation to obey for Christ's sake, constitute the framework in which man is addressed within his communal relationships.

Of course the Bible does not give us a theory of sphere-sovereignty. To expect such would be the highest of folly. The term is nowhere to be found. But when once aware of the creation-principle for the organization of society, we do find in the Bible a self-evident harmony with that principle; in agreement, of course, with the historical development of social practice. The Bible addresses us from and about its own time. It does not give evidence of the variety which we know. Sphere-sovereignty is a principle, a guidepost at the beginning of the history of humanity. It has to be brought into practice, unfolded, in the course of history. If the exegesis is correct, the text in Genesis, "In the days of Enos men began to call upon the name of the Lord," means that an independent community of worship, the first church, freed itself from an undifferentiated family life. In the course of history different associations of society split off and become independent according to their respective natures.

From the Mosaic legislation and its proclamation, it is evident, e.g., that the community of Israel was then to a large extent undifferentiated. But hundreds of years later when Israel has a king reigning over the entire nation, including Samuel, the latter respects Saul's

81

office, but proclaims the Word of God to Saul
with his own authority, (1 Sam. 8:19; 12:14;
13:13).

The lesson of history

The course of history has not been as simple
as here indicated. The liberation of life and
the formation of independent associations of
society have frequently been retarded by the
rulers, chiefs, priests, kings and emperors. A
society so liberated has again frequently been
tyrannized and cast into bonds by some potentate.
History shows not only a continuous unfolding
but also a retarding and reactionary concentration of power. To many a culture, decline and
fall has come in such a phase of its history.
Of course too great haste is also possible. Perhaps this was the case when Israel asked for a
king (1 Sam. 8). The story makes it plain that
such was a wrong desire because Israel occupied
a privileged and special position. By asking
for a king it gave evidence of having rejected
God. In its folly it now begged for the yoke of
a king.

Kuyper arrived at the idea of sphere-sovereignty because he observed in history that where
this principle was violated, life was brought
into distress and society reached a dead end.
Sometimes he gives the impression that he dreads
danger only from the state. "Sphere-sovereignty"
is opposed to "State-sovereignty": there you have
the long and the short of world-history. It will
become evident that even in his time the danger
was not from the state, but from the economic
realm. Bavinck understood something of this in
1905.

Undoubtedly, however, Kuyper also viewed the
concentration of economic power as a danger; he
also saw a threat to the sphere-sovereignty of
science by the church, in the Middle Ages and
long thereafter.

Danger can indeed come from very different quarters. Bruno's imprisonment by the inquisition and burning in 1600 was mainly because of his scientific critique of the Aristotelian-Ptolomaic world theory held by the church. And in the same manner the sphere-sovereignty of science was assailed when in 1663 Galileo was forced to promise never to teach that the earth moved around the sun. Sassen defends Galileo really only on the ground that he was later proved to be right. His condemnation is explained in the setting of the time, since Galileo assumed an individual position against collective opinions. In my opinion it is this latter point that needs to be criticized.

Kuyper was right in thinking that in history it was mostly the state that oppressed the various organizations of society. We think of Caesarism, the tyranny of Philip II, Louis XIV, Napoleon, Hitler and Stalin. In the last instance, however, we must be cautious, because at the center of power in communism, politics, technique, and economy are inextricably braided together, contending for primacy.

The religious background

To understand the principles of the balance of authority and freedom, and sphere-sovereignty, it is necessary to trace their religious significance. Only if such is kept in view, can a merely formal manipulation be avoided.

According to the first chapter of Genesis, God created nature in an orderly fashion, endowing each facet with its own distinct nature. He then created man in His own image. Man was created as a masterbuilder. Man's duty was not only to maintain the creation but also to add to it by developing its latent possibilities. Man's official task was to cultivate the potentialities inherent in creation. Reflection on this state of affairs in the light of Scripture

83

discloses much that is perplexing. And the
fall into sin renders the situation still harder
to understand. And yet a few things are intelli-
gible.

Everything that is created is of a religious
meaning-structure, i.e., it has to serve God.
It exists for God's glory and for His unsearch-
able good pleasure; and unto that end He has
subjected it to His laws. Man is also subject
to the latter, but God granted him freedom, that
he might be responsible for his deeds. An important manifestation of his freedom is that man
may unfold the plan of creation. The wealth of
creation forbids us to think of it as being rigid
and simple. But it must be remembered that man
in his freedom does not make anything wholly
new; he unveils in the course of history such
works as God has laid out for him at creation.
In all probability man performs only part of
this task and what he does is still faulty and
misshapen, and there is sure to be a good deal
of possible work undetected. Nevertheless, no
other possibility is open to him than to follow
the main lines of the plan of creation. In nature everything has its own peculiar character.
Likewise what man constructs in the sphere of
culture has its own peculiar nature. Sin may
hinder the production of a sound structure; its
infection may cause deformity. Sin may blind
man to the latent potentialities of culture,
but all that man does and leaves undone is
directed by the structures of creation. He may
establish a disorderly family, but it is still
a family; he may form a totalitarian state, but
it is still a state; a powerless church, nevertheless a church; an a-social project, still a
project; a useless bridge, but a bridge; an
insipid novel, withal a novel.

Among such structures the relationships of
society occupy an important place. In his responsibility to God, man stands together with others.
It is here that the idea of human community is

84

encountered.

At this point one must guard against a
dangerous misconception. Such a fellowship is
not an equalizing collection, embracing all of
humanity, or a race or nation. It is in such a
sense that the alternative between the individual and a community is forced upon us; the
individual is then secondary and the community
is primary. Such a view commits idolatry with
respect to the community (as aforetime - perhaps
in America still at present - the individual was
idolized), and it leads already in thought to
a totalitarian society, in which the life of
man is regarded as a service to the community
rather than as a religious devotion to God. The
criticism of this idea of a community is one of
the main features of this book. Such an idea
of a community would liquidate sphere-sovereignty.

A community is always qualified by a determining meaning-function. It is never something
indefinite. Accordingly each relationship has
of necessity a specific structure, and this
structure depends upon the meaning of such a
community. This holds even in experiments with
groups. William Foote Whyte blames the failure
of some of the experiments of group-discussion
by the Research Center of Group Dynamics at the
University of Michigan on a lack of group structure and of corresponding tasks. A community
is always determined and limited by the nature
of the activity jointly performed, e.g. family
life, union work, technical production, scientific research. Such a limitation concerns the
number of people constituting the group, the
reason for their grouping, and the duration of
the group. Man functions is a group in a
qualified sense, without the loss of his personal
identity. His personal identity is not to be
merged in any single relationship nor in the
totality of his relationships. Man does not
exist for the sake of any form of society.

Within the limits of a lasting social relationship, however, man shares a common task.

Such cooperation and communal living does not originate automatically. Affairs must be regulated and order maintained; unto that end, authority is instituted, "That we may lead a quiet and peaceable life" (1 Tim. 2:2). On Paul's return after his circuit through Asia-Minor, he establishes order by officially ordaining elders over the congregations (Act 14:23).

The bearers of authority in such a social unit do not derive their competence from their own volition, nor from the will of the people in their social unit. The Lord endows them with authority. On the other hand they don't have such authority for their own sake, nor are they in every respect the link between the original source of their charge and their subordinates. They occupy their office in order that, in a qualified cooperation or communal life, men may come to the fulfilment of their function, to their cultural calling, in direct free responsibility to God, who calls them into His service. That is the key to the principle of authority and freedom. Authority and freedom constitute a balance, aiming in a constructive sense at the coordination of a qualified cultural mandate. Such a balance would moreover protect human labor in such a social unit from the permeation of sin, especially from individualism. It would ward off the arbitrary and improper use of freedom through the usurpation of power. A despot does not understand that his authority ought to establish an environment in which, with the greatest possible freedom of action, men may follow their combined calling to carry out their qualified cultural task.

There is something more to be said concerning authority. It can be localized, it ought to have real power, and it may not be confused with leadership in general. Authority can be localized in a person, in a group or in a very complicated hierarchical structure. But it must always be distinguished from the people upon which authority is exerted. A so-called "democratic leadership," that according to Group Dynamics theory diffuses all leadership through the whole group, has nothing to do with authority, leadership, or democracy. When the discussion-leader in the afore-cited group-discussion experiments changes his role to a mere resource person, the group is confused and is paralyzed in its functioning. Democracy in a group or in a community does not mean that decisions are taken without an authorized leader, but it means decisions of the group under the guidance of a leader, provided a proper balance of authority and freedom is established. Leadership belongs to the created structure of groups or qualified communities, or, otherwise stated, it belongs to the freedom of men operating together in a qualified sense.

But to be effective, leadership ought to have power. Only if power is derived from a constitution can such leadership be called authority. The personal aspect is of course not irrelevant in the obedience to parents, the government, or a supervisor, but this obedience depends fundamentally upon the constitution by which authority is established as a delegation from the authority of Christ.

Even if such constituted leadership is not effective due to a serious lack of personal power or wisdom, e.g., in a factory, other, and in that case informal leadership will emerge and take over. Such leadership and, in general, leadership without a constitution, will depend solely upon personal qualities. It has no real authority, although it may be of use.

From the fact that each form of society is so qualified, that it is endowed with its own peculiar nature, (the qualified structure of the social units), it is clearly evident that the organ of authority in one relationship cannot rightly seek to exert itself in a relationship

of another nature. In other words the authority
in one sphere cannot rightly be transferred to
that of another; it cannot rightly regulate the
other sphere. Sphere-sovereignty is inherent
in the created structure of things. And it is
an expression of God's absolute sovereignty over
His creation in Christ. The subordination of
a qualified authority to another of a different
kind, e.g., the subordination of parents to a
consistory, of the direction of an enterprise to
the government, deforms the order of creation.
Moreover, it shifts to human institutions the
responsibility the office bearers owe to God.
The maintenance of sphere-sovereignty concerns
the sovereignty of God over life, the authority
granted to Christ.

This order of creation, moreover, restrains
the influence of sin. The distribution of power
in many independent forms of society prevents
the concentration of power. And it is the
accumulation of power that man is tempted to
abuse. Popes and despots have taught us that
much.

In practical life sphere-sovereignty also
leads to a balance. The various organized units
of society constitute an equilibrium of many
social forces. When one begins to attain preponderance and to endanger the independent existence
of the others, forces are thereby aroused which
tend to restore equilibrium. The process is
(apart from the question of responsibility)
analogous to the way in which disease bacilli
activate forces of resistance in a body.

It should be clear that neigher of these principles is the result of an abstract theory.
They are fruits of Scriptural reflection upon
the formation of society.

The relation between the various societal relationships.

Up until now only the independent existence
of the various societal units or relationships
has been treated. Such forms of society are,
however, also related to each other. Lines of
influence run back and forth, intermingling and
inspiring each other. Well then, such influence
is properly exercised if it conforms to the nature
of the social organization exerting it. The church
ought to remind the state, parents, and all other
persons in authority, together with those owing
allegiance, of what the Word of God demands from
them. The products of an enterprise and their
economic value exert an influence, e.g., upon
circumstances within the family. In virtue of
their special calling with regard to their children, parents have a right to make demands in
school or in the military service. The state
properly takes cognizance of economic life by
providing public legal protection in its commerce
and business enterprises.

There is, however, another influence. Each
authority is responsible for the affairs of its
own sphere. The protection and development of
this sphere affects demands and conditions valid
for other spheres. The state may properly develop
and maintain national conditions favorable to an
equitable commercial life, e.g., the guarantee
of the value of its currency. The state exceeds
its function when it interferes in economic life
by determining individual conditions affecting
credit that properly belong to the individual
decision of the enterprise concerned. The digging
of canals and public power projects, such as
Boulder Dam, concern national conditions affecting
the economic life, but also have a broader reach.
For the digging of canals, and the reclamation
and cultivation of inundated territory, e.g., are
not limited solely to economic life; they enable
life to unfold in all its rich variety of facets
and relationships. Confusion arises on this point,
because in keeping with the time, the content of

the economic sphere is taken in too wide a sense.

Our society is at present so deformed that it is difficult to make our meaning completely clear. An example taken from a sphere that is still somewhat normal may help. Parents have the right and the duty to control and to regulate matters in their family, in order to make possible the free development of their children for their life's vocation. The state has nothing to regulate within a family, between families, or between a family and a business, because this is not in accordance with its meaning. It has its own domain to regulate; it ought to care for the public milieu by maintaining and cultivating public conditions favorable to national life (e.g., work on pavements, sidewalks, and the development of public territory). Consequently, among other things, the state, in keeping with its proper and necessary function, thereby provides the family with a structure in which it can function. The economic spheres for their part accordingly condition the family, e.g. with wages and labor hours.

Moreover, public authorities may be properly concerned with a family, with its relation to other families, and with the relation of family and industry. Their task is not with a family's internal order and affairs, nor with the external relations with other families in general, however, but with the establishment of justice. Even its preoccupation with justice is not universal. Not all injustice is a matter for the state. Only in border situations is it proper for the state to establish justice by interfering in the private lives of its citizens, as individuals and as members of groups; that is, in such instances where injustice and need would otherwise be intolerable (e.g., extensive unemployment, cruelty to a child, insufferable neighborhood rows, etc.).

Summarizing, we can conclude that the family is governed by its parents; and that the government of the nation acts in various border situations of the family. In the first place the government provides the public conditions for family life. Then the government has to act in case of an emergency caused by acts of injustice or by serious distress. The state may act, for example, in severe unemployment threatening a family with dissolution; the state may interfere to protect a family's right to exist, or to protect the rights of its members (e.g., in divorce cases). An emergency may also arise where it may become necessary to protect society against the family, as in the case of infectious disease. And in cases of cruelty the rights of a child may need to be protected by its removal from parental control. It is easy to understand that in some of these examples it is also possible for the government to have a right and a duty to act, viz., if the national well-being is at stake (unemployment, infectious disease, etc.).

The relation between the state and economic life should be conceived of analogously. The state ought not to regulate or direct economic life in such a way that it places its own authority above the authorities proper to the economic sphere. But the state ought to maintain and develop favorable national and local public conditions in which the economic sphere can properly flourish. And in borderline cases of distress, emergency or injustice, the state ought protectively to put matters aright. The government may have to deal with some intolerable distress or injustice concerning private persons or social units, and even at times with some menace to its own sphere.

I have yet to hear an argument, biblical or otherwise, in support of the contention that unlike the coordinate relation between the family and the state, the economic sphere ought to be subordinate to the state. An appeal to a factual situation is no argument for the correctness of the situation; it implies no more than that we must put up with it until we are able to restore the proper relation of coordination.

If a person has a million dollars, in general
that is no business of mine, nor of the government. A man owes responsibility to God for his
stewardship. But when he uses it to perpetrate
an injustice, the government has the right to
step in. And if an emergency arises the government may make a coercive appeal to such a person
for assistance. If the government wants to go
any further, e.g., arbitrary appropriations, an
ideal society is not thereby obtained; man simply
loses his accountability to God and total power
is granted to the state.

Our exposition and the example cited here do
not pretend to provide exhaustive instruction
for general application. Such instruction cannot
be drawn up. Every problem concerning the inter-
relations between social groups is new. It
requires continual reflection upon and interpretation of the peculiar nature of the social relationships involved.

And even if such reflection is successful, the
question is still not solved. For example, even
if we know what the authorities may rightly
do and what they ought to forego, the question
still persists, whether under the given circumstances the government ought here to exercise
its right to interfere in the life of another
sphere. There is always a spectrum of emergen-
cies. And likewise, it holds that even if we
understand the significance of authority and
freedom in social relationships, it must still
be determined in each separate instance where the
balance ought to lie.

Man is continually placed before such practical decisions, connected not only with particular circumstances, but also with the historical
moment. After weighing all the factors, a compromise conclusion must be reached. Such is life,
and luckily so; it would be of small interest if
every solution to life's problems were written in

a field manual.

Well-meaning practical people are, therefore, often inclined to trust their common sense exclusively. They uproot the guideposts of principles and rely on their keen nose. The risk of a keen nose, however, is that it can with equal ease adapt itself to a perfumery or to a cowbarn. Without the anchorage provided by principles we drift along with the stream of social events. But, someone will say, what is the use of a principle such as sphere-sovereignty? It may teach in a general way the nature of the state and of some other organized social units, but in a borderline situation, where decisions are made, the clarity of our distinctions grows vague. Let us answer with an example.

In a spectrum various tints lie between red and orange, concerning which it is impossible to say if they are one or the other. Such obscurity might lead us to the faulty denial of the existence of red and orange. But the little that can be said about such a borderline situation can be said only because of the distinction between red and orange.

The degeneration of society

A respect for the sovereignty of God over His creation is expressed - insofar as the forms of a community are concerned, and especially the lasting forms - in the principles of a proper balance between authority and freedom, and sphere-sovereignty. Such principles constitute the pattern within which man can attain his divinely ordained destiny in the different areas of life. The redeeming and re-creating work of Christ signifies for society its liberation through the realization of the principle of sphere-sovereignty and of the principle of authority and liberty. It is in this way that Christ wants to be its Sovereign.

On this earth it has pleased God that people living
in the faith in His Son should actualize that
society. When the tension of faith slackens, and
spheres of life are withdrawn from the direction
of that faith when unbelief gets the upper hand,
that actualization will wholly or partially cease.
The unfolding of society is then not only inter-
rupted, but it is deflected toward deformation.
The equilibrium guaranteed by the above mentioned
principles is then disturbed.

There the balance between authority and liberty
is disturbed and when authority loses power, the
danger of confusion and revolution arises. When
authority acquires power at the expense of liberty,
the danger of oppression and tyranny threatens.
Such situations are encountered in all relations
of life, in the state, in the family, in schools,
and in factories. It often happens, however,
that a situation of confusion and revolution is
abrogated by swinging to the other extreme of
tyranny.

The equilibrium of forces corresponding to
sphere-sovereignty is also frequently disturbed.
Society then generally threatens to become
collective or even totalitarian because of the
preponderance of one of the societal relationships. And when a sphere loses its independence
its internal cohesion is also lost. It then
begins to disintegrate.

Such disturbances of the balance between the
spheres may be occasioned through a particular
sphere's abuse of power or by the loss of spiritual intensity on the part of various spheres.
As to the balance of authority and freedom within the spheres, it may be caused by a concentration of power due to over anxious bearers of
authority or by a shirking of responsibility on
the part of individual members or citizens. Very
often more than one factor is present.

In my opinion many do not sufficiently discern

the principles in question and thus do not even
notice if they are no longer in practice. There
also exists the inclination to relate problems
to the principle of authority and freedom, and
to forget sphere-sovereignty. This is simply a
cause of confusion; the importance of developments deserving attention is overlooked. Our
present social order is primarily engaged in
rendering relative the independence of the various
forms of society. It is replacing coordination
by subordination. This hierarchical collectivization, beginning with economic life, is leading
to an all-embracing union through the state or
even through a supernational organization. For
the present it is especially concerned with economic tendency that accompanies the disturbance
of equilibrium between authority and freedom.

Much more can be said. A communal ideology
is everywhere rampant. If, because of the community formation by the state the church should
try to engage in the socialistic formation of
society by providing a superstructure, so that
a spiritual socialism may thus come about, it
would also wander from the way. Reference to
the Middle Ages, which knew such an all-embracing
community, will not avail; what stood then at
the beginning of the liberation of life now
signifies a hindrance to such a liberation, and
is a mere reaction.

Between medieval times and our own lies the Reformation, followed by the secularization of Western
civilization; the latter has thrown the above
named liberation out of joint. A hierarchical
integration of the community under the guidance
of the church will not help matters; on the contrary it can only remove the conditions of restoration. Under the present curcumstances it can
result only in a secularized spiritual bond.

One more observation. Collectivization is
always accompanied by the formation of an elite
group. Two classes of people arise: the thought-

ful, provident, and responsible elite, and the
looked-after and dependent masses. The position
of the masses is an obstacle to any return to
Christianization.

The appearance of the elite and of the masses
is always a proof that the independence of the
various associations of society has been lost,
and the balance of authority and liberty disturbed. In a collectivized society there are
two kinds of people. The one constitutes the
elite and provides the leadership. Such are the
organizers of today. In a Christian society the
authority granted and sustained by Christ is
all important; the person of the office-bearer
is rather irrelevant. Sphere-sovereignty may
also be viewed in this way. An engineer prescribes with authority to the man who mounts
the machinery in a factory; but as the elder
of a church, the latter may that very evening
authoritatively admonish the engineer about his
religious life. Likewise a minister may be
admonished by a member of his congregation pre-
siding at a political meeting. Christian thinking refuses to recogaize an elite; it views the
actual appearance of such as the derailment of
the social processes.

As far as the actual situation is concerned,
we live in a time in which the principles discussed are out of joint. Characteristic of our
day is the shifting of the responsibility of
freedom toward central control and the wrecking
of the independence of the social relationships.
The considerations of the following chapters
will revolve around these problems.

The causes of this anti-normative development in society are at present to be sought in
a perverse view of the function of authority.
Some bearers of authority would make it absolute,
others, on the contrary, would make it merely
relative. An equal perversity is present in
the current insight into the destiny of man and

into the function of the organized units of society. In consequence man abandons his divine cultural mandate and his own freedom; he discards the freedom of relationships in which he works and lives. And we should bear in mind that every freedom results from the fact that man owes his deepest responsibility to God. (I have in mind the mass-formation, the disintegration of families, and similar issues).

No authority is safe unless it recognizes, is rooted in, and is limited by the sovereignty of Christ. No freedom can flourish and be preserved except upon the foundation of the work of redemption of Christ (Gal. 5:1).

Of special interest in connection with the degeneration of society is the fact that the development of science and technique has already done much to bind humanity. It still can do much more. But already a few people in authority have an enormous concentration of power.

An observation

The relation between societal relationships of the same kind has not entered into the discussion. Insofar as these relations are regulated, varying situations are encountered, e.g., the autonomy of municipalities within the state, the agreement between churches in their synods, and the contracts and trusts of enterprise. Socioeconomic organs for coordination in course of development also acquire a regulating position in respect to enterprises. This relation may best be compared to that between churches and their synod. We may also think of the federative movement in Europe.

Except in the first instance, we may not speak of an over-arching societal unit nor likewise of the ordinary relations of authority and freedom. We must speak rather of a binding agreement entered into by parties of equal standing.

The main feature in all such instances, the
meaning of such agreements, regulations, and the
like, and of the super-organizations, ought to
be that the freedom of the societal relationships
involved, in view of the development of their
activity, is served by these agreements.

THE ANABAPTIST ALTERNATIVE

By Arthur Gish

The movement began with intellectuals who were trained in the humanist tradition of Erasmus, and who had worked closely with Zwingli's reformation attempt. Probably most important was the humanist emphasis on biblical studies. The most obvious factor was that they began to take the Christian tradition seriously and soon saw that the Catholic Church and the Reformation were not meeting the standards of biblical faith. They were not anti-Christian, but they thought the established church was. They were convinced that the Christian message was relevant, and that it should be lived rather than compromised for political expediency. They believed what their Bible study had forced them to conclude, and thus began to put their faith into action.

They were people who had tried to bring reforms, but their suggestions were rejected. They sought public discussions (disputations) whenever possible; but their reforms would have meant disestablishment, as will be noted below. They soon learned that meaningful change was not possible within the system. Soon they, like the New Left, were forced to take the sectarian route of working outside the establishment.

There has been much debate regarding what was the central concern of the Anabaptists. Littell sees it as the attempt to reinstitute the "True Chruch," patterned after the life style of the early church. The restitution of New Testament Christianity then would be the center of the movement. Harold S. Bender, the Mennonite historian, sees the central thrust as discipleship and obedience to Christ, which results in a church that is a brotherhood and in an ethic of love and nonresistance. Bender is more accurate, for it seems that the attempt to recover primitive

99

Christianity is actually a result of discipleship. While orthodoxy implied that the Bible
is ambiguous, the Anabaptists taught that it
is clear in regard to both the content of Christian faith and the demands on a Christian community. They believed the biblical vision to be
worth living, and they proceeded to live it.

The Anabaptist Analysis of Society

As has been noted above, the Anabaptists were
disturbed by the condition of the church. They
accepted the view that the church had "fallen"
and was no longer the true church described in
the New Testament. The basis for Littell's
argument, that restitution was at the center of
Anabaptist thought, is that they saw the church
as fallen. They adapted the fall of man to the
history of the church. Most Anabaptists dated
the fall of the church with the reign of Constan-
tine (313-337), although some would put the date
earlier. The important issue here is the union
of church and state and the end of the church as
a voluntary association of believers. It was
the transformation of Christianity from a personal
faith and a movement into an obligatory state
religion. They were protesting the transformation of religion into an establishment serving
the ends of the state.

The Anabaptists had a clear doctrine of the
state. There was little doubt among most of
them that the state (Obrigkeit) is ordained by
God. The task of the state was considered to
be closely connected with its origin. It had
existed from the beginning of creation with God
as the ruler. After the fall of man, however,
this office was given to man. The state, then,
must be understood in light of man's sin. God
gave man the state because of his sin. Riedemann,
an early Hutterite, puts this quite strongly.

It is therefore obvious that the state
is not given out of grace, but out of

100

punishment and wrath. And this is due
to the alienation of the people when
they forsook God and followed the flesh.
Therefore they must be ruled by the
flesh.

Most Anabaptists, however, did not feel quite
this negative about the authorities. Most would
say the state was given as an act of grace, for
the giving of the state was seen as God's desire
not to allow man to go to the last consequence
of his sin. As one Anabaptist put it, "Where
there was no state, it would be impossible to
live." Thus government is for man's protection,
for the preservation of order. Its purpose was
seen to be to protect the innocent and weak from
evildoers, to maintain peace and order. In the
Zofingen disputation· of 1532, the spokesman for
the Swiss Brethren stated:

We grant that in the non-Christian world
state authorities have a legitimate place,
to keep order, to punish the evil, and
to protect the good. But we as Christians
live according to the Gospel and our only
authority and Lord is Jesus Christ.

They made no theological distinction between
a just and unjust government, for their relation
to the state was independent from the moral
nature of the government. The government itself was not the judge of their relation to it.
They maintained that a godless government is
just as ordained of God as is a "good" government, but that a good government also stands
outside the "fullness of Christ."

However, for the Anabaptists, the authority
of the state was limited. They were agreed that
the state had no authority in matters of faith.
It could have nothing to do with the inner man.
At this point there was a sharp disagreement
between them and the mainline reformers. During
Sattler's trial he referred to the judges as
the servants of God. Thus he recognized their
authority, but at the same time maintained that

they had no authority over religious matters.
We see here a very firm basis for their position
of separation of church and state, a very radical
position for that day, and a view they never gave
up. As late as 1589, they declared in the Zurich
City Council: "The state authorities have no
place in the Church of God, no right to control
and persecute the conscience." We see then
that the state was recognized as having authority
in an evil world, but that the authority for
the Anabaptists was not the state, but Christ.
As will be noted below, the Anabaptists felt no
responsibility for the state.

The Anabaptist doctrine of the state rests on
a two-kingdom dualism which makes a sharp distinction between the kingdom of Christ and the
kingdom of this world. To understand it better,
let us first look at Luther's two kingdoms. This
view acknowledges both Christ's rule and the
kingdom of this world, but maintains that the
two cannot be distinguished. Luther's two kingdoms are really one. They are "two different
modes of divine rule." Of those who accept
Christ's rule, Luther states:

> These need neither worldly sword nor law.
> And if all the world were made up of true
> Christians, there would be no need for
> ruler, king, lord, sword or law - for
> the Holy Spirit which they have in their
> hearts teaches them and brings it about
> that they wrong no one, but love all
> and suffer evil voluntarily and cheer-
> fully from anyone. Therefore it is
> impossible that worldly sword and law
> would have anything to do among Chris-
> tians.

With this statement, any Anabaptist could agree.
The big difference between the two comes when
Luther states that God rules over both kingdoms
with different standards. The Christian for
Luther has dual citizenship and thus must live
by two sets of standards. The Christian must

live in both realms.

The Anabaptists, however, separate the two
realms. For them, Christ brought in a new kingdom and a new life for those who follow him.
Those who wish to follow him cannot be in both
kingdoms at the same time. This is an important
distinction between Luther and the Anabaptists.
This is expressed in the covenantal theology of
Pilgram Marpeck, who drew a sharp distinction
between the Old Covenant and the New. The
Christian is called to live in the New Covenant,
not the Old. Therefore he cannot live by the
standards of the Old, or of the world that
still lives in the Old. The Anabaptist view
of the two kingdoms and their sharp separation
applies not only to one's relationship to the
state, but to all relationships. Christian
discipleship involves all of life. The whole
Christian life must be lived under the New
Covenant, separated from the world. He no
longer lives by the standards of the fallen
world.

The Anabaptist Value System

The Anabaptists, like most sectarian groups,
were seen as troublemakers more interested in
destroying than in building. The reason these
groups appear so negative, however, is that
they have values which they consider so important that they must reject the corruption of the
status quo. It was because of radical obedience
to Christ and their vision of the kingdom of God
that the Anabaptists were forced to reject the
dominant values of the sixteenth century. As
was noted above, they saw the need for people
to live now as if the kingdom of God were already
here. This was at the heart of their value
system.

The Anabaptists were more interested in living
a Christian life than in speculating about it.
As Littell has noted,

...In contrast to many groups in history
and in contemporary Christianity the Anabaptists actually meant what they said.
The separation between verbalization and
action which has been so marked in contemporary church groups can mislead us
in our approach to the Anabaptist movement:
the Anabaptists meant just what they said,
and their teaching is unimportant apart
from the direct attempt to give it embodi-
ment in actual groups living in history.

They saw grace and salvation not as theoretical
doctrines, but as something known from personal
experience. They were uninterested in theological speculation. As Marpeck stated,

> We recognize as true Christian faith only
> such a faith through which the Holy Spirit
> and the love of God came into the heart,
> and which is active, powerful, and oper-
> ative in all outward obedience and com-
> manded works.

This is seen in their rejection of sacramentalism
(the belief that grace is objectively present
in the bread and cup) and other practices. Thus
the bread and cup were seen as a "remembrance"
of Christ. For the same reason they denied the
validity of the Mass and the special office of
the clergy. Thus the important word for them
was not faith as with Luther, but discipleship
(Nachfolge Christi). While Luther stood in
the Augustinian tradition which emphasized man's
being totally lost in sin, the Anabaptists began
with conversion and the new life of the Christian. Rather than focusing on personal salvation,
they stressed living in the new kingdom, living
by a new set of values (love, peace, forgiveness,
etc.). Hans Denck, a South German Anabaptist,
stated that "No one can truly know Christ, except
he follow Him in life." This meant commitment
of one's whole life to Christ.

The Anabaptists had an emphasis on moral

purity, as seen in their stress on integrity, noncompromise, and the simple life. The integrity of the Christian life was very important for them. They strongly opposed the forms of religion that did not come from the heart. Menno Simons, the leader of the Anabaptists in Northern Germany and the Netherlands after 1536, illustrates this concern.

> The regenerate, therefore, lead a penitent and new life, for they are renewed in Christ and have received a new heart and Spirit...And they live no longer after the old corrupted nature of the first earthly Adam, but after the new upright nature of the new and heavenly Adam; Christ Jesus... Hatred and vengeance they do not know. Avarice, pride, unchastity, and pomp they hate and oppose...They seek righteousness with all their might...In short they are fruit-bearing branches of the true vine.

This life style was affirmed even by their enemies. Franz Agricola, a Roman Catholic theologian, wrote in 1582:

> Among the existing heretical sects there is none which in appearance leads a more modest or pious life than the Anabaptists. As concerns their outward public life they are irreproachable. No lying, deception, swearing, strife, harsh language, no intemperate eating and drinking, no outward personal display, is found among them, but humility, patience, uprightness, neatness, honesty, temperance, straightforwardness in such measure that one would suppose that they had the Holy Spirit of God.

While Luther said that since we live in a sinful world we must compromise with it, the Anabaptists rejected compromise. They felt called to live by the standards of the kingdom, not the standards of this world. Bender describes this view of the Christian life.

Since for him no compromise dare be made
with evil, the Christian may in no circum-
stance participate in any conduct in the
existing social order which is contrary
to the spirit and teaching of Christ and
the apostolic practice. He must consequently withdraw from the worldly system
and create a Christian social order within
the fellowship of the church brotherhood.

The simple life was also stressed. They
urged people to avoid anything that would lead
to pride, and opposed living on a high economic
plane. This was because the New Testament
criticized wealth, and because wealth destroys
community when one has more than another.
Kessler, a contemporary Reformation leader and
chronicler of the Swiss Reformation, wrote:

Their conversation and bearing shine forth
as entirely pious, holy and unpunishable.
They avoid ostentatious clothes, despise
delicate food and drink, clothe themselves
with coarse cloth, decking their heads
with broad felt hats, their way and conversation quite humble.

They urged their people to refuse to participate
in the commercial and financial institutions and
were highly critical of the developing capitalism
of that time. In criticism of usury, Menno
wrote: "The whole world is so contaminated and
involved with the accursed...finance, usury, and
self interest that I scarcely know how it could
be worse." He listed among those who "live
openly in sin...all financiers and bankers, all
who love money." Ridemann puts it even more
strongly.

This only we regard as wrong: when one
buyeth a ware and selleth and same again
even as he bought it, taking to himself
profit, making the ware dearer thereby for
the poor, taking bread from their very
mouths, and thus making the poor man

nothing but the bondman of the rich...
They (the traders) say, however, "But the
poor also profit in that one bringeth
goods from one hand to another!" There
they use poverty as a pretext, seeking
all the time their own profit first, and
thinking only of the poor as having an
occasional penny in their purse.

Freedom was especially important for the Anabaptists, since they struggled so hard and
suffered so much for their religious beliefs.
Their concept of freedom must be seen from
several perspectives. First was their call
for separation of church and state, which meant
that everyone should have the right to a free,
private interpretation of faith within a pluralistic society. No government should have any
authority in matters of faith. This was their
alternative to the medieval structure. It has
been suggested that the Anabaptists were the
first to proclaim religious liberty in the way
we think of it now. Hans Denck, a South German Anabaptist, illustrates this view of religious
freedom.

Such a security will exist, also in outward
things, with practice of the true Gospel
that each will let the other move and dwell
in peace - be he Turk or heathen believing
what he will - through and in his land,
not submitting to a magistrate (in matters
of faith). Is there anything more to be
desired? I stand fast on what the prophet
says here. Everyone among all peoples may
move around in the name of his God. That
is to say, no one shall deprive another -
whether heathen or Jew or Christian, but
rather allow everyone to move in all territories in the name of his God. So may we
benefit in the peace which God gives.

Secondly, freedom meant that the church must
be a voluntary association of believers. Whoever
did join the group was to do so by his own free

choice. Thus they had to reject infant baptism,
for if Christian faith is to be voluntary, then
so must be baptism. The most radical act of
the Anabaptists was baptism. Even though adult
baptism was punishable by death, they continued
to baptize any who would take that step. This
was a direct defiance of the system and soon
become the symbol of the movement. This was the
act that struck to the core of the authoritarian
Corpus Christianum. It was similar to the burning
of a draft card today or the early church's
refusal to put a pinch of incense on the fire
as a symbol of support for Caesar. Baptism soon
became the real issue dividing the establishment
men from those seeking a voluntary, believers'
church. For Zwingli the main issue was no
longer theological, but political. He wrote:
"The issue is not baptism, but revolt, faction,
heresy."

For this reason, Baul Peachey can state:

> The Reformers therefore fought the Anabap-
> tists, not because they considered them an
> immediate revolutionary threat, nor yet
> because they misunderstood their position,
> but because the "totalitarian" social
> order in which they stood and for which
> they had decided, simply could not tolerate
> in its midst an autonomous, voluntary,
> noninclusive social grouping.

We see then that the Anabaptists became early
proclaimers of the disestablishment of the church.
With the exception of the Hutterite colonies they
did not equate the church with the political
community. Here we see the beginning of a new
era of freedom.

Freedom was based on a profound understanding
of community. This meant rejection of the individualism of the Spiritualists, who rejected any
church, and of the totalitarianism of the established churches. The Anabaptist vision can never
be lived out individually, but must be lived within

the context of a group. Friedmann, an Anabaptist scholar, sees this as most important.

Now then, the central idea of Anabaptism, the real dynamite in the age of Reformation, as I see it, was this, that one cannot find salvation without caring for his brother, that this "brother" actually matters in the personal life...This interdependence of men gives life and salvation a new meaning. It is not "faith alone" which matters...but it is brotherhood, this intimate caring for each other, as it was commanded to the disciples of Christ as the way to God's kingdom.

Discipleship includes one's brother. Thus they saw the essence of the church to be found within a community of believers. Zschabitz sees the important fact of Anabaptism in its coming together in communities outside of the established church.

Even though they rejected an elaborate system of church government, they did recognize the need for some type of organization and leadership. Because of their acceptance of the priesthood of all believers, they needed no hierarchical structure. Since the missionary mandate applied to every Christian, the distinction between laity and clergy almost disappeared. Littell rightly points out that theologically they were not self-governing, but insofar as they developed free discussion for decision making and rejected external political and ecclesiastical pressures, they developed a democratic form of government.

The social scientist may be justified in considering this one of the first manifestations of government by consensus. The church historian finds it one of the first patterns of lay government in Christian history, a historical moment when the professional monopoly of theologians and canon lawyers was broken in favor of the priesthood of all believers.

One could call it the beginning of participatory democracy.

Love was very much at the center of the community. There was a genuine caring for the neighbor. As Burkholder, a Mennonite scholar, describes it, "Love was not a mere turning of the cheek from time to time, but the creation of a continuous network of relationships in which love was intrinsic." However, this was not seen as an easy-going sentimentalism. It also involved discipline: what they called the ban. They rejected any other use of compulsion, for they recognized that faith cannot be forced. As Claus Felbinger, a Hutterite, stated in his confession, "God wants no compulsory service. On the contrary, He loves a free, willing heart that serves him with a joyful soul and does what is right joyfully." But since they saw the church as composed of committed Christians, those who strayed from the faith had to be dealt with. For this they used only the threat of loss of privileges within the fellowship and sometimes social ostracism. The Schleitheim Confession recommends the use of the ban, but only after there have been two private confrontations with the offender and one public hearing. Here we see a practice that maintained a disciplined community, and a form of confrontation that had great therapeutic potential for all involved. Peachey sees Anabaptism as "a synthesis between Christian freedom and discipline rare in history."

Free discussion was important for the Anabaptists. Since the Bible was their rule of faith rather than creeds, they depended upon each other for instruction. They were always eager to discuss theological issues with their opponents. This attitude of openness to truth is portrayed by Hubmaier, an early Anabaptist leader.

I can err, for I am a man, but I cannot
be a heretic, for I am willing to be
taught better by anybody. And if anyone
will teach me better, I acknowledge that
I shall owe him great thanks.

This attitude is very much at the heart of their
desire to live with others in freedom and is a
sound basis for democracy. It should be remembered, however, that their concept of religious
liberty was based not on abstract theories of
freedom, but on their doctrine of the voluntary
church with only Christ as Lord and Master.
Staughton Lynd has noted this Anabaptist view
of freedom.

Few groups have been more devoted to personal freedom than the sixteenth-century
Anabaptists, who "when asked their trade
and location and station in life in court
actions...replied, 'No master!' (kein
Vorsteer), for in the New Age only Christ
was Master."

Their sense of community also had implications for their economic life. This has been
noted above in the discussion of the simple
life and their rejection of wealth and capitalism. Zschabitz is right in describing them as
rejecting selfish, capitalistic motives.[40] They
were early socialists. Each member of the community was considered equal and was expected
to share what he had. Spittelmaier's "Seven
Decrees of Scripture" illustrates their view of
economics.

Nobody can inherit the kingdom unless he
is here poor with Christ, for a Christian
has nothing of his own: no place where he
can lay his head. A real Christian should
not even have enough property on earth to
be able to stand on it with one foot. This
does not mean that he should go and lie
down in the woods and not have a trade or
that he should not work, but only that he

might not think they are for his own use,
and be tempted to say: This house is
mine, this field is mine, this money is
mine, but rather ours, even as we pray:
Our Father. In brief, a Christian should
not have anything of his own, but should
have all things in common with his brother,
not allow him to suffer need. In other
words, I do not work that my house may be
filled, that my larder be supplied with
meat, but rather I see to it that my
brother has enough, for a Christian looks
more to his brother than to himself.
(I Cor. ch. 13).

There was no agreement, however, how this ideal
should be lived out. For the Hutterites, it
meant a structured form of a community of goods
with no private property. For most of the other
groups it took a voluntaristic form, with a
clear teaching of sharing with anyone who was
in need. They were all agreed, however, that no
Christian should consider his property his own
and that he should always respond to the need
of his brother as if it were his own need.

Important also is their view of man, which
contrasts sharply with the mainline reformers.
Over against the predestination of Luther and
Calvin, the Anabaptists affirmed man's free will
and responsibility. They still considered man
a sinner, but rejected the view that man is
totally depraved, for there can be no discipleship without man's ability to respond. They
had an especially deep sense of responsibility
to both God and to their fellow man. This is
also reflected in their view of salvation, which
is seen not as some spiritual effect on man, but
a renewal of all of life, for discipleship includes every area of life. It affects both the
personal and social dimensions of life. This
assumes that through the grace of God man is able
to be faithful and to live in the light of the
kingdom. In fact, he is commanded to do so.

We must also briefly look at their view of
history. In this respect, they were also not
pessimistic, but lived in hope. They expected
the kingdom to come on earth. This did not
mean that they could bring it in themselves,
but that they lived with the hope that is was
about to come. This is especially important
for understanding their whole ethical position.
They desired to live by the standards of the
kingdom, for they saw the end of history not in
the powers of this world, but in the kingdom
which was to come.

Strategy for Social Change

One of the significant differences between
the Anabaptists and the leaders of the Reformation was the unwillingness of the Anabaptists to
work through the magistrates to achieve their
goals of reforming the church. This was the
point of division between them and Zwingli.
Zwingli took a compromising approach, trying
gradually to bring his reforms through the
establishment. This does not mean, however, that
they were narrow-minded separatists. They had
tried to work through the structure and bring
the established church to change, but soon
realized that this was not possible. They then
withdrew from the church, but continued to relate
to it and call for its reformation. Important
for the Anabaptists was the conviction that the
Christian must be different from the non-Christian. The Hutterite Article Book of 1577 states:

> There is a great difference between Christ
> and the world, like that between heaven
> and earth. World is world and remains
> always world. The Christian, however, is
> called away from this world and is called
> never to conform to this world. Whoever
> is a friend of this world and is liked
> by her is no servant of Christ who is ever
> being contradicted on all sides...

We must now consider what this separation
from the world meant for their relation to the

establishment. Since they accepted the authorities as ordained by God, they believed in obedience to the government. Since they did not distinguish between a good or bad government, their obedience was independent of the morality of the government. Hans Hillerbrand points out:

Obedience to the established authorities is an expression of thankfulness to God, who through the appointment of the office of the authority declared his kindness... Disobedience to the authorities is therefore not only disobedience, but above all also thankfulness to God.

This obedience, however, related only to those functions of government that they considered legitimate for the state. Sattler, during his trial, tried to show that he was a loyal citizen, that he had not defied the authorities in anything that was under their jurisdiction. But they were very clear what that jurisdiction did not include. They first acknowledged the primacy of God's claims over the claims of the authorities. They considered it more important to obey God than men. Thus they were ready to disobey any ruling that conflicted with their beliefs. Claus Felbinger stated in his confession,

Therefore we are gladly and willingly subject to the government for the Lord's sake, and in all just matters we will in no way oppose it. When, however, the government requires of us what is contrary to our faith and conscience - as swearing oaths and paying hangman's dues or taxes for war - then we do not obey its command.

The Anabaptists were also opposed to a Christian holding public office, although there were various shades of opinion on this. Erland Waltner, a Mennonite, maintains that Menno Simons was not as strict as were the Swiss Brethren in separating the Christian from the state. He states that while the Swiss Brethren saw the state only as a punitive institution, Menno believed if the state is administered rightly, it can be an aid to the kingdom of God. The main reason for excluding the Christian from public office was because the ethos of the state conflicted with redemptive love. The Handbuchlein of 1558, the Anabaptist answer to Melanchthon, states that no Christian can take up an office which involves vengeance and killing. The Anabaptists saw the use of force and revenge as inherent in the role of government. Hillerbrand quotes the Alteste Chronik der Hutterischen Bruder in answer to the question whether the state can be Christian.

If it would deny itself, give up every-thing, take the cross upon itself, rid itself of violence and pomp, and follow Christ, then it could be Christian.

Hillerbrand writes that stated negatively this means: "The state must resist evil and use the sword for punishment. If it does not do that, then it ceases to be the state." The Schleit-heim Confession also opposes participation in government.

Finally it will be observed that it is not appropriate for a Christian to serve as a magistrate because of these points: The government magistracy is according to the flesh, but the Christians' is according to the Spirit; their citizen-ship is in this world, but the Christians' citizenship is in heaven...

Thus because they were convinced that the state cannot be Christian, they believed that the Christian should not take part in it. First of all the Christian must be obedient to Christ.

Another aspect of noncooperation with the authorities was their refusal to take an oath. Three main reasons were given. First, it is unnecessary because the Christian is always ob-ligated to tell the truth; second, it was for-

bidden by Christ; and third, it is impossible
because man does not know if he can keep it since
he does not control the future.   The Schleit-
heim Confession stated the same position.
Another reason may have been the political implications of the oath.   In Strasbourg every year
the citizens were required to assemble and take
the oath of allegiance to the city constitution.
It is clear why the Anabaptists refused to follow
this directive.

Their position on paying taxes is unclear,
since there was disagreement.   Some claimed that
the authorities have scriptural authority to
exact taxes and that the Christian is not responsible for how they are spent.   In the
Handbuchlein of 1558, it is stated that they
would pay toll and taxes, but not taxes for war,
executions or other injustices.   Claus Felbinger
in his confession rejects paying hangman's dues
or taxes for war, as quoted above.   At least we
can say that there were those who were selective
in what taxes they would agree to pay.

Were the Anabaptists basically anarchists?
If everyone were Christian, would there still be
a need for government?   Felix Mantz is supposed
to have said that there should be no government.   It could be that they would have seen
Christ as the only authority necessary.   Certainly there is an element of anarchism.   The question
must remain open, however.

We see then that the Anabaptists rejected the
notion of bringing change from the top down.   They
agreed neither with the notion of the state controlling or bringing change into the church, nor
with the idea of the church dominating the state.
Rather, change must start with communities of
believers who live changed lives.   Friedmann notes
that,

> To the Anabaptists "salvation" (or rather
> redemption) means the newly-acquired
> strength to walk the narrow path and to

know oneself as a part of the divine drama
which will eventually lead to the kingdom
of God on earth. It means also the awareness of being a fighter in the incessant
warfare between the powers of light and of
darkness.

Change comes when people begin to live in the
kingdom, and are obedient to Christ. But they
went one step farther and said that we can bring
in the kingdom neither through institutional
forces nor through our own efforts. We must
simply begin living in the kingdom. It cannot
be forced. For this reason the Anabaptists were
dropouts from society, choosing to separate
themselves and create their own parallel structures, their own obedient communities where they
could live in the kingdom. The real agents of
social change were seen as those who accepted
the Lordship of Christ and were obedient to him.
The community did not live by force, but believed that those who were faithful would be
victorious.

Possibly the best-known characteristic of
the Anabaptists was their emphasis on nonresistance. They did not believe in the use of force
or participation in war. According to Bullinger, the Anabaptists believed that "war is the
worst evil that one can conceive." This concept
of nonresistance must be seen as coming from
their doctrine of the cross, which means a willingness to suffer in the face of evil. Bullinger
states:

They believe that Christians should stand
ready to suffer (rather than strike back)..
.Christians do not resist violence and do
not take recourse to law...They do not defend
themselves, therefore they do not go to war
and are not obedient to the government on
this point.

This position should not be confused with modern
pacifism, nor was it basically political. As

Littell rightly points out,

> For them, pacifism was narrowed to the
> testimony of the nonresistant martyrs;
> the atmosphere was eschatological rather
> than utopian, the pattern of behavior one
> of discipleship rather than social strate-
> gy.

It had its political implications, however.
According to Zurich court records, Andreas
Castelberger was

> ...saying much about war; how the divine
> teaching is so strong against it and how
> it is sin. And he expressed the idea
> that the soldier who had plenty at home
> in his fatherly inheritance and goods and
> yet went to war, and received money and
> pay to kill innocent persons and to take
> their possessions from people who had never
> done him any harm, such a soldier was
> before Almighty God, and according to the
> content of Gospel teaching, a murderer and
> not better than one who would murder and
> steal on account of his poverty, regardless
> of the fact that this might not be so
> according to human laws, and might not be
> counted so bad.

A few did advocate the defensive use of the sword,
including Hubmaier, but these were a small minority. In spite of severe persecution, the Anabaptists were able to maintain this nonviolent
witness. Clemens Adler in a manuscript of 1529
sums up their position.

> (They) also have peace with everyone, harm
> no one in any respect, neigher in body nor
> in goods, but endure at the hands of all
> men all kinds of injustice which may be
> done to them; yea, for the love of Christ
> they love their enemies, do good to them
> and pray for them, as Christ teaches them,
> and thus hearken to the voice of their

shepherd. Even if the world rises up
against them, rages and storms against
them, yet they rage and.storm against
none; and if the world lifts up its
sword against them, yet they take no
sword against it nor against anyone...

Evaluation and Comparison

Because of intensive persecution, the Anabaptists were not able to make the contribution
to society that the free churches in England
and America could make. We do not know what the
effects would have been had Anabaptism been
left free to develop and spread. However, in
spite of this, Anabaptism has had and is having
its impact. The heritage is being kept alive in
the Mennonite churches and the Church of the
Brethren. But its influence is much broader
than this. Bender claims that

There can be no question but that the
great principles of freedom of conscience,
separation of church and state, and volun-
tarism in religion, so basic in American
Protestantism, and so essential to democracy, ultimately are derived from the
Anabaptists of the Reformation period...

Staughton Lynd believes the "vision of a coven-
anted community" had an influence on the Declaration of Independence and the American tradition.
Williams writes that

...in looking both to the apostolic past
and the apocalyptic future, the Radical
Reformation induced currents in history
and the interpretation thereof...ranging
from explicitly Christian theologies of
history, through democratic progressivism,
to Marxism.

Littell points out that

...it has been customary even for many

119

latter-day friends of the movement to
assume that the Anabaptists contributed
nothing to social and political thought
as such. I long thought that study of
the contribution of the free churches to
democratic development as such must be
postponed until the Commonwealth Period
in England. However, the implications
for a constitutional and just government
are also there and some of the direct
teaching as well.

There is also evidence to suggest that the Anabaptists had an impact on the English Puritan
Left. More research needs to be done to study
the true impact of Anabaptism on our modern
world and radical movements in particular. In
the meantime, it can be affirmed that the Anabaptists have made a significant contribution.

III. The Nature of the State

The Bible is full of pictures of persons dealing with the State. Saul is annointed King. Nathan points his finger at King David as a prophet. Pilate asks the mob, "What shall I do with this Jesus, you call the King of the Jews?"

Reading any chapter in the Bible turns up words like this: law, liberty, kingdom, rebellion, slavery; all of which originally found their context on a political horizon. Paul, in fact, used the word redemption in his day because his readers knew that military captives or legal slaves found a new life when their freedom was purchased. The reason for this transfer of vocabulary is obvious. Christianity is a series of relationships between God, man, and other people. Political life is also a series of relationships between the ruler and the ruled. The most important institution of political life - the center of activity - is the State.

Any science of politics must then study life in the organized community. But just what is the state? Is it natural or artificial? Where did it come from? Could man do without it? How much power should it have? Who should rule? These bewildering questions have been the concern of political thinkers, including Christians, from the earliest days. Down through the centuries, man has wrestled with these same questions over and over again: they are, in other words, perennial.

What have Christians added to this time-honored discussion? In "Contemporary Christian Views of the State", Nicholas Wolterstorff asks "what is the nature of the state, and how does it fit into God's ordering of his creation?" Looking at what Catholic, Reformed, Lutheran, and Anabaptist have in common, and how they part company, Wolterstorff is guided by the normative issue of what a "properly-formed state" is. This Christian understanding of the state and its specific tasks is the greatest service Christian citizens can render the state in which they find themselves.

James Skillen's article, "Toward an Understanding of Politics and Government from a Christian Point of View", makes clear why in the twentieth century Christians lack a unified political standpoint. Our predicament is caused not only by a care-less attitude, but also by a tendency to synthesize a uniquely Christian position with one or more non-Christian views. This accomodating spirit has had disastrous effects. So, can a Christian political position be articulated? Skillen tries to do so in a biblically sensitive way--a way which has concrete and practical implications for the situations in which we find ourselves.

Marxists, Liberals, Conservatives, Socialists all have developed theories of the State; all use man and rationality as their guiding star. What would a Christian theory of the State look like? What would shine light on its path? In "The Bible, Justice, and the State", Bernard Zylstra attempts to answer these questions. He argues that the state can be both something good and creationally fruitful when it is normed by the gospel. The state never stands actually outside of the gospel's call to obedience. In other words, the call of the gospel republishes for government and politics the norm or standard by which we must work here and now.

Looking at the relation between the Bible and social concern, Zylstra focuses on four items: Jesus as Reformer, the social concern of Christ's disciples, government as the Lord's servant, and public justice in society. Here we have a sketch which graphically shows what it means to take seriously God's word for all of life, including political life in the State.

CONTEMPORARY CHRISTIAN VIEWS OF THE STATE

By Nicholas Wolterstorff

What is the nature of the State, and how does it fit into God's ordering of His creation?

Once upon a time - until the 1930s to be more exact - one knew what the Catholic, the Reformed, the Lutheran, the Anabaptist, the Anglo-Saxon Evangelical, and the Liberal traditions would each say to those questions. Each of the main Christian traditions had worked out its views on the State and built up its rejoinders to those of the others. Each had marshalled its claims to biblical support and its rebuttals of the claims of the others.

That familiar stalemate has now been upset, that comfortable equilibrium destroyed. Catholics have refused on grounds of conscience to enter military service. Reformed persons have argued that the chief function of the State is to make possible the proclamation of the Gospel. Lutherans have participated in revolutionary assassination attempts. And Anglo-Saxon Evangelicals have publically enlisted support for McGovern for President.

There are many reasons for this shifting of positions and mingling of lines. I wish to call attention to just two.

The Christian community came into the twentieth century with the confident belief that all states are ordained by God for the good of men, and that accordingly we are to obey them out of conscientious support for their repression of evil and encouragement of good. Within the community there were disagreements concerning the limits to one's duty of obedience. But these disagreements had a thoroughly speculative quality about them, since nobody was actually proposing acts of disobedience. Then too, the Anabaptists continued to say that Christians should not actively participate in the functioning of the State. But they were by now saying this very quietly indeed. The only issue still being discussed with vigor was this: What is that good which the State should perform, and what that evil which it should thwart?

Today we are all aware of living in the aftermath of Auschwitz and Viet Nam and the collapse of the Great Society. The political events of our century have profoundly shaken us all. We have all undergone reality therapy. Our sanguine attitude toward the State has been destroyed.

A second fundamental reason for the fluidity of our current situation is that important new biblical studies have forced us to reconsider all the old lines of exegesis. I have in mind here particularly those studies into the New Testament teaching concerning the powers - those elements of reality which, though created by God, continue in demonic fashion to enslave men even though they are on the way to being overcome by Jesus Christ. The teaching of the New Testament concerning angels, principalities, rulers of this present age, powers, etc., once seemed on the edge of New Testament doctrine, harmlessly excisable from the Gospel. Now it seems very near the center, and astoundingly relevant to our twentieth-century experience. Romans 13, which once looked like a simple statement of God's authorization of the State, with its opening reference to "supreme powers," now looks rather different - and much less simple.

The shifting of old familiar positions induced by twentieth-century political experience and by new biblical insights has given us all a feeling of insecurity. Guideposts have disappeared. But we would not be true to our high calling as God's agents in the world if we

dwelt on that feeling. For the shifting of
positions provides us with an opportunity such
as we have not had for centuries - the opportunity to work out a common Christian doctrine
of the State. I do not think it is unrealistic
to hope that the traumas of our century will
provoke us into something near a common position.
My hope is that this paper can make a contribution to that future event, by digging beneath
the surface of our disagreements to the basic
issues that together we must discuss, and by
pointing a way out of the impasses that so long
have plagued us.

I

The basic issue which political events in
our century have posed to Christians is not
which candidates to support, nor which legislative programs to promote. Today the basic
issue is that of the nature of the State itself
and its place in God's order. Because of our
confusions and disagreements on this point we
are in confusion and disagreement about officials and programs. Our experience has made the
nature of the State a deeply existential issue
for all of us. And that, of course, is why this
issue is also at the center of all those theories
of the State which have been worked out by contemporary Christian thinkers.

I must offer a word of explanation as to what
I mean when I speak of the "nature of the State."
I do not mean that complex of features which all
states do as a matter of fact display. Nor do I
mean that complex of features which are essential
to states - those features which something must
possess if it is to be state at all. I mean
rather that complex of features necessary to
something's being a properly-formed state. That
is what contemporary Christian theories of the
State have mainly been about. The question as
to the nature of the State is a normative issue.

When I remarked, above, that political events

in our century have forced us all to reflect on the nature of the State, what I had in mind was that our century has confronted us not only with the passing of bad legislation and the accession to power of bad officials. It has confronted us with states which have themselves become monsters. Our states have become grossly malformed, their structure seriously misshapen. Perhaps the greatest service we Christians can render the states in which we live is reminding them of what a properly-formed state is like.

I dare say that most political theorists would reject with scorn this talk of a properly-formed state. Here I cannot enter into a defense. It must suffice to remark, first, that a delineation of the features necessary to a properly-formed state is indeed what contemporary Christian theories of the State are centrally about. If you and I today reject this concept we shall have to work out entirely new lines of thought from those of our predecessors. Secondly, it is worth remarking that even those theorists most scornful on the concept of a properly-formed state operate with counterpart distinctions throughout their lives. Think, for example, of what the botanical taxonomist tells us about, say, the Shingle Oak (quercus imbricaria). He does not tell us which features all shingle oaks have in common, nor does he tell us which features are necessary to something's being a properly-formed shingle oak. He knows very well that there are malformed shingle oaks, and that his description will not wholly fit those. Similarly, all of us in dealing with our pets distinguish between some undesirable action that the animal performs and some malformation in the animal itself. There is nothing apriori absurd about applying counterpart distinctions to the State by delineating the features necessary to a properly-formed state.

II

I begin with what all Christians would hold

in common.

States are institutions. While God-ordained,
they are actualized by men. They are not, like
rocks and trees, part of the world in which we
are placed by God. Rather, they are brought into
existence by human activity. Further, they
are governmental institutions, comprising a
structure of governing and governed, of authorities and subjects. And they are historical governmental institutions. They are not, like
families, foundational to the whole pattern of
human historical development. Rather, they
arise within the course of human history. They
are elements of human culture, appearing at
certain points in the development of human societies.

To each state belongs a certain territory,
that territory, namely, over whose inhabitants
the state in question has the power of the
sword. That phrase, "the power of the sword,"
is of course a metaphor. What the metaphor
points to is the fact that states are not only
governmental institutions which make demands
over certain people, but that they back up those
demands with coercive power. The State does not
permit its members the choice of resigning from
membership if they do not wish to obey. The subjects of a given state are those people over whom
the state makes demands and over whom it is
effective in backing up those demands with its
coercive power. And the territory which belongs
to a state is then that area over whose inhabitants the state has this power of the sword. In
thus having a certain territory which belongs
to it, a state is strikingly different from the
Church.[2]

What is especially worth noting is that one's
subjection to the State is not a voluntary
matter. Of course one can become a subject
of a different state by moving. Yet we are all
born subjects. This makes the State almost
unique among historical institutions. Further-

more, today it is no longer possible to escape being a subject of some state or other. There are no longer any unclaimed lands. The combination of the fact that one is subject to a certain state just be virtue of dwelling within its territory, with the fact that all states have the power of the sword over their subjects, has always troubled the Christian. What is the place of this non-voluntary coercive institution in God's order? And how should we who are members of Christ's body participate in it?

So much, then, all Christians hold in common.

III

Christian thinkers have also believed that a certain proper function belongs to the nature of the State. But it is here that our disagreements begin. While we all hold that the proper function of the State is set by God, we disagree as to what that function is.

If we dig down to fundamentals, there are, I think, three basic views on this matter which have been defended and articulated by Christian thinkers in the twentieth century. These are also, I believe, the views which are most alive as patterns and options in the Christian community as a whole. Of course most of us probably don't have any clear views on the proper function of the State - either that or we have inconsistent views. But these three are the basic views which both pattern our thought in subtle ways and confront us as options when we try to think clearly and consistently. These are the basic types around which our thinking gravitates.

As background it will be convenient to have before us the medieval and traditional Catholic view of Thomas Aquinas. For all three contemporary views have been carved out in opposition to the main features of that traditional view.

Aquinas repeatedly described man as "a social

and political animal" (D'Entreves anthology, 3).
What he had in mind by that was, first, that
existence in society is necessary if man's
created nature is to find fulfillment. In that
way man is a social creature, "destined more than
other animals to live in community" (3). Secondly, Aquinas argued that no society can exist
unless there is some government within that society - unless, that is, someone has a care for the
common good of the society and the others render
to him obedience. In this way man is by nature
a political creature (5).

Within every body politic there is a whole
fabric of institutions. Aquinas thinks of the
State as part of such a fabric, as one of the
institutions of the body politic. To explain
which part, we must first distinguish between
religious matters and secular matters. In
Aquinas' view the concern of the State is wholly
with secular matters. Religious matters belong
within the competence of the Church. Secondly,
the State is that one, among all the institutions in the body politic dealing with secular
matters, which is topmost. It is the one having
supreme authority. With the possible exception
of the family all the others are, so far as
authority is concerned, subordinate to the State.
The proper function of this topmost part of the
entire institutional fabric is to care for the
secular common good - that is, for the secular
good of the body politic as a whole. It does
this, in part, by ordering those other social
institutions which are properly subordinate to
it.

Viewed from our vantage point in the twentieth
century, the most striking feature of this view
of the State is that it sets so few limits to
the totalitarian tendencies of states. Aquinas
does of course say that the proper function of
the State is limited to secular matters. And
he does say that within the domain of the secular, the proper function of the State is limited
to the common good of the body politic. Yet within

the domain of the secular common good the State
may properly act wherever it deems such action
donducive to the common good. In many circumstances it may well be bad policy for the State
itself to make medical decisions, educational
decisions, economic decisions, etc. But if it
did so, it would not by virtue of so doing be
a malformed state.

A totalitarian state is of course not necessarily an evil state. Its laws may be good
ones, and its administration may be just. Yet
biblical reflection and twentieth-century experience have sufficed to convince contemporary
Christian political thinkers that a state so
near-totalitarian as Aquinas' theory would allow
is inherently malformed. Accordingly, contemporary Christian political theories can all be
viewed as forged in opposition to the extremely
comprehensive scope which the Thomistic theory
assigns to the State's proper function. All have
tried to formulate limits, structurally comparable
to those which Aquinas set with respect to religious matters, to the proper function of the
State. Of course all have gone along with Aquinas
in saying that the proper function of the State
is limited to the common good of the body
politic; that is already an extremely important
limitation. And all have gon along with Aquinas
in ascribing autonomy within its own domain to
the Church. But all have also attempted to go
well beyond this and form a theory in which the
proper function of the State is confined to
some definite domain within the common good.
They have not been content to say that the
State differs from all other institutions concerned with the common good in that, except for
the Church, it is topmost.

IV

Let us begin with the most comprehensive of
these contemporary theories - that which I shall
call the law, justice, and welfare view of the
proper function of the State. This view is most

130

characteristically found among Catholics and
Liberal Protestants. It is the view to which
the Catholic Jacques Maritain gravitates. I
shall expound the general view by looking at
Maritain's specific version of it.

Mariatain vigorously argues the point that a
well-ordered body politic will not be a collection of individuals having just one important
institution, the State. Rather, it will to be
high degree be what he calls pluralistic society.
His own words describe well what he has in mind:
"...the body politic...contains in its superior
unity...a multiplicity of...particular societies
which proceed from the free initiative of citizens
and should be as autonomous as possible. Such
is the element of pluralsim inherent in every
truly political society. Family, economic,
cultural, educational, religious life matter as
much as does political life to the very existence
and prosperity of the body politic. Every kind
of law, from the spontaneous, unformulated group
regulations to customary law and to law in the
full sense of the term, contributes to the vital
order of political society...Finally, the public
welfare and the general order of law are essential parts of the common good of the body politic,
but this common good has far larger and richer,
more concretely human implications...(11)" In
short, a well-ordered body politic will have
within it a large number of institutions each
of which has its own distinct domain of proper
functioning.

Where is the State in this array of institutions? What is its proper function? Maritain's
answer seems to be that the State has a threefold proper function. For one thing, it is the
State's proper function to regulate the activities of members of the body politic - both individuals and societies - by a system of law based
on justice and good order. Secondly, it is the
State's proper function actively to promote social
justice among the citizens and societies of the
body politic. Sometimes when the basic struc-

tures of society "are not up to the mark with regard to justice," the State may itself have to step in and provide benefits of one sort and another. But that is malformation. In general, it is the proper function of the State actively to promote the satisfaction of the right to education without itself providing it. Thirdly, Maritain holds that in the area of economics it is the State's proper function to engage in whatever activities are necessary to secure economic welfare.

Even in the domain of economics, however, Maritain wishes to protect his principle of pluralism. He argues that normally it is good policy for the State to promote and support the efforts of business and labor institutions rather than itself to perform the economic functions necessary to the public welfare. He cites the TVA as a good example of what he has in mind (22-23). Still, he does not hold that the State is necessarily malformed it, for example, it nationalizes certain industries or provides a guaranteed annual income. In the domain of economic welfare, but only in this domain, it is within the State's proper function to act as a service organization.

The main question that must be put to the law, justice and welfare view of the State is this: Why should the service function of the State be limited to economic welfare? Is this not a purely arbitrary limitation? What is it that is fundamentally different between the sphere of economics and that, say, of art? To this question Maritain has no answer. The attempt to give a theoretical safeguard against the totalitarian state proves, at least in Maritain's version of the law, justice and welfare view, to have no structural basis. And this, I think, is characteristic. Those who hold such a view characteristically have no principle to offer in objection to the State's becoming a service institution in other domains than the economic. And thereby they have no principle

to offer in objection to the State's becoming a
service institution in other domains than the
economic. And thereby they have no principle
to offer in objection to the State's becoming
totalitarian. The chief task for anyone
attracted to the law, justice, and welfare view
would be to find such a principle.

V

   In strong contrast to the law, justice and
welfare view is what I shall call the law and
order view. This is the most constricted of
contemporary Christian views as to the domain
of the State's proper function. It has been
found mainly among Anabaptists and Anglo-
Saxon Evangelicals - though of course these two
traditions differ sharply from each other on
the related but distinct issue as to whether
Christians may actively participate in that
coercive non-voluntary institution which is
the State, an issue which, unfortunately, we
will not have time to treat. To give some
specificity to the general view I shall expound
it by considering Carl Henry's statement of it
in his book Aspects of Christian Social Ethics;
for this is the view to which Henry quite consistently gravitates.

   A theme which also pervades Henry's thought
is that of abhorrence for the totalitarian tendency of contemporary states. He remarks that
"when the power of the State becomes the means
for compelling people to do their whole duty,
this power can easily be employed to force
people to do what is not their duty at all" (118).
In his discussion Henry singles out especially
two connected causes for the self-aggrandizement
of contemporary states: The belief that the
State should act out of benevolence toward the
desires of its citizens (154 ff.), and the belief
that the State can and should be an instrument
of social transformation and renewal (108 ff.).
He sees these beliefs as the principal culprits
behind the encroaching welfare state which "is

no longer dedicated to justice and order, encouraging and enforcing human rights and responsibilities under God, but is benevolently bent toward people's socio-economic wants" (169).

Henry is himself deeply convinced that our society needs renewal. Equally he is convinced that Christians must work for such renewal. But he argues that such renewal will come about if and only if there is a religious change in the hearts of individual men. Evangelism and not legislation is the road to social betterment. "The reliance on political means to lift all the burdens of mankind...is characteristic of contemporary social theory in which secular concerns wholly replace the spiritual...Such secular proposals, while claiming to promote social justice, tend in the long run simply to readjust the existing disorders along new lines" (124). The "aim of the Christian's political activity," he goes on to say, "is not to produce a utopia, but to preserve justice and promote order in a fallen world" (96). For, he asks rhetorically, "Is not the State's obligation in preserving justice to provide what is due (as corresponding to the rights of men) rather than to implement agape by acts of mercy or love?" (166).

From these quotations it is already clear how Henry views the proper function of the state. The State's proper function is to maintain a system of laws regulating the activities of the members of society, a system of laws which secure good order and protect the rights of the members of the body politic. As he puts it, "The justification of civil law is that it protects my rights (and my neighbor's)...The role of government is but to declare, to apply, and to enforce rights which are given of God and therefore inalienable...The purpose of law is to prevent one person from injuring another; my rights end and become my duty where my neighbor's rights begin" (92). The same point could be put in terms of justice rather than in terms of rights: The laws must be based on principles of

good order and justice. For "justice considers
every person a subject of rights and an object
of duties..." (92)

On reflection this point of view will quite
inevitably stimulate the following line of
questioning: Do not the members of our society
have a right to education, to fire protection,
to decent medical care, to enough income to
live decently if disabled? And so will not a
system of laws based on justice secure these
rights to the citizenry? Why then should the
securing of these rights be prejudicially described as the benevolent satisfaction of
wants? But if the State does actually secure
these rights, will it not then become what
Henry so abhors - namely, a service-state distributing benefits? In short, does not Henry's
own principle of justice lead to a vastly more
comprehensive state than he wants? No doubt
some thinkers have justified a comprehensive
service-state by the principle of benevolence.
But does not Henry's own principle of justice
lead to the same destination by a different
road?

I think not; and it is of utmost importance
to see why not. I do not know whether Henry
holds that in our well-to-do society citizens
have a right to education. But it is clear
that even if he does, he does not believe that
it is the State's business to provide education.
For this is not the kind of right he is speaking
of. Henry is speaking of what I shall call
freedom-rights - the right to act without coercion in one area or another. Examples of freedom-rights are the right to free assembly, the
right to free speech, the right to private
property, and the babeas corpus right to one's
own body. But when men speak of the right to
education, they do not mean the absence of coercive threats against getting educated. They do
not mean the right freely to pursue an education
if one so chooses. They mean rather the right
to receive an education. Similarly the right

of the disabled to a decent income is not the
right freely to go about securing such an
income for oneself. It is the right to receive
such an income. We might accordingly call such
rights as these, benefit-rights. Freedom-
rights call for protection. Benefit-rights
call for provision. A freedom-right is a claim
on everyone to respect that right. A benefit-
right is a claim on someone or other to satisfy
that right.

I think it virtually certain that when Henry
speaks of rights it is freedom-rights and not
benefit-rights that he has in mind. Correspondingly when he speaks of justice as consisting
in establishing a man's rights by securing what
is due to him, he has freedom-rights and not
benefit-rights in mind (154-171). It is not
social justice but regulative justice that he
is thinking of. Henry's view is that the
State's proper function is to regulate the
activities of its citizens by maintaining a
system of laws based on regulative justice and
good order. It is not the State's proper function actively to promote social justice, i.e.,
actively to promote the satisfaction of benefit-
rights. And certainly it is not its proper
function itself to dispense services, in any
area whatsoever. This Henry takes to be the
biblical view on the matter: "The Bible," he
says, "views government as a means of preserving
justice in a fallen and sinful order" (93).

Parenthetically it may be remarked that what
I mean by social justice - namely, the satisfaction of benefit-rights - is not to be identified with what has traditionally been called
distributive justice or equity. Distributive
justice consists of treating people equitably
in the distribution of benefits or burdens. It
does not speak to the issue of whether someone
has a right to such-and-such a benefit, but only
to the mode of distribution of benefits. Social
justice, however, consists in the satisfaction
of someone's right to some benefit. And the

right to some benefit is of course different from the right to be treated equitably if that or some other benefit is to be distributed at all. For benefits may be distributed to which no one has any right. In that situation distributive justice pertains but social justice does not.

It is worth adding to our discussion of Henry's views that in the course of developing his law and order view of the State Henry expouses an extremely individualistic view of human society. This would seem not to be a necessary accompaniment of the law and order view. The Anabaptist after all shares the law and order view while holding a non-individualistic view of at least the Church. On the other hand, the law and order view does quite inevitably accompany an individualistic view of society. Henry seems to regard all institutions apart from the Family, the State, and the Church, as purely instrumental and contractual. No other institutions are regarded as having a definite domain of proper functioning. Thus no other institutions are regarded as having independent authority within a definite domain. And so no other institutions are regarded as entering into the fabric of rights and duties. When Henry speaks of rights he speaks exclusively of the rights of one individual vis a vis another (though of course his disoussion assumes the right of the State to the obedience of its subjects).

What should chiefly give us pause before the law and order view of the State is its radical exclusion of social justice from the domain of the State's proper function. It is impossible to read the Old Testament prophets without seeing that is was social justice they were calling for. It was the deprivation of benefit-rights that evoked their denunciation. The Christian cannot possibly regard justice as confined to regulative justice. Of course it is one thing to say this, and quite another to say that social justice belongs to the proper function of the State. But still, what reason might be offered for not moving to this conclusion?

Henry's defense is that social justice can be secured only if hearts are changed, and conversely, that it will be secured if hearts are changed (15-16, 72). But this seems just false. It is true of course that in a society of sanctified men social justice will flow forth. So too will regulative justice. And we must indeed beware of the utopian heresy that the Kingdom of God will be inaugurated by the State and its coercive devices. But what concerns us here is not the society of sanctified men but our mixed society. And it is simply not true that benefit-rights cannot be secured in such a society. The freedom-right to hold private property is protected in our mixed society. And in that very same society the benefit-right to fire protection is secured. Further, it is not secured by conversion of the hearts of men but by the very device that Henry suggests cannot be used to secure benefit-rights - by legislative action of the State. It must of course be acknowledged that in our mixed society we will never succeed in fully securing all benefit-rights, neither by legislation nor any other means. But that is scarcely a reason for not even trying to do so. We will also never fully protect all freedom-rights.

St. Paul's statement in Romans 13 that the State is for restraining wrong-doing has also sometimes been used to support the conclusion that the State is to be limited to regulative justice. But surely the deprivation of benefit-rights is also a matter of wrongdoing, both individual and collective: a matter of perversity, and of dereliction in duty. Amos would not tolerate the suggestion that the deprivation of benefit-rights in Old Israel somehow occurred without wrongdoing on anyone's part. The wrong-doing which underlies social injustice, as well as that which underlies regulative injustice, must be restrained and punished. But what other

138

institution than the State is authorized to exercise the power of the sword over the entire citizenry?

There is no escaping the conclusion that all justice which falls within the common good - social as well as regulative - belongs within the proper function of the State.

But once again we are faced with what now looks like the other horn of inescapable dilemma: If the State seeks to secure social justice, does it not then become a distributor of services, and that not only in the area of economics but in all other areas as well? And is not a comprehensive service-state inevitably a totalitarian state?

We have here touched on one of the most basic polarities confronting the community of evangelical Christians today. We seem to have to choose between blinking our eyes to the deprivation of social justice, and acquiescing in the monstrosity of the comprehensive service-state. Some of us choose one way, some the other. Some of us cannot ignore the cry for social justice so we put up with the evils of the comprehensive service-state. Some of us cannot ignore the evils of the comprehensive service-state so we put up with the absence of justice. That is our agony. Is there no escape?

VI

There is, I am convinced. To see what it is, we must sketch out the third major view as to the proper function of the State which has been developed by Christian thinkers in our century, what I shall call the law and justice view. To the best of my knowledge this view has never been characteristic of any one Christian tradition. It has received its finest expression, however, by two thinkers in the Reformed tradition - Emil Brunner in his book <u>Justice and the Social Order</u>, and Herman Dooyeweerd in the third

volume of his New Critique of Theoretical
Thought. I shall depend on their expositions
in sketching out the general view.

Brunner and Dooyeweerd have also expressed
their alarm at the totalitarian totalitarian
state exceeds the State's proper function -
exceeds God's ordering for the State. The
thought of both is in good measure shaped by
their attempt to work out the limits of the
State's proper function. Brunner says that

> The monstrosity which bears the name of the
> totalitarian state has at last succeeded
> in reminding us that there are not only
> primal rights of individuals and of commun-
> ities, but that there is a just and unjust
> order of the state itself. The totalitarian
> state is not, like a dictatorship, a form
> of the state. It is the absorption of all
> institutions and all rights by the state.
> The totalitarian state is the inevitable
> consequence of the view that...all rights
> obtaining among the people issue from the
> state. The totalitarian state must of
> necessity come into being wherever politi-
> cal thought is centralistic, and all organ-
> ization is regarded as issuing from above
> from state centre...(134. See also 203).

And Dooyeweerd remarks that

> In whatever shape the absolutist idea of the
> body politic is set forth, it does not
> recognize any intrinsic legal limits to the
> authority of the State. This idea implies
> an absorption of the entire juridical posi-
> tion of man by his position as citizen or
> as subject of the government (441).

But at the same time that Brunner and Dooyeweerd
express their alarm over the totalitarian tendencies in modern states, both also express their
conviction that the State is charged by God with
the function of promoting social justice.

140

Central to the thought of both is the vision
of a well-ordered society as being what Brunner
calls a federal society - that is, a society
whose institutional fabric contains a large
number of distinct autonomous institutions.
Brunner's federal society is obviously similar
to Maritain's pluralist society, and it is
interesting that there should be this coalescence
between Catholic and Reformed thinkers. Yet they
cannot be identified, if only because Maritain
is hazy as to the nature of his pluralistic
society - more hazy than in my exposition I made
him out to be. Maritain clearly thought that
the Church and the Family each have a proper
function within a definite domain, and that consequently each has an authority not derived from
the State and rights to be protected by the State.
But Maritain can be read as saying that all institutions except these are subordinate to the State.
His recommendation that the State grant each a
considerable degree of independence can be read
as having no deeper basis than what is good
policy in most circumstances.

On this crucial issue Brunner and Dooyeweerd
are clear. They hold that the institutional
fabric of a well-ordered society will cantain
a great many institutions having a proper function within a definite domain, each of such
institutions accordingly possessing both authority in that particular domain and rights which
ought to be respected by the state. The institutions of society are not purely instrumental
and contractual. "In the Christian understanding
of man," says Brunner, "communities are just as
much established in the divine order of creation
as the independence of the individual. They are
innate in the God-created individual with his
capacity and need for completion" (83).

Thus it is not the proper function of the
State to make educational decisions for society,
nor of schools to make business decisions for
society. Each of these God-ordained institutions has autonomy in its own domain, sover-

eignty in its own sphere. The State too is
sovereign. But like every other institution
it is sovereign only in its own sphere. Hence
even

the standards of justice obtaining in these
forms of community are antecedent to the
state; they are formed in manners and cus-
toms, agreements, contracts, rites and
ceremonies, established rights to which, in
the first instance, no state pays heed. It
is not the state which sets this life in
motion, not the state which determines by
which rules it shall proceed, not the
state which can pronounce on its justice
or injustice...The state, in all this,
comes late, protecting, preserving, regulating, but not as a creative or constitu-
tive agent (Brunner 137).

What then is the sphere of the State's action?
What is the domain of its proper function? A
two-fold one. The State's proper function is to
regulate the activities of the members of society-
both individual and institutional-by a system of
laws based on good order and regulative justice.
And secondly, the State's proper function is
actively to promote social justice.

The phrase "actively promote" is crucial here.
When at all possible, the State is not itself
to provide the services and engage in the
activities which will satisfy our benefit-rights.
Rather, its function is actively to promote a
society containing institutions which will and
can satisfy those rights. For remember, in all
its actions the State must respect the autonomy,
the sovereignty, of the other institutions in
society:

The State may promote the interests of science
and the fine arts, education, public health,
trade, agriculture and industry, popular
morality, and so on. But every governmental interference with the life of the nation

is subject to the inner vital law of the body politic, implied in its structural principle. This vital law delimits the State's task of integration according to the political criterion of the 'public interest,' bound to the principle in sphere-sovereignty of the individuality structures of human soceity (Dooyeweerd, 445-446).

Here then we have an escape from the dilemma pressed upon us: How can the cry for social justice be answered without making of the State a comprehensive service-institution? The State is properly concerned with social justice. Yet insofar as possible it must not itself become a service institution distributing all sorts of benefits. That would violate the principle of federalism. Its fundamental role in the area of social justice is instead that of actively promoting a federal society containing non-state institutions which satisfy the genuine benefit-rights of the citizenry.

A real public legal integration of a country and people is, therefore only possible within the internal limits set by the structural principle of the State-institution itself. This integration can only be accomplished within the juridical limits set by this structural principle to the competence of the body politic, and with due regard to the internal sphere-sovereigntyof the other societal structures. Every political theory denying these limits is in principle a theory of the 'power-State,' even though it masks its absolutization of the State's power by a law-State ideology (Dooyeweerd, 441).

VII

This theory, of course, needs a good deal more elaboration than I can give it here - and more than either Brunner or Dooyeweerd have given it. The theory does not imply that the State may not use its taxing powers to support non-State institutions. Nor does it imply that the State may never render anything which can be regarded as a service. For example, the maintenance of a system of good roads is a service, and is perhaps to be justified by the principle of good order - that which makes it possible for the citizens to go about their tasks. And perhaps some benefit-rights are such that it is impossible for anything but the State to satisfy them; maybe that is true of the right to a decent income if disabled. One would like these and other distinctions more carefully articulated. Yet it seems to me that this theory does, in its main lineaments, promise us an escape from the dilemma pressing upon us.

Our American legal structure does, to a gratifying degree, recognize the domain autonomy of our many non-State institutions. Insofar as that is true, our legal structure is resistant to totalitarianism. And for that we should be thankful. Yet undoubtedly our state has been drifting in the direction of becoming more and more an entrepreneur and a distributor of services in a multitude of areas. For this there are many reasons, some no doubt insidious. Yet it would be wrong glibly to say that in every case the right thing for the State to do is to resist itself acting to secure social justice. Brunner states well the predicament to which we as Christians must be sensitive:

The fundamental Christian realization is that the state has only to intervene where individuals, families, free social groups, the churches, the municipalities, cannot perform their tasks. Any justice created by the state is a makeshift, a substitute for the justice which human society should create of itself...And vice versa, the greater the decline in the moral vigour of society, the more tasks the state must take upon itself, and the greater the expansion of the element of compulsion in justice, the nearer

144

the approach of the totalitarian state.
Hence the rise of the totalitarian state is
in the first instance quite simply a judgment on the wretched moral condition of modern
society. We must not fear to add - a judgment too on the Christian church and its
powerlessness to direct the moral forces
of society in the sense of the justice of
creation. Let us take as an example the welfare work of the state, which has already
assumed monstrous proportions. This would
not have been necessary if the family in
the narrower and wider sense of the word,
the social community, the Christian community and the economic community of labour
had not so conspicuously broken down (205-206).

VIII

We have probed some of the issues involved in
the nature of the State. With this as background let us consider, lastly, how the State
fits into God's ordering of His creation.

Christians have traditionally affirmed that
the existence of states among men is authorized
by God, that their existence conforms to God's
will for our human condition. But what is the
fundamental status of that authorization? Is
it part of God's creation decrees for the life
of man, no matter what man's condition? Or is
it rather part of His providence decrees for the
life of fallen man?

The Catholic tradition has favored the former
view, the Protestant tradition, the latter.
Yet, passionate though the dispute has often
been, it is hard to avoid the conclusion that
there is no genuine issue here. The Catholic
emphasizes the fact that the State is a governmental institution in charge, for all the inhabitants of a certain territory, of some domain
within the common good. And he rightly insists
that the Christian neither views governance in
general as an evil or necessitated solely by

145

evil, nor does he view such governance thus.
The Protestant on the other hand stresses the
embeddedness of our states within our present
fallen age. Our states exact obedience from the
inhabitants of a certain area by their power
of the sword; and given our sinful condition,
how else could they exact it? And our states
maintain a system of laws whose purpose and
effect is in large measure to restrain wrongdoing. No one should hold that this is the sole
purpose and effect of our laws. In part they
have a purely regulative, ordering purpose and
function. Still there is no denying that our
political structure is in large measure devoted
to restraining wrongdoing.

What makes it hard to see any genuine issue
here is that the coin of the State simply does
have these two faces. The State is a governmental institution, responsible for some domain
within the common good of all those who inhabit
a certain territory. The Protestant need not
deny this, nor need he deny that God's authorization of such an institution can be seen as
belonging to His creational decrees. But the
State is also an institution which acts to
restrain wrongdoing, and it does so by exer-
cising the power of the sword. The Catholic
will scarcely deny this, nor will he deny that
God's authorization of such an institution
belongs to His providential decrees for a fallen
world.

Protestants have sometimes cited Romans 13
as support for their side in the dispute. But
a close scrutiny of what Paul is saying makes
clear that he provides no support whatever for
the view that the State is wholly a negative
institution. Civil authorities, Paul says to
the Roman Christians, are "God's agents working
for your good." And he adds, "it is not for
nothing that they hold the power of the sword,
for they are God's agents of punishment, for
retribution on the offender." It is clear that
what is here uppermost in Paul's mind are the

related facts that the State is called to deal
with wrongdoing and that it is authorized to
do so coercively. But as to whether the State
also has a positive side, Paul here says nothing
one way or the other. He is not here giving a
general statement as to the nature of the State.
He does not say that the whole of the State's
proper function consists of restraining by constraining. This becomes especially clear if one
considers the context; the only side of the
State which is relevant in the content is its
negative side.

The opening eight verses of Romans 13 are
embedded in a larger passage which Paul begins
by imploring the Roman Christians "by God's
mercy to offer your very selves to him: a living
sacrifice, dedicated and fit for his acceptance,
the worship offered by mind and heart" (12:1),
and which he closes by saying "love cannot wrong
a neighbor; therefore the whole law is summed
up in love" (13:10). Paul's comments on the
State are set in the context of a discussion of
the duties of Christians.

Within that context Paul says, near the end
of chapter 12, "never avenge yourselves, but
leave it to the wrath of God; for it is written,
'Vengeance is mine. ˎI will repay, says the Lord'"
(12:19). Obviously this injunction raises a
serious problem for Paul's readers when they
reflect on their relation to the State - a
problem, however, only with respect·to the
negative side of the State. The officers of
the State characteristically do exactly what Paul
urges the Roman Christians not to do; they
avenge themselves. Paul's solution is bold and
striking. He does not say that State officials
should cease doing this; nor does he say that
Christians should on account of this feature of
the State renounce all contact with it. Quite
to the contrary. In its very act of avenging,
the State is to be seen as "the servant of God
to execute his wrath on the wrong-doer" (13:4).
The officers of the State are executants of

God, and must on that account be obeyed.[5] But
the other side of the situation must also be
kept in view: The State as we know it, an institution which restrains by constraining, is
destined to pass away. Such actions have no
place in the Kingdom of God. Restraining and
constraining belong solely to this present age.
So if one keeps in mind the context it is easy
to see that Paul in Romans 13 is not denying
that the State has a positive side.

The traditional debate between creationalists
and providentialists is not only based on a
pseudo-issue. What is perhaps even more important to notice is that the issue it raises is,
at best, on the margin of New Testament concern.
That has been quite decisively shown by those who
have espoused the so-called Christological view
of the State. The Christological view does not-
contrary to what is sometimes suggested-offer a
distinct position on the issue we were discussing
earlier, namely, the proper function of the State.
Rather, it offers a new and important view on
the place of the State in God's ordering of
creation, and correspondingly, on the ground of
Christian obedience to the State. We shall
focus on the former of these two issues.

Our discussion up to this point has in a
certain way been "unreal." We have been discussing the proper function of the State. And
we have just observed that the State in its
proper functioning has both a positive and a
negative side - the Catholic emphasizing the
former, the Protestant, the latter. All this
is surely profoundly relevant for Christian
political action. Yet it has about it an air of
unreality. For you and I are seldom if ever
presented with states which confine their
actions to the domain of their proper functioning. And neither you nor I nor anyone else has
ever been presented with a state all of whose
actions were right ones. So not only do the
actions of States consist, in large measure, in
trying to cope with the results of our corrupted

condition, states are themselves corrupted. And that is what concerned the New Testament writers. It is one thing to discuss whether God's will that there shall be states belongs to His creational decrees or to His providential decrees or both. It is quite a different thing to discuss God's way of dealing with our actual states - these malformed misshapen institutions confronting us in history. That is the issue on which the writers of the New Testament speak.

The central claim of the Christological view is that one cannot understand the New Testament thought concerning the place of the State in God's ordering of His creation apart from understanding the New Testament thought concerning the relation of our actual fallen states to the work of Jesus Christ. The New Testament writers neither assert nor deny some abstract authorization by God of the existence of states - some decree on God's part. Nor do they ground the injunction to their fellow Christians to be obedient to the State on any such authorization (Cf. Romans 13:1-8; I Peter 2:13-17, 23-25; Titus 3:1-8). They ground it on what God in Christ has done and is doing in history.

In the opening sentence of Romans 13 Paul speaks not of the State as that which we ought to subordinate ourselves to, but rather of the supreme authorities. The word he uses (exousiai) in the form in which he uses it (plural) is one which he invariably uses to refer to invisible, angelic or demonic powers that make themselves manifest on earth. Thus we must relate Romans 13:1 to I Corinthians 2:8, where Paul speaks of Christ as being crucified by "the rulers of this present age"; and to I Corinthians 6:1-7, where in defending his view that Christians should not use the civil law courts, he says that we "are to judge angels." The proper conclusion seems to be that in speaking of authorities and rulers Paul is referring at one and the same time to civil authorities and to certain cosmic powers backing up those civil authorities. Behind the

actions of the civil authorities Paul sees the
influence, and in their actions the manifestation, of angelic and demonic powers.

These powers were all created by God. In
Christ, says Paul, "everything in heaven and on
earth was created, not only things visible but
also the invisible orders of thrones, sovereign-
ties, authorities, and powers" (Col. 1:16). But
the powers fell. And in opposition to God they
enslaved humanity. Paul speaks of men as being
within "reach of the elemental powers" (Col.
2:20), as obeying "the commander of the spiritual
powers of the air" (Eph. 2:2), and as being
"slaves to the elemental spirits of the universe"
(Gal. 4:3). Ultimately these powers try to turn
men away from the true service of God. Thus they
try to separate us from the love of God (Romans
8:38).

All of this will strike some as calling for
the sharp scissors of the demythologizer. But
remember, Paul is pointing to the enslaving,
God-alienating, qualities of various factors in
our ordinary existence as well as suggesting
that in our struggle to be freed from these
factors, we are dealing with powers of which
these factors are only the instruments. The
powers use such ordinary things as institutions
to do their work. Further, Paul's list in
Romans 8 of things once capable of separating
us from the love of Christ suggests that he
saw the powers as in turn belonging to a far
larger group of factors - including along with
cosmic powers the various contextual structures
of human life - which can alienate men from
God.[8] To speak more specifically of the State:
Paul discerned the enslaving tendencies of our
actual states. He saw how they force us into
living lives alienated from God, even to the
extent of setting up themselves as idolatrous
alternatives to God. So much is "empirical."
But behind these phenomena Paul saw demonic
powers at work. This for him would explain how
a state could become like that depicted in

Revelation 13: a beast out of the sea, with
power and rule and great authority conferred
on it by the Dragon, demanding that men worship
it, blaspheming God, waging war on God's people,
grasping for universal authority.

These enslaving powers were conquered by the
Cross and the Resurrection of Christ. It must
be said emphatically that Paul does not see the
work of Christ as consisting merely in the revelation of God's law, His will. Nor does he see
it as merely the salvation of a few individuals
from the burning. Nor even does he see it as
merely the creation of a new community, the
Church. Rather, he sees Christ's work as including the conquering of the powers and the placing
of them at the disposal of God. Christ on
his cross, he says, "discarded the cosmic powers
and authorities like a garment; he made a public
his triumphal procession" (Col. 2:15. Cf. Eph.
1:20-23; 2:8; Romans 8:31-39; Hebrews 1:7-8,
I Peter 3:22).

The binding of the powers means that we can
look forward to the reconciliation of all things
through Christ. For "through him God chose to
reconcile the whole world to himself, making
peace through the shedding of his blook upon the
cross - to reconcile all things, whether on
earth or in heaven, through him alone" (Col.
1:20. Cf. Phil. 2:7-10; Eph. 1:10; Romans
8:18-25). But the day of total reconciliation
has not yet arrived. When it does arrive, then
"comes the end, when Christ delivers up the kingdom to God the Father, after abolishing every
kind of domination, authority, and power. For
he is destined to reign until God has put all
enemies under his feet" (Cor. 15:24-26). In
the meanwhile the mopping-up operation and the
skirmishes go on, though the battle has essentially been won. In

Christ the angelic powers are called to order
and, so far as they need it, they are restored
to their original order. Therefore any further

151

only take place in accordance with their creation, and within Christ's order, in the form of unwilling service to the Kingdom of Christ, until even that rebellion, within the boundaries of the Kingdom of Christ, is broken down in His Resurrection and Parousia.

The demonic quality of the powers still exists. But even the demonic powers are now instruments, albeit often unwilling ones, in God's order.

What follows when all this is applied to the political angelic power? Clearly this: that that power, the State as such, belongs originally and ultimately to Jesus Christ...The State can of course become 'demonic,' and the New Testament makes no attempt to conceal the fact that at all times the Church may, and actually does, have to deal with the 'demonic' State. From this point of view the State becomes 'demonic' not so much by an unwarrantable assumption of autonomy...as by the loss of its legitimate, relative independence, as by a renunciation which works out in Caesar-worship, the myth of the State and the like. We should add that, in the view of the New Testament, in no circumstances can this 'demonic' State finally achieve what it desires; with gnashing of teeth it will have to serve where it wants to dominate; it will have to build where it wishes to destroy; it will have to testify to God's justice where it wishes to display the injustice of men.

When we now return to Romans 13 it wears a very different aspect indeed from the traditional one. Paul says there that the authorities are 'instituted' (NEB) or 'appointed' (RSV) or 'ordained' (ASV) by God. In all likelihood what he means is that they have been ordered, placed into order, by God. They have been subjected to Christ's Lordship. By virtue of Christ's work they have been placed, willingly or not, at the

152

disposal of God in the working of His purposes. They are now God's agents, His servants, His ministers - usually no doubt unwittingly so - working for our good by restraining evil and making it possible to "lead a tranquil and quiet life in full observance of religion and high standards of morality" (I Tim. 2:2).[12] Thus these authorities deserve our subordination - not our unquestioning obedience but rather our subordination. We must give them their due - no more, but also no less. We must give them that which their office calls for (Rom. 13:8).

So Paul, in speaking of God's ordering of the State, is probably not speaking of some decree of creation nor of some decree of providence. He is speaking of what God has done and is doing in our actual history by way of Christ's work.

What does this all mean for those of use who engage in politics?[14] What it means, at its deepest level, is that we must always regard our actual states with a dual attitude. We must give thanks to God for the tranquility which they insure. We must pray for them (I Tim. 2:1), and as with all sincere prayers, we must follow up those prayers by working within and for our states.[13] But at the same time we must regard our states with a watchful eye, seeing to it that they retain their place in God's ordering and that they do not, by overstepping the bounds of their proper function, move in the direction of totalitarianism. For the totalitarian state always carries within it the live danger of becoming the demonic state - the state which turns men away from the true service of God, ultimately even to the extent of setting itself up as an idolatrous alternative to God. And there, finally, we see what is ultimately so threatening in the totalitarian state: In overstepping God's ordering it verges on the demonic. It is this demonizing of the State that the Christian must above all be on the watch for. Neither democracy nor any other form of government is insurance

153

against it. Indeed, the characteristic loose-
ness of governmental bonds within a democracy
constantly tempts the democratic state into
trying to secure unity among its citizenry by
elevating patriotism to an idolatrous level.

Yet even when confronted with demonic states
we can give thanks to God that all is now under
the Lordship of Christ and that we are therefore
more than conquerors in Him. In the face even
of the demonic we can act as freed men. Above
all, we can in our freedom confront even the
demonic state with a society distinct from every
state, a society which is a true community, one
from which coercion has been banished - a society
which is a reminder of love lost and the first
fruit of a harvest to come: The Church, an abiding
testimony to the State of the ultimate subjection
of all powers to their Lord, Jesus Christ.

TOWARD AN UNDERSTANDING OF POLITICS AND GOVERNMENT FROM A CHRISTIAN POINT OF VIEW

By James W. Skillen

Introduction

Today the adjectives "liberal," "conservative," "socialist," and "marxist" are not unambigious in themselves. There are several varieties of each of these political brands. Unfortunately the word "Christian" when used in connection with politics is no less problematic. In fact, there may be a greater variety of so-called Christian political positions or viewpoints than of liberal, conservative, socialist, and marxist positions put together. This historical reality means that great care and caution must guide the enuciation of a Christian view of politics and government, especially when the author is convinced that a truly Christian view can be developed force-fully and with a minimum of ambiguity.

The first thing we should try to do, there-fore, is to explain why at present there is so little agreement among Christians about the nature of a Christian political standpoint. This in turn will help to explain why it is so difficult to outline the basic elements or prin-ciples of such a position in a way that will com-pel the assent and support of a large body of Christians.

The next step will be to attempt the very task that seems, at first glance, to be so difficult and impossible. We will set forth those basic elements of a Christian political position which appear to be both biblically necessary and allow-able. This articulation of a Christian view-point will be done with as much sensitivity to different historical traditions as possible in order to spotlight the most serious divisions and differences that exist among Christians.

The third major section of the essay will be devoted to some of the concrete and practical implications of a Christian political standpoint for the present American political situation. In particular we will suggest some activities that Christians ought to be engaged in right now - activities which are not, however, being carried out with any degree of urgency, consistency, depth, or breadth by a significant body of confessing Christians.

The Lack of a Christian Political Standpoint

Perhaps it is not at all remarkable that Christians lack a common political mind when they do not even possess a common ecclesiastical mind. Yet it does seem to be significant that whereas ecclesiastical splinteredness has almost always led, on the one hand, to ecumenical efforts to overcome the divisions, and on the other hand, to efforts of the separate wings to defend themselves as the only true church, the lack of a common Christian political mind, by contrast, has usually been accepted without much complaint and with little effort either to overcome the splintered diversity or to develop and defend a uniquely Christian political position. This state of affairs is especially true in twentieth-century America.

The basic cause of this predicament can be identified as the twofold willingness of the Christian community to synthesize its unique position and view of life with non-Christian positions and views - (synthesis) - and to relinquish its responsibility for a truly Christian cultrual calling in this world - (care-lessness). For anyone who will take time to look, the evidence is available to show the tremendous influence of Platonic, Aristotelian, gnostic, stoic and modern humanistic influences on the formation of so-called "Christian" political ideas and programs. And also available is the evidence of an absence

of any powerful and long-standing Christian
political tradition manifesting a passion for
serving the Master according to His Word in the
political activities of this age. The different
views of political life in America today held
by Roman Catholics, Eastern Orthodox, Lutheran,
Reformed, Quaker, Anabaptist, and other Christian
traditions, manifest both the great variety of
non-Christian influences just mentioned as well
as the careless, passive, haphazard, and relatively inconsequential character of Christian
involvement in and concern with the political
world.

Professor Herman Dooyeweerd, who stands in
a most unusual tradition of Christian political
activity in the Netherlands, summarizes our
point here when he insists that the differences
among Christians about political life are due
to the "monster-marriage of Christianity with
the movements of the age, which arise from the
spirits of this world." That is "synthesis."
And synthesis springs from and leads to the
relinquishing of a distinctively Christian
approach to culture - "carelessness."

The fundamental cause of the inner weakening
of Christian political thought, yes, of the
entire Christian mode of life among Christians in our day, lies not so much in external factors but in inner decay, threatening
Christianity from the beginning in its
positive endeavor regarding culture, learning,
political life and social movement...

As soon as Christianity began to compromise
learning, culture, and political life with
pagan and humanistic philosophy, with its
view of state and culture, Christianity's
inner strength was broken.

American political life reveals a peculiar
character in all of this, even though the Christian communities of America do display the above

mentioned attitudes of "synthesis" and "care-
lessness." The peculiarity is that while a
separate and distinctive "Christian political
movement" has always been rejected by American
Christians, the conviction has remained deeply
rooted that our "secular" political system
(parties and policies included) is truly from
God and well pleasing in His sight. To understand this fact requires that we understand the
nature of the "American civil religion." Our
purpose here does not include tackling that subject, but we need only mention it in order to
make the point that any effort to deal with
"Christian politics" in America must come to
grips not only with splinteredness due to a
"synthetic" and "care-less" mindset on the part
of Christians, but also with the American quirck
of an ecumenical faith in the "Christianness"
of our "secular" system.

What this means is that we will have a difficult time sorting out the "Christian" and the
"non-Christian" elements or influences in our
American political tradition if we are unable
to get beyond the contradictory attitude which
holds that a distinctively Christian political
position is unAmerican while at the same time
holding that the American political system is
basically "Christian."

The point that we want to argue is that despite
much Christian influence in American politics
from the beginning, our system has been far
more dependent, from the beginning, on the modern,
secular, humanistic (not biblical) assumptions
and actions of John Locke, Charles Montesquieu,
Adam Smith, Tom Paine, Thomas Jefferson, Jeremy
Bentham, John Stuart Mill, and countless others,
than on the assumptions and actions of confessedly
Christian political thinkers and statesmen.
Christians in varying degrees have wedded themselves sythetically and uncritically to our
emerging system with the historical result that
they have "sanctified" as "Christian" a political
way of life that is in many respects anti-thetical

to biblical Christianity. At the same time the traditional divergent Christian views of politics and government have been kept locked up in the churches away from the concrete political structures and activities of our parties and government, bearing testimony to the fact that Christians as a visible body do not believe that an identifiable and actual Christian political movement is either possible or legitimate. In sum, synthesis built upon cultural care-lessness has led in American Christianity to the sanctification of secularized politics and to the rejection of a distinctively Christian political option.

Precisely at this point we uncover the heart of our difficulty in coming up with a Christian political position in contemporary America. The deepest religious agreement that American Christians have about politics come not from the Christian faith but from their secular ecumenical faith in the American political way of life. If we were simply to avoid the word "Christian" in our political discussions, then we would face only the less difficult problem of debating Republican-Democratic conservative-liberal divergencies which are evidently the same for Christians and non-Christians alike and which presuppose, afterall, a prior ecumenical agreement about the sanctity of the political system as it now exists - secular "neutrality," popular sovereignty, two parties, and single-member district electoral system majority rule, etc., etc.

When we begin to try to define a Christian view of politics, therefore, it is not first of all the differing historical traditions within Christianity (Lutheran, Catholic, Reformed, Anabaptist, etc.) that present the major difficulty. Rather, the most severe problem we discover is that a radically Christian political position threatens the deepest political faith already held by both Christians and non-Christians - a secular ecumenical faith that does not even claim biblical foundations. The challenge of Christian politics in America is seldom met with the criticism that it is "unbiblical" or "anti-Reformed," or "unLutheran," or "not Anabaptistic enough." The criticisms almost always take the following form: "A Christian political movement would lead to the destruction of our two-party system;" or "It would bring dissension in the midst of our great American melting pot;" or "It wouldn't work here because we could never get a majority to support it;" or "American politics and government are already 'Christian' and the very act of calling that into question would reveal the non-Christian (read: unAmerican) character of any separate, so-called Christian political movement."

How has it been possible for this situation to emerge in America? It has been possible, fundamentally, because American Christians along with most of the rest of the Christian world have grounded their cultural care-lessness in an unbiblical, dualistic view of life - usually expressed in such polarities as "sacred-secular," "holy-profane," "supernatural-natural," "religion-politics," "church-state." In other words, Americans have attempted to institutionalize religion in the church in such a way that politics by definition is considered non-religious or irreligious. But as we have just seen, this attempt to keep religion over to one side of life (locked up in the so-called sacred, holy, supernatural, ecclesiastical affairs) has only led to the need for another religious faith in the political, secular, natural domain.

The truth is that religion is life - all of life - and it cannot be compartmentalized. State, family, school, business are equally as religious as the church - they are all dimensions of man's service to the true God or to false gods. Christianity has not been kept pure and clean in America by keeping it out of politics. To the contrary, Christians have simply dethroned Christ in the public world of politics

160

and replace Him with other gods - the gods of "economic progress," "keeping America No. 1," "majority rule," "popular sovereignty," and so forth. And the outcome of this dualism is that the secular religion has come to dominate and destroy much of the Christian religion.

The history of Christianity in America shows that, almost without exception, Christians have not tried to take politics as politics seriously in a systematic and integrally Christian way. Instead political life has been viewed as an external secular domain which may, from time to time, require ecclesiastical, moral and theological attention, control, or tampering from the outside - from Christians and Christian institutions that see themselves as standing outside or above politics. In this regard, even the New England Puritans lacked an integrally Christian view of the state. Thus, a distinctively Christian concern has almost always expressed itself only in limited, ad hoc, moralistic movements for prohibition, for abolition, against abortion, against war, etc. The inner structure and functioning of the political system as a whole has been left untouched by Christian communal efforts so that it can be dealt with in the "neutral," secular, ecumenical, two-party way where Christians see themselves as having no special responsibility, identity, or insight different from anyone else.

The following outline of a Christian political standpoint seeks to break with this false bifurcation of religion; it seeks to break with "synthesis," "care-lessness," "secularism," "moralism," and other fruits of the dualism of sacred-secular religion-politics, church-state. The tentativeness of the proposal is due to the fact that one fallible American Christian cannot guarantee a final, perfect, and total break with a long tradition of which he is very much a part. On the other hand, it should now be clear how he will respond to traditional objections offered against what follows.

The Basics of a Christian Political Standpoint

In his important book, The Myth of the State,
Ernst Cassirer has shown that from ancient times
to the present day political life has been guided
by deep religious impulses which come to expression in communal symbols and language. He calls
this religious - emotional - intellectual -
symbolic complex "mythical thought." He believes,
however, that at least from the time of Socrates
another mode of communal expression has been
developing, namely "rational thought." The latter
he assumes is superior but it is locked into a
never ending battle with mythical thought.

Cassirer seems to suggest that there was a
brief interlude in modern times when rational
thought gained the ascendancy in politics. But
in the twentieth century, particularly with the
rise of Hitler's Third Reich, mythical thought
came storming back.

Perhaps the most important and the most
alarming feature in this development of
modern political thought is the appearance
of a new power: the power of mythical thought.
The preponderance of mythical thought over
rational thought in some of our modern
political systems is obvious.

What Cassirer fails to see, however, is that
so-called "rational thought" is itself rooted
in a deeper religious-symbolic myth. Socrates'
ideal of rationality presupposed faith in human
self-reflection as the ultimate starting point
for truth. Plato's rational philosophy was
totally bounded by his faith in the ideal polis
as the macrocosm of individual microcosmic man
and by his faith in the mythical "Idea of the
Good." Stoic natural law philosophy was rooted
in the "myth" of an original order of mankind.
Machiavelli's secular politics made sense only
if one believed the new myth that politics is
everything. Thomas Carlyle's hero worship and
Gobineau's racism, as well as the political

philosophies of those whom Cassirer would type as "rational" thinkers, all arose from new religious myths - even if the myth was simply that man can be secularly rational.

The Christian view of politics begins without apology as a religious response to the only true God Who has revealed Himself in Jesus Christ. It rejects the starting points of the dominant political ideologies of our day - the religious myths of "popular sovereignty," "the withering away of the state," "nationalism," "economic progress," "pragmatism," "balance of power," and so forth. But Christian politics is not thereby "mythical-religious" as over against the supposed "secular-rational" character of modern democratic constitutional politics. Christian politics simply expresses its deep religious roots openly in contrast to the humanistic political standpoints which seek to hide their deepest religious presuppositions under the cover of the myth of "neutrality," "secularity," and "a-religiousness."

A Christian understanding of politics, therefore, is not strange or peculiar because it is religious but because its religiosity is openly Christian. Likewise, Christian politics does not imply the confession of some unearthly ideal or utopian dream that has only incidental contact with the real world. It is not a pious hope for unrealizable principles over against the real world of pragmatic, compromising, "rational" politics. A Christian political standpoint has everything to do with the present world in its actual political configurations. It is concerned with the distribution of justice on earth, nothing more, nothing less. But as a real political option it has its roots in Christ's Lordship over this earth not in some humanistic myth whether that myth be "rational" or "irrational."

Our Christian political standpoint, which begins with the confession of Christ's Lordship, begins at that point with a very specific conception. God's rule over all things in Christ is an integral, total, non-dualistic, creational, redemptive lordship. (See for example: Gen. 1; Lev. 25; Job 38-42; Isa. 42; Dan. 4:1-3; 6:25-27; Luke 1:30-33, 46-55; 4:16-30; Jn. 1:1-5; Rom. 8:18-39; I Cor. 15:20-28; Col. 1:15-19; Heb. 1:1-4; Rev. 1:4-8, 4:1-11, 20-22). We reject the medieval idea of an independent natural realm ruled by natural law and natural reason existing along side a supernatural realm ruled by Christ and the church. We cannot find in the biblical revelation any basis to support Luther's idea of two kingdoms - one of law and one of love, one of nature and one of grace, one ruled by thw sword and another ruled by mercy and peace, one in which Christians serve the Gospel inwardly and another in which all men serve the world outwardly. Nor does the confession of the integral and total lordship of Christ over all things coincide with the Anabaptist view that "the sword is ordained of God outside the perfection of Christ," so that even though a political ruler "serves as God's instrument...he is not truly righteous." Likewise the idea of the separation of church and state, when that idea implies the a-religious character of the state, must be rejected. And we find the biblical proclamation of Christ's Lordship incompatible with every nation that Christianity is primarily a moral and ecclesiastical force which Christians must then apply to the secular state for the latter's transformation.

Instead of the above dualistic conceptions we want to affirm the biblical announcement of the single and all-embracing Kingdom of God in Christ - the Kingdom which is

the rule of the Lord over the entire creation by His Word. The Kingdom of God is the Creator's constitutional order for every creature...the kingdom is also that creation itself in the measure that it follows the King's orders.

164

With Bernard Zylstra we argue:

> In the light of the Gospel we can safely conclude that no human organization may escape the realm of Christ's Lordship... The power and authority of the state is subject to the power and authority of Jesus Christ. That means it must establish a social order where love between human beings is given a political shape.

God's command to men to establish justice not injustice is not a lesser word or a contradictory word or an incompatible word with respect to His evangelical command that men should love and not hate one another.

> Justice is one of the ways in which we are to love our fellow man. Justice is one of the many commands or words which the Lord addresses to mankind. Justice is an inherent element of the Gospel. For this reason the restoration of the human community in terms of the covenant between God and man implies the restoration of a just society.

If we deny that there is any dualism in God's kingdom-rule over His creation in Christ, do we thereby imply that there is no diversity on earth? By no means! We explicitly affirm the biblical revelation about different offices, communities, and spheres of stewardship and authority which God has instituted among men on earth. (See for example, Ex. 18:13-26, 30:30-35; Numb. 3:5-10; I Cor. 12:1-31; Eph. 5:17-35, 6:1-10; Col. 3:17-25; Rom. 13:1-7; I Pet. 2:13-17). We believe that the very possibility for the existence of any political order (as distinct from ecclesiastical, economic, scientific, educational, and familial orders) is due only to God's gracious rule in Christ through which He also upholds marriage, family, business, education, and everything else. The fact that many states reveal so much injustice, or that many marriages end in divorce, or that many families

165

are warped by hatred, or that many businesses
harm the environment, the consumer, and the
workers, or that many schools are not doing much
educating - all of these distortions manifest
man's sinfulness which is his deaf disobedience
to God's gracious Word of life which holds the
legitimate diversity of life together for good.
But the very possibility of such human malformation is due to the fact that the good creation
order redeemed by Christ (the single Kingdom
covenant which sustains the earthly diversity
of offices) remains there to be malformed by
sinners.

The creation does indeed reveal a manifold
order of creatures, associations, communities,
institutions, and so forth. But this total
diversity of good things exists by the creative
and redeeming Word of God which holds for all
of human life. Thus, we deny the typical humanistic confession that man is the completely
autonomous creator of the diverse non-bodily,
cultural components of his existence. According to Michael Landmann, for example, there are
no mandatory norms anchored in man's nature "for
family, marriage, religion, art, or science."
"All this is culture," he says. "And by definition culture is created by man's own free initiative, and that is why he gives it such a
multiplicity of forms, differing from people to
people and from age to age...But in creating
culture, man creates himself."

Contrary to this perspective, we believe that
human life in all its diverse dimensions is
structured normatively by divine ordinances.
Man is not the autonomous and arbitrary creator
of earthly society.

It is crucial then for us to discover, and
to live obediently in accord with, the divine
norm for public justice that holds for every
political community. And this requires that we
discover the normative difference of a political
community from a marriage, a family, a school,

166

a business, a church, a voluntary association, and an informal interpersonal relationship, because the different character of these communities and relationships is not accidental or arbitrary. We agree that the church must not be made over into a political party, and that the state must not attempt to function as a universal church in the territory of its dominion. The state ought to be limited to its divinely given task, and business, art, science, education, and worship ought to be free to unfold according to their own distinct, nonpolitical characters.

The above conception of political, ecclesiastical, educational, economic, and cultural freedom in diversity is grounded in the two-fold idea of the God-ordained diversity of earthly offices, on the one hand, and of the total unity and integrality of religion in God's one Kingdom, on the other hand. All of the diversity is embraced by and grounded in the religious unity of life. God's people, redeemed in Christ, have been called to serve Him totally in all things, not just in personal and ecclesiastical life (Deut. 10L12-22; Mk. 12:30; I Cor. 10:31). Therefore, true obedience to God in Christ, true religion, requires truly Christian education, truly Christian marriage, truly Christian family life, truly Christian economics, and truly Christian politics. But the basis for Christian politics cannot be ecclesiastical sponsorship of political proclamations and pressure groups. Nor can it be simply the independent establishment of an association of Christians who want to influence politics. It is neither the ecclesiastical nor individual identity of persons as Christians that makes politics Christian. Christian politics is based upon and determined solely by God's creative, redemptive Word of justice as that is obeyed by men in the actual political formations and activities that they carry out. Christian politics must be real politics and it exists only as political obedience to God's Word of justice.

Moreover, the only alternative to Christian politics is not "neutral," or "a-religious," politics, but politics of another religious drive and persuasion that is not Christian.

This idea of a distinct political sphere with an internal character and purpose different from a church, a school, a business enterprise, and a family (an idea which we can call "sphere-sovereignty"), is not the same as the old liberal (now conservative) idea of the separation of church and state.

According to Dooyeweerd,

Insofar as liberalism wished to safeguard the freedom of church-life over against the state it would not do otherwise than (1) effect a watertight division between state and church, and (2) introduce the "religionless state", where faith is completely excluded. The freedom of the church was then derived from the absolute constitutional rights of the "religious individual". The church became a private association, and in it the "general will" of the members was declared sovereign.

Scriptural Christianity, on the other hand, can never take over this liberalistic slogan of separation of church and state without spiritual suicide. Sphere-sovereignty does not yield a watertight compartment or mechanical division among the areas of life. It is, as we have seen, an organically most deeply cohering principle, for it begins with the religious root-unity of the life-spheres.

Religion, as we have emphasized, cannot be identified solely with church life. But the fact that all of life is religious does not mean the obliteration of important structural differences among God-ordained communities, institutions, and relationships. All of the spheres of earthly life are closely interwoven because

they are all part of one divine creation. At
the same time the diversity is guaranteed by
the same divine Creator Who holds all things
together. Consequently we see neither the
obliteration and amalgamation of the different
spheres of life nor their isolation and total
separation from one another. "The various social
structures by which sphere-sovereignty is internally guaranteed" Dooyeweerd explains, "do not
stand alongside each other in isolation."

In temporal life they are intertwined and
interwoven. All other societal relationships also have a function within the state,
just as conversely the state functions in
all other societal relationships. But all
these structural interplays remain in the
final analysis of an external character with
respect to sphere-sovereignty. Members of
a family, a congregation, or a business
enterprise are at the same time citizens.
And conversely, the state is always dealing
with families, churches, and business enterprises. But the competence, the sphere of
jurisdiction of the state can never be
expanded into the internal, structurally
determined concerns that are proper to these
societal relationships without thereby
violating in an revolutionary way the cosmic
constitution of sphere-sovereignty.

But here one might well ask about the difference between a church where all the members
confess Christ's Lordship and a state where
many (perhaps most) citizens do not confess
Christ's Lordship. Does the Christian confession
of Christ's Lordship over the political sphere
imply that it is the responsibility of Christians
to transform the state into a commonwealth of
confession Christians even if that requires the
expulsion or forced "conversion" of those who
do not confess Christ's Lordship? It is understandable that much confusion exists over this
matter since the Western world has endured centuries of different Constantinian and eccles-

iastical efforts to make a certain territory
"Christian" by various means that have not
recognized either the importance of religious
freedom or the proper relation between church
and state. It is also understandable that
many evangelical Christians distrust the idea
of "political transformationism" after the
efforts of liberal social gospelers earlier in
this century.

The biblical picture seems to be quite clear
that whereas God constituted Israel of the old
covenant in a compact religious way that included
a political territorial organization. He has,
in the revelation of Jesus Christ, fulfilled His
promise to inaugurate the universal Kingdom of
peace and glory that cannot be embraced by or
identified with any earthly political state as
such. The commands of Christ do not include
any directive to Christians to rebuild the walls
of Jerusalem, or to crusade later on in the
old territory of Israel to destroy Islam, or
to establish on some new continent in the seventeenth century a "true" nation of God's people
as over against all false nations.

We can only interpret this fact (together
with Christ's claim to possess all authority
in heaven and on earth) as a further revelation
of His grace during the time until He returns.
In other words, the responsibility for men to
establish political communities of justice on
earth does not include the task of compelling
men within those communities to confess a particular faith or of punishing men for idolatrous
worship. Such judgment is now in the hands of
Christ, the risen One, and He has chosen, for
a time, to restrain the final judgment which
will indeed separate the confessing members of
His Father's Kingdom from those rebellious ones
who have no part in it.

From a Christian point of view, therefore,
political communities are explicitly limited by
this measure of Christ's gracious restraint of

judgment; they may not attempt to reconstruct
the present earth by means which Christ has
not delegated to them. The state is not to be
a community guided by a uniform confession of
faith on the part of all its citizens. Here
we can appreciate the Anabaptist contribution
which has emphasized Christ's parable of the
wheat and the tares. Balthasar Hubmaier argued
in 1524 that:

the slayers of heretics are the worst heretics
of all, in that they, contrary to Christ's
teaching practice, condemn heretics to the
fire. By pulling up the harvest prematurely
they destroy the wheat along with the tares.

God's grace as it expresses itself in the
political sphere extends by implication not
only to the protection of heretics from the death
penalty but also to the evenhanded distribution
of public care, protection, and welfare to all,
no matter what the religious confession. A
Christian political position, therefore, is not
one which seeks to make men confess Christ or
to elevate Christian persons and institutions
over non-Christian persons and institutions.
That is the self-seeking deformation of public
justice, not Christian transformation. Rather,
Christian politics should seek to implement
the gracious divine norm of justice for every
person and social community within the state,
including non-Christian persons and communities, even where and when the Christian view of
life is held by a majority of citizens within
that political community.

Here we can begin to see the unique shape and
character that the political sphere ought to
have in this age of grace. Quite unlike a
family, a school, an industry, a church, or a
personal friendship, the state is an all-embracing
public community which ought to integrate all
of the non-political communities as well as individuals and interpersonal relationships within
its territory into a legal relationship of even-

171

handed justice for all. It is not personal
friendship or familial love or economic purpose
or ecclesiastical faith that can define the
nature of citizenship in a state. Nor may a
state seek to turn its "power for public justice"
into a "power for totalitarian control." The
fact is that an all-embracing public legal
community - a state - does not own or possess
the families, churches, schools, businesses,
and individuals within its borders. Its em-
brace is solely one of guaranteeing public
justice. It has no authority whatever to define
or interfere internally with these non-political
relationships, communities, and persons. Its
sole task is to see that justice rules all the
relationships among these persons and diverse
communities. Christian politics is certainly
concerned with the Christian transormation of
earthly society ("Thy will be done on earth as
it is in Heaven"). But the only kind of political transformation which should interest Christians is the transformation which comes by God's
grace working through our obedience to His norm
of justice and mercy for every man. The norm
for politics is not: "Christians transforming
the state into a church for God by force," But:
"God transforming politics into true justice
for men through Christian obedience." Christ
is the One Who is redeeming and transforming
politics by the power of His resurrection. No
group of men, no earthly nation, may claim to
be God's unique, transorming, political instrument since the only transforming instrument has
already been revealed - Jesus Christ. But every
group of Christians in every earthly nation ought
to be acting together communally, in obedience
to Christ's gracious, resurrection rule, for the
transformation of public injustice into public
justice in the earthly political communities.

In the light of what has just been said we may
now point out three important interconnected
elements of Christian politics: (1) historical
development, (2) the relation of actual political
structures to divine normativity, and (3) human

responsibility.

From the initial chapters of Genesis on through the Bible, we are made conscious of the fact that God has given men responsibility for which He holds them accountable. That is, He has given men the stewardly job of forming and shaping life on earth. Among other things this has meant that with the unfolding of human generations and of human culture, including agriculture, art, science, technology, architecture, trade, education, and so on, new social relations have grown apace. In this creational pattern of historical development or unfolding, God did not reveal some "ideal" form of human government (a monarchy or a democracy or whatever), which men were supposed to aim for and, after achieving, hold on to forever without change. The ideal of "frozen cultural forms" comes from those ancient civilizations which did not obey God's command to go forward and follow Him into the promised land.

The biblical picture of stewardship, of human historical responsibility, means for us that in Christ we have been called to renewed service before God here on earth. We have been called to assume responsibility for the historical unfolding of human culture and society. We have not been given some frozen ideal form of political society such as David's monarchy or the original constitutional order of American federalism as our "Christian" norm. To the contrary, the Gospel norm of live, including public justice for political society, requires that we give actual responsible attention to the current social configurations and circumstances of the political communities in which we live and of the world political order as a whole. Today in the United States we face social-historical realities such as nuclear weapons, complex industrial technology, multinational corporations, severe natural resource depletion, pollution, organized crime, institutionalized racism, urban decay, and many others, which were unknown or less problematic to the organizers of our political system at the end of the eighteenth century. As Christians we must face this state of affairs and seek new ways to obey the Lord in our political responsibilities.

Human responsibility for historical development according to divine norms means, therefore, that we look not to some frozen ideal of the past for our political guidance but to the normative Word of God as it illumines the actual situations of our time. Christian politics is not an ideological program of humanly constructed ideals imposed upon other men as though it were a final revelation from God. To the contrary, Christian politics is the humble, frequently repenting effort to obey the divine norm of public justice in the historically unfolding political circumstances of our time - circumstances for which we are responsible and accountable. Every actual political, economic, and social formation - including the U.S. constitution, the two party system, the laws about trade and business and education and health care, etc. - all these established laws and structures are subject to the judgment of God's normative Word which calls men to change, to repent, to overthrow, to reform the existing order where it is unjust so that His will might be done on earth in the political arena.

Bob Goudzwaard address himself to this matter in the following way.

How often have people not tortured themselves to bridge the 'gap' between an ancient Bible and a complex of contemporary political realities! Some have attempted to build bridges by means of eternal principles and derived principles; but hardly had a 'derived' principle been constructed (free trade, rugged individualism, rejection of all birth control) before one had to break one's own principle in certain respects. More than this, the radius of activity of these prin-

174

ciples turned out to be so limited that whole areas of political life were not touched by them at all - and hence these areas were relegated to bleak neutrality. In these political areas one often had to make do with the motto: relying on common sense.

But this is not the biblical approach. The Bible is not an ancient frozen form, and there are no neutral issues. God's Word, Christ's evangel, and the power of the resurrection are not lifeless, abstract "truths" which are left to Christians to apply to politics. The Gospel of Christ is the living power of life which is normative even for political justice. It grabs us; we don't make use of it. "Christian evangelical politics," says Goudzwaard, "comes into being when we let ourselves be used by the gospel. Evangelical politics does not rest on our active reaching out to God's Word, but on the active reaching out of God's Word to us and to the whole world." Human historical responsibility, as a consequence, is related to God's normative Word for politics in a very dynamic way. Goudzwaard brings this to sharp focus.

Those who believe that truly scriptural principles for the state can be obtained solely from explicit Bible texts, base their beliefs on a completely wrong view of scripture. They merely see words, but forget that God's Word is Spirit and Power, and that this Word has to bear upon all of life. God's Word-revelation puts you to work. It wants to influence your whole existence, it wants to bring new life where death and spiritual laziness rule. You who'd like to take it easy hope the ripe fruits of God's Word-revelation will be given to you without any efforts on your part. But Christ Jesus tells you that you yourself have to bear fruit when the seed of God's Word has fallen in fertile soil.

175

What this means for a Christian political position is that Christians must work together in the light of the Gospel according to the principles and norms which that good news allow them to see and articulate now. But their work together must be a humble, repenting, reforming effort to gain clearer insight and to establish greater justice with each new day. The articulation of a principle like "sphere-sovereignty" is not to be taken as a final frozen revelation from God, but as a Christian response to God's gracious revelation - a revelation which continues to transcend and bring into judgment all of our human articulations and responses.

Christian politics is thus principled politics as over against the relativistic pragmatism of modern humanistic politics. But the only firm principles for Christians are God's principles not man's. By contrast the relativists have first rejected all divine principles and then have gone ahead and frozen their own "relativism" and "pragmatism" as the ultimate rules of the game.

Christian politics is also based on an "intolerant" faith in God - a faith which is revealed in Christ as the only way of life. But that very intolerance is grounded in graciousness on God's part which must lead Christians to work for true justice for all men in the political community. By contrast humanistic "tolerance" of all faiths has turned into a public intolerance of any faith that will not accommodate itself to the "neutral", "secular" game of politics as it is now being played.

Finally we must emphasize again that Christian politics is politics, not ecclesiastical or moralistic tampering with certain political issues from the outside. Christians should, once and for all, relinquish every self-serving pressure and lobby effort to impose Christian faith and morality on others through the forceful means of the state. Instead, Christians should join together within the political process

to labor for a system of real public justice
that will open society to all men.

Practical Implications of a Christian Political Standpoint

In a very important book just off the press,
Political Change in the United States: A Framework for Analysis, Kenneth M. Dolbeare concludes this study with this startling assessment:

Perhaps the most important point (about
political change) is still the preliminary
one regarding the nature of the problem of
change in the United States. I have argued
from the start that the question of fundamental change is first and foremost a concep-
tual or epistemological one - a problem of
how to think and what to think about - before
it is a problem of social action. The proper
answer to the insistent American question,
"What do I do, right now?" is not a list of
strategies and tactics for poeple to under-
take. It is that what you do first is to
understand why most "organizing" and other
activity is either irrelevant or self-
defeating, and why some image of a total
process, starting with consciousness change
as the centerpiece and reaching past the
transfer of state power to the construction
of a wholly new society, is the indispensable
prerequisite. To fully absorb this point is
action: one has changed oneself profoundly
and achieved the potential to similarly
change the world. It is far from inconsequential, isolated, or asocial; it is doing in
a vital sense, for it initiates the essential
continuing process of reflection, action, and
reflection...Of course social action is necessary for any individual or societal transformation of this kind, but such action must
be with this context - a component in a consciousness change process in which we first
see and understand differently, and then

177

reshape our world and ourselves accordingly. There has been no lack of mere action in search of change in the United States. But there has been a lack of action in the context of a new consciousness and its associated theory of change.

The message of these two paragraphs should not be missed by Christians concerned with political reformation. The very worst thing for a Christian political movement to do would be to ignore the most crucial and fundamental questions about the nature of the contemporary American political system, in an anxious effort to forge ahead as countless organizations have done in the past with some activistic program of superficial slogans calling for quick and superficial change. The great problems confronting modern political systems are not superficial and they will not be solved in a hurry even by the most sincere efforts of those who imagine that minor adjustments in the system will provide the answers.

A very serious and concerted effort must be made on the part of Christians to act by way of listening to what the Word of God has to say about divine love and justice and about the fundamental structures and direction of our contemporary republic. Apart from such action subsequent actions will be relatively worthless. But the activity of critical reflection and analysis, of investigation and prayerful foundation-laying, requires such an immense amount of energy and patience that there is reason to believe that American Christians are hardly ready to act in this way.

In view of the existing political consciousness of American Christians and of the need for basic political reform, it seems clear at the moment, then, that a three-pronged long-range program of action will be required of any serious Christian political movement. All three prongs have to develop at the same time

but there does seem to be a relation of "founda-
tion-second level-third level" among the three.
First, at the foundation, there must be a sturdy
and sustained program aimed at the development
of a Christian political mind rooted in a biblical world and life view. Second, a program of
critical historical evaluation must aim to uncover
the roots and development of our contemporary
political system so that the problems and injustices which we see on the surface can be under-
stook in their full interrelationship in terms
of basic religious-historical motives that have
been at odds with God's normative, life-giving
Word. Thirdly, the implications of the emerging
Christian political standpoint, as it confronts
the present malformations and political injustices
through its historical critique, must be worked
out in terms of concrete, alternative programs
and policies. The combination of all three
levels of development will lead, by God's grace,
to the eventual determination of additional
tactics for attempting to bring about the desired
political change. Let us look briefly at this
three-pronged program of action.

(1) If our discussion at the beginning about
the lack of a Christian political standpoint
was accurate, then there appears to be no alternative to the development of serious discussion
among Christians about the nature of Christian
politics. We simply cannot assume at the moment
that the phrase "Christian politics" has any
common identifiable meaning among Christians.
But if we lack a common Christian political
mind, the cause is surely the lack of a common
Christian view of cultural life as a whole.

One point of departure for dealing with this
lack will have to be the renewed, and in some
cases entirely new, effort to debate and discuss
politics among communities of Christians that
have different traditions and different views of
political life. Open forums, small group discussions, college and university courses, new
publications, elaborate research seminars, large

179

and small conferences, and much more will be needed if Christians are to gain a common mind in politics. It will not be enough for Christians to get together only briefly or occasionally to work out some common denominator program that will remain general, vague, activistic, and open to all the unresolved disagreements of the past. Serious principled differences will have to be exposed and pitted against one another in an honest effort to let God's Word judge all historic differences and errors. Much time, patience, and research will be required for this effort to lead Christian to maturity.

Another point of departure for dealing with the lack of a Christian political standpoint will have to be the evangelistic, educational propagation of the Gospel as it relates to political life. Non-Christians coming to know the Lord personally, along with Christians who now know little about what the, Gospel has to do with politics, will need to be, instructed in the way of the Gospel until they reach maturity. That maturity will necessarily include an understanding of Christian political responsibility, as well as an understanding of the government's responsibility for establishign justice in earthly political communities. One cannot have a mature knowledge of God without knowing what God's servants and ministers are supposed to be doing.

(2) Built on the foundation of a common Christian communal consciousness in politics will have to come the intricate, penetrating, thorough, and critical evaluation of the actual historical development and present condition of the American republic. We will have to uncover the roots of modern "nationalism" as it dominates world politics, including American politics. We will have to analyze the philosophical, social, and historical background of the legal thinking which led to such great emphasis in our early history on constitution-making. And we must come to grips with the almost worshipful attitude that is now fixed on our federal constitution and its

main institutions. We will have to penetrate the failure of America to make room for a true diversity of cultures, races, and peoples in public life. All those elements of individual rights, separation and balance of powers, democratic and representative government, economic and religious freedom, and so forth, that have gone into the make-up of our American way of life are factors with deep historical roots in a view of life which does not always coincide with a biblical view.

Particularly during the last one hundred years the dominating influences of positivism, evolutionary progressivism, relativism, economism, and pragmatism have so altered the pattern of political life that our old ideas inherited from the middle ages and from Franklin, Jefferson, Adams and others simply do not put us in touch with reality. And in general American evangelical Christians have been so narrowly busy (as self-conscious Christians) with personal evangelism, church work, and foreign missions that the major economic and political developments of this century have unfolded without our awareness of critical evaluation much less our organized communal effort to deal directly with political and economic life.

The forced humanistic tolerance which dominates our two party system, coupled with general "Christian" acquiescence in the idea of the neutrality and secularity of politics, government, economics, and education, means that without a penetrating, critical evaluation of the present state of affairs, any so-called Christian political movement will remain caught in a predicament of ignorance, superficiality, and secularism since its activities will simply carry forward much of what now exists as part of the problem.

Naturally such a program of critical historical analysis will require the talents of trained specialists in history, economics, and political

science. But the program is not one solely for
"intellectuals." All of us together must enter
into the reading, discussing, and questioning
enterprise that will lead us: (1) to investi-
gate the operations and motivations of our elected
officials and of their political parties; (2) to
collect information from newspapers, books, and
other sources on how our political system now
functions; (3) to organize small and large groups
for the discussion of critical issues such as
tax reform, racism, penal reforms, defense
spending, educational freedom and equality, environment and energy, housing and welfare, etc.; (4)
to work together on learning how to be self-
critical about our dualistic misconception of
life so that we can learn to think in a more
consistently Christian way about political matters
and so that we can begin to see alternatives to
present political policies; (5) to seek for new
ways to train our children with Christian minds
instead of with secularistic minds when it comes
to politics; (6) to find ways to acquaint others
with the movement toward a Christian political
option; and (7) to coordinate efforts which, at
the beginning, will undoubtedly be dispersed
across the country among small groups interested
in quite different issues, until we can all
benefit from the work of everyone else.

(3) The confidence that Christian political
action, if truly obedient to God's will, can
lead to fundamental and significant political
reform should not lead us to imagine that at
the present time a considerable body of Christians is working together with such a confidence.
To the contrary, without major steps forward on
the first two levels of development, it seems
unlikely that social action leading to fundamental
political reformation is possible. Consequently,
it is not possible now to suggest what policies,
programs, strategies, and tactics might be adopted
by a Christian political movement two, five, ten,
or twenty years from now. Such developments
await the action of Christians already engaged in
the careful critical analysis of the status quo

and in the building up of a Christian political consciousness.

However, we can say something about what must transpire between the beginning of a Christian political awakening and its coming to maturity.

First, a concrete political action strategy will not emerge automatically somewhere down the line without the conscious effort now to think in terms of the actual alternatives that are necessary to existing programs and policies. In other words, historical criticism and Christian consciousness development require the growth of a truly concrete political understanding that can function in Congress, in the courts, in the Executive Office of the President, and in the political process generally. A Christian political mind can find itself at home only in the actual political affairs of life. Thus we cannot put off policy and program developments until later as though they were not important now. It is just that we must be sensitive to the timing of all three levels of the development process so that we do not attempt to build the third stage on weak or non-existent earlier stages.

Secondly, and in conclusion, it appears that the present historical situation might provide Christians with something of a developmental timing device. The celebration of the American Revolution of 1776 will be taking place in 1976. Undoubtedly that year of attention to our historical foundations will display much patriotism and naivete, along with little criticism and a short-lived concern with "revolution".

A Christian political movement, by contrast, should take 1976 as the point of departure for a long-range program of development, as suggested above, that would aim at 1989 for its climax. One of the main themes underlying this thirteen year program would be that the new American states went through a period of great instability after the revolution during the era of confederation before the U.S. federal constitution went into effect in 1789. A Christian movement could use the thirteen year period between 1976 and 1989 to draw attention to all of the problems that the American states faced and dealt with during the period from 1776-1789. But the Christian political movement would also aim for a radical reformation of contemporary American politics, including reform of the present constitution, by elucidating the various problems, injustices, and causes of instability that grip our nation now.

The fact that this period of historical consciousness raising is almost upon us means that a Christian political movement should have a greater opportunity to gain the ear of both Christians and non-Christians concerning the unfolding of true justice in our republic. Perhaps by God's grace, if His people will repent and learn obedience, the time is at hand for a great blessing of God's judgment and mercy in the political affairs of this and other nations.

THE BIBLE, JUSTICE AND THE STATE

By Bernard Zylstra

Wherever one turns today, the question is
asked whether we can live a meaningful human
existence in the kind of society that has developed in the twentieth century. For it is evident
that the kind of society we live in brings with
it many seemingly unsolvable problems: inflation,
unemployment, crime, inner city decay, urban
sprawl, corruption in places high and low, stagna-
tion in the process of democratic government,
dehumanizing work conditions, fantastic riches
next to frightful poverty, the elimination of
nature from the cities where most of use reside,
progress in industrial production alongside of
regress in cultural refinement, development of
nature and underdevelopment of personality, etc.

So many ask the question: Have we lost the
quality of life because of our preoccupation
with the quantity of material goods? If so, how
can quality be regained? To paraphrase the title
of Theodore Roszak's latest book: Where does
the wasteland end?

It is necessary to explore the various answers
to this question that are being suggested by
neo-capitalists, neo-liberals, and neo-marxists.
It is not my intention to do that in the present
essay. Instead, I will proceed from the assumption that the quality of life can be regained if
the Biblical vision of man and society is regained
and infused into our political, economic, and
educational institutions.

I. Was Jesus A Social Reformer?

One way of entering our problematics is to ask
a traditional question: If a Christian gets
involved in social and political matters, doesn't
he become entangled in matters of this world so

that he may easily become of it? What was the
attitude of Christ Himself to these matters?

There are many today who argue that Christians must be active in society because Jesus
Himself was a social reformer. Is that really
true? A social reformer tries to change relationships in society in order to improve conditions of human life. A social reformer directs
his attention to the problems cited above, problems of poverty and riches, slavery and war,
racial tensions and housing, etc.

Jesus was not a social reformer. When one
of His listeners asked Him to settle a problem
of inheritance, Christ's reply was brief and to
the point: "Man, who made me a judge or divider
over you?" (Luke 12:14). No, Christ's central
office lay elsewhere because God the Father had
given Him a far more significant assignment:
"I must preach the good news of the Kingdom of
God...for I was sent for this purpose" (Luke
4:43).

So, quite clearly, if we want to establish a
connection between Jesus Christ and social concern we must find out 'if there is a connection
between the Kingdom of God and social life. That
connection exists, radically, integrally, indis-
pensably.

The Kingdom and the goodness of life

The Kingdom of God, as I indicated in "Thy
Word Our Life," can be circumscribed from two
vantage points. In the first place, it is the
rule of the Lord over the entire creation by
His Word. The Kingdom of God is the Creator's
constitutional order for every creature. In
the second place, the Kingdom is also that creation itself in the measure that it follows the
King's orders. The quality of human life lies
in the rapport between the order of the King and
the obedience of men. As a matter of fact, the
very life of every creature is that order, that

186

Word of the master, Who has the say over us all.
Creatures simply are servants. When they serve,
their life is good as citizens of the Kingdom.

This brings us directly to the problems of
our society. If we have lost the quality of
life, it is because we do not obey the Creator's
constitutional order for society. I know that
this is not a particularly popular thing to say
today, for we have been taught by our philosophers, our artists, our political leaders, and
by our schools that the quality of human life
depends upon getting rid of the phenomenon of
obedience. Service, we are told, is sub-human.
How can we rid our society of the necessity of
obedience? By **abolishing** authority, both divine
and institutional. Consistently pursued, this
tenet of humanism leads to social anarchy.
Anarchy means: no rule or authority of any kind.
In order to avoid social chaos following anarchy,
the most significant modern social thinkers and
politicians suggest a compromise in the form of
the social contract: autonomous individuals can
establish social connections and institutions
on the basis of consent. They can agree to be
governed by rules of their own making. For this
reason the foundation of the state is popular
sovereignty, the consent of the governed, or -
to use a more contemporary expression - participatory democracy. This basic conception of
social order is shared by John Locke, Rousseau,
Thomas Jefferson, and Karl Marx. They will
start from the notion of human autonomy as the
basis for building the Kingdom of Man.

The Bible unmasks the notion of human autonomy
as one expression of sin. Sin breaks the harmonious life of God's good creation into bits and
pieces. It is the underlying cause of the disintegration in human life. That disintegration
is the curse of which we see so many symptoms
today. Right at the outset the Bible **reveals**
that sin has a fourfold disintegrating effect
on the harmony of life.

1. It makes us strangers to God. It separates us from Christ, the living Word (cf. Eph. 2:12). Since the bond between God and man includes the entirety of man's existence, this primordial alienation suptures the following relationships.

2. Sin destroys the unity within man's personality which is now caught up in tension, frustration, in service of the creature rather than the creator (Rom. 1:25). Since the very nature of man's being is to serve, the rejection of the true God makes him look for substitutes elsewhere. These substitutes are deifications of one facet of the creation, at the expense of other facets. The idols thus imagined can never give peace to men. There is no rest for the 'wicked' in the search for a new idol after the former has proved his failings. This restlessness explains the aimless speed of contemporary culture, with men and women yearning for one cure after the other without ever finding any that satisfies. The Bible describes this predicament of inner tensions and endless pursuits as man's being brokenhearted (Ps. 147:3).

3. Sin makes us seek ourselves at the expense of our neighbour. If man is alone in the universe, self-preservation (John Locke) or enlightened self-interest (Adam Smith) is the key to the social fabric. The apostle Paul tells us what we can expect to find in a society like ours: If men are not lovers of God their society will be one of lovers of self, lovers of pleasure, lovers of money, haters of good, inhuman. Understand this, he writes, that in the last days there will come times of stress. Well, these are our times (II Tim. 3:1-7).

4. Finally, sin causes us to lose our home, our paradise on this earth. Because of man's sin, the earth will bring forth thorns and thistles. In other words, the relationship between man and nature is disrupted. The evidence of that is clearly present in today's ecological and energy crises. As a result of our

188

enlightened self-interest we have lost the sense
of stewardship over the earth's potentials so
that we exploit this planet's limited resources
in an entirely unbalanced manner.

Christ cures the heart of the disease

When John the Baptist, the last of the old
testament prophets, introduced Jesus, he said:
"behold, the Lamb of God, who takes away the
sin of the world" (John 1:29). Here we are faced
with another description of Jesus' office. At
this juncture we must avoid falling into the
dilemma of either the 'individual gospel' or
the 'social gospel.'

The proponents of the individual gospel hold
that the 'sin of the world' which Jesus came to
take away in effect amounts to the sum total of
the sins of isolated individuals. The proponents
of the social gospel argue that the sin of the
world is the sum total of inhuman disruptions
in social institutions. The former look upon
Jesus as the Saviour of souls; the latter consider him to be a social reformer, a social
saviour. In the light of the above I would
suggest that both are mistaken since both disregard the totality of the covenantal context
within which man's place on earth is situated
in the Scriptures.

Jesus indeed is a Saviour; that's the very
meaning of His name: Jesus means Healer. He is
the Prince of Peace (Isa. 9:6). He is a peace-
maker, a reconciler. But we should be scrip-
turally clear about the scope of His peacemaking
office. Paul makes that clear in the letters to
the Ephesians and Colossians, from which we can
cite one decisive passage: "For in Christ all
the fullness of God was pleased to dwell, and
through Him to reconcile all things, whether on
earth or in heaven, making peace by the blood
of His cross" (Col. 1:19f).

The crucifixion of Christ is the central and

189

decisive event in human history. For there
Christ made things right again between the
Creator and the creation. Moreover, since
Christ rose from the dead, He is the Resurrec-
tion and the Life.

This is not a matter merely of theology.
This is a matter of the foundation of human
life and the social order. For at the cross
the basic disease disrupting human life and the
social order is cured. Christ came to take away
the sin, the disharmony and disintegration, from
human life and the social order.

Indeed, Christ was not a social reformer. His
task and office was much more basic and radical.
His task was to get to the root of all ill,
social ills included. Since God so loved the
world He sent His Son to take away the sin of
that world. The Good Shepherd lays down His life
so that men and women, in faith, may have life,
and have it abundantly (John 10:10). Christ -
that is the name of His office - is the redeemer
of the universe and, by His Spirit, a renewer
of hearts. In that light we begin to understand
the central task of His brief ministry, the proclamation of the Good News of the Kingdom (Luke
4:43). In that Kingdom lies our life, also of
our social and political and economic life.

How can we have that life? There is only one
way, a narrow way, the way of conversion. This
is the message of Christ to those who cause and
to those who suffer the alienation and dehumanization of today's social order: "Repent, for
the kingdom of God is at hand" (Matt. 4:17).
Conversion, repentance from sin, that is, a
radical turn-about in one's conviction, allegiance,
and life's direction, is the avenue which Christ
procliams as a healing of the social order.

The all-embracing scope of the Gospel is
clearly evident in Christ's ministry. His salvation brings healing and renewal and hope in
the whole of human life. When John the Baptist

entertained some doubts about Christ's work, Jesus has this message for him: "Go and tell John what you hear and see: the blind receive their sight and the lame walk, lepers are cleansed and the deaf hear, and the dead are raised up, and the poor have good news preached to them" (Matt. 11:4f). The proclamation of the Gospel and the healing of misery go hand in hand. Christ's miracles are signs and pointers of the new life. When the crowds are hungry, Jesus has compassion on them, and commissions His disciples to give them to eat (Mark 8:2; 6:37). That brings us to the place of Christ's disciples in the history of reconciliation and peace-making.

II. The Social Concern Of Christ's Disciples

Christ's redeeming compassion over the hungry multitude, the poor, the suffering ones, must be expressed also by Christ's Body, the spiritual community of His followers. Is is part and parcel of the Christian way of life that love of God implies love on one's neighbor. We cannot understand the meaning of Christianity if love of God is separated from love of our fellow man, and vice versa. The Old Testament was clear on this (cf. Deut. 6:5 and Lev. 19:18), and the New Testament throughout posits the inseparable conjunction of the two loves (Matt. 22:36f). "Love does no wrong to a neighbor; therefore love is the fulfilling of the law;" (Rom. 13:10). "He who does not love does not know God" (I John 4:7). It's as simple as that!

The two love commandments sum up whatever God requires of human beings. They are the creation order for men. Earlier I said that all creatures are servants. Human beings are servant of God in the measure that they love God above all and neighbor as self. This service-of-love expresses their creatureliness, their very humanness.

If life is indeed religion, if the service-of-love embraces all that is required of men, then all other requirements must be expressions of love. In **that** way, I think we should understand the integral relation between love on the one hand and justice and stewardship on the other hand. Justice and stewardship are not commandments from God that stand next to the commandment of love. Rather, they are specific instances of the way in which our love to our neighbor ought to be channeled.

Divine justice

Let us briefly try to catch a glimpse of the Biblical perspectives on justice. The first thing to note is that the word 'justice' is frequently used in the Scriptures to describe God's relations with men. Someone has remarked that only a religion whose God is just can make a contribution to social justice, that is, to a 'right' relation among people. The Bible unmistakably tells us that Yahweh is a just God. All His ways are justice (Deut. 32:4). How are we to understand this?

If the covenant is the totality of the relationship between God and creation, especially the relationship between God and men, then justice is a **fiber** of the covenantal fabric. The covenant consists of two parts: God's command and man's obedience. If man obeys, his life will be blessed; it will be a good life. This two-sided character of the covenant is stressed again and again: "I will be your God, and you shall be my people, and walk in all the ways that I command you, that it may be well with you" (Jer. 7:23)

God's justice consists in His faithfulness to the terms of the covenant. God is just in that He gives His people what He has promised. For this reason I believe that we should not look upon God's grace and God's justice as two relationships which stand in tension with each other. God's grace is not in conflict with, but an expression of, God's justice. This is involved

also in Paul's teachings on justification. God
will make sinners just again because of Christ's
work of reconciliation. One way of looking at
the doctrine of justification lies herein, that
God will rehabilitate sinners to their original
position as loving servants. From the human
point of view, we can say that when men accept
this justification by faith they can count on
it' that their life will be made whole again. For
God in Christ will now deal with men as restored
human creatures who will begin to experience the
blessings of the good life that the Spirit gives.

God's justice is revealed in Jesus Christ,
Whose name already in the Old Testament is: "The
Lord is our Righteousness" (Jer. 23:6). This
name describes the office of the Messiah Who,
especially in the prophecies of Isaiah, is pic-
tured as the One Who will establish a Kingdom
of justice. With righteousness He shall judge
the poor, and decide with equity for the meek
of the earth (11:4). "He will bring forth justice of the nations" (42:1). This brings us to
justice in the affairs of men.

Human justice

Justice is one of the ways in which we are
to love our fellow man. Justice is one of the
many commands or words which the Lord addresses
to mankind. Justice is an inherent element of
the Gospel. For this reason the restoration of
the human community in terms of the covenant
between God and man implies the restoration of
a just society. This is clearly evident in the
books of Moses, in the Psalms, in Proverbs, and
in the major and minor prophets.

It is impossible to define precisely what the
content of the norm of justice is. We face a
similar difficulty in defining the content of
other fundamental norms like beauty, moral love,
and stewardship. Words like equity, fairness,
and right hint at the meaning of justice. I
find Emil Brunner's attempts at a description

helpful here.

> The Christian conception of justice...
> is determined by the conception of God's
> order of creation. What corresponds to
> the Creator's ordinance is just - to that
> ordinance which bestows on every creature,
> with its being, the law of its being and
> its relationships to other creatures.
> The 'primal order' to which every one
> refers in using the words 'just' or 'un-
> just,' the 'due' which is rendered to
> each man, is the order of creation, which
> is the will of the Creator made manifest.

The South African philosopher H.G. Stoker
relates justice to the status of man in the
cosmos. In a recent study entitled "The Nature
and Role of Law: A Philosophical **Reflections**" **he**
writes:

> God's Word-revelation sheds an even keener
> light on the status of man. Viewed in its
> divine context and in religious perspec-
> tive we note the following concerning
> man's status. Man alone is created as
> God's image. Man has been given a calling
> which he must fulfill, for which he is
> responsible and for which he must give an
> account. Man has an appointment. He has
> been appointed as mandator dei, as a crea-
> turely vicegerent of God to act as ruler
> within the cosmos in the name of the Lord.
> He has been appointed as ambassador of the
> Most High. And as such he is entrusted
> with an office to contribute, as a crea-
> turely means in the hands of God, to the
> realization of God's council and plan in
> and with the cosmos. In all this man is
> responsible to God. In other words, with
> reference to all this, including the func-
> tion and purpose of his status, man has
> been given a special mandate. He is called
> to be a child of the King and in his royal
> status he is at the same time a servant of

God. All of this is characteristic of his
appointment and the mandate that goes with
it, presented to him as man. Must we not
find human justice and law here, that is,
human rights, legal norms and the legal
order?

Both Brunner and Stoker are trying to formulate
in the Biblical setting what the traditional definition of justice intended with 'rendering to
each his due' (suum cuique tribuere). What is
due to man is a status in the social context which
makes his unique creatureliness possible. For
this reason the Biblical norm of justice must be
based on the Biblical teachings of creation. For
insight into man's specific nature or creatureliness presents the clue to 'what is just.' Now
man has been created as God's image.

So we can arrive at this provisional summation:
the norm of justice requires a social order in
which men can express themselves as God's imagers.
To put it in different words: the norm of justice
requires social space for human personality. By
personality I then mean the human self whose
calling lies in love of God and love of fellowman.
That calling entails the realization of a multiplicity of tasks in history. Justice therefore
also requires societal space for man's cultural
tasks. Moreover, the realization of man's central
calling also entails the establishment of social
institutions, like marriage, the family, schools,
industries, and the like. Hence justice requires
societal space for these institutions as long as
they contribute of meaningful, harmonious, and
an opened up human existence. Finally, the realization of man's many tasks and callings involves
the use of 'nature' and its resources. In view
of this, justice also requires such an allocation
of material goods that human life is made possible,
protected, and enhanced in accordance with its
creaturely character, status, and end. In short,
justice requires freedom for man's service. In
this context we dare to speak of human rights.
That is one of the fruits of Christ's work of

redemption, which in principle entails the restoration of creation, also of man's authentic creatureliness as God's imager in the realization of his social and cultural tasks or offices.

Biblical pointers

The Bible was written during a time different from ours. The numerous ways in which the Lord told His people about how a just society is to be established are oriented to a largely agricultural setting. Nevertheless, there is much for us to learn.

1. To begin with, the Bible rejects the modern notion of private property. When the Psalmist sings, "The earth is the Lord's and the fulness thereof," he means what he says (Ps. 24:1). In effect, the Lord owns the earth; man can only inherit it from Him and use it subject to certain conditions. When the people of Israel entered the land of Canaan, it was divided among the various tribes according to their families (Josh. 13). Quite clearly the intent was to make sure that each tribe and sub-group would receive enough to live on. Moreover, if for some reason or another land was sold, it had to be returned in the Year of Jubilee to its original possessor so that no class distinctions would develop between haves and have-nots (Cf. Lev. 25:8f). In the buying and selling of land our notion of land speculation for profit was entirely absent. "When you sell or buy land amongst yourselves, neither party shall drive a hard bargain...You must not victimize one another, but you shall fear your God...The land is mine" (Lev. 25:14-23).

2. The blessings of the Lord to one person were looked upon as avenues of stewardship to those in need. In the light of what we said about justice in general it comes as no surprise that both in the laws of Moses and later in the books of the prophets the deprived persons were given special attention. The Lord as it were said

to His people: "Make room in your society for
all my creatures. They are made in my image;
they are not blocks or stones or beasts but persons with their own tasks and responsibilities.
Now make very sure that they can indeed express
themselves as such, that they have elbow room
for the fulfillment of their tasks. Make sure
that the high are brought low and that the lowly
ones among you are protected, restored to new
opportunities, to service in my vineyard." Quite
concretely this meant that four groups of needy
persons are constantly singled out as the special
recipients of justice and stewardship: the widows,
aliens, the poor and the orphans. We recall how
Ruth found food for herself and Naomi. But this
did not depend upon the personal philanthrophy
of Boaz: social concern was built into the fabric
of the covenant community. "When you reap your
harvests in your field, and have forgotten a
sheaf in the field, you shall not go back to get
it; it shall be for the sojourner, the fatherless,
and the widow; that the Lord your God may bless
you in all the work of your hands" (Deut. 24:19).

The same approach is taken with reference to
the relations between rich and poor. The former
was clearly told never to exploit the latter.
As a matter of fact, being wealthy only increased
one's responsibility for those in need. "If you
lend money to any of my people with you who is
poor, you shall not be to him as a creditor, and
you shall not exact interest from him" (Ex. 22:25).
In the same passage we read how concrete love becomes in the otherwise humiliating circumstances
of the person who gives his coat in pledge for
a loan. The creditor is told to bring to back
before the sun goes down, before it gets cold -
"for this is his only covering." The financial
dealings between rich and poor could never be
such that the poor man might lose the base of
his livelihood. "No man shall take a mill or an
upper millstone in pledge; for he would be taking
a life in pledge" (Deut. 24:6). How could the
miller make a living without his tools?

3. The earth could be used but not exploited.
There is the notion abroad today that Christianity
is responsible for the ecological crisis. Lynn
White has formulated this notion thus: "Christianity...not only established a dualism of man
and nature but also insisted that it is God's will
that man exploit nature for his proper ends."
Whatever role Christians may have played in the
development of modern natural science, technology,
industrial production, and environmental exploitation - the destructive effect of this development
is not a consequence of the Biblical view of
nature. Precisely because nature is also God's
creation man's relationship towards it must be
one of stewardly concern, of custodianship. Man
is God's trustee in creation. This implies that
man's interaction with nature must be conditioned
by the creaturely structure and limits of nature
(inorganic matter, plants, and animals). Man
must be just not only to his fellow man; he must
also be just to non-human creatures. He must
respect their potentials and their limits.

An illustration of this can be found in the
Sabbath Year described in Lev. 25:1-7, where we
read that every seventh year the land must be
given a rest. Man indeed is distinguished from
nature in the Bible; human creatureliness is
structurally different from the creatureliness
of matter, plants, and animals. But this distinction does not warrant exploitation; it implies
man's stewardship over available but finite resources. The energy and ecological crisis of
our day are not a result of Biblical motifs
but a consequence of the rejection of these motifs
in the Renaissance and the Enlightenment. For in
these distinctly post-Biblical movements of the
modern era the finitude that belongs to reality
as creation is replaced with the notion of man's
infinite potentials and nature's infinite - and
therefore exploitable - resources. This notion
is foreign to the Bible. The Lord has indeed
given man dominion over the works of His hand.
He is instructed to 'till' the garden but at the
same time to 'keep it,' to preserve it, to protect

it (Cf. Gen. 1:28; 2:15; Ps. 8:6).

III. The Government is The Lord's Servant

A good deal more needs to be said about justice
and stewardship than present space allows. But I
believe that enough has been said to move on to
the next theme, viz., the Biblical conception of
the state. The state arises in a society when
the interrelationships between tribes and clans
and cities within a particular territory requires
a central administration for the dispensation of
justice. The people of Israel were surrounded
by states' and empires in which the basis of political unity generally was more a matter of absolute
power than justice. When something like a national state appeared within Israel itself we detect
immediately the liberating force of the Gospel
for politics. For in the light of the Gospel
the king has but one main task, that is, the fur-
therance of a just society. "Give the king thy
justice, O God, and thy righteousness to the
royal son!" "May he defend the cause of the
poor of the people, give deliverance to the
needy, and crush the oppressor!" (Ps. 72).

Authority is an avenue of service

It is in this light that we must interpret
Paul's famous passage about "governing authorities" in Romans 13. Authority is social power,
that is, power exercised by one group of persons
over other persons. The Bible clearly recognizes the need of authority in the social order.
It speaks freely of the authority of priests,
kings, parents, even masters. But it sheds
indispensable light on the nature of authority.
Authority is office, that is, a channel for the
realization of divine norms in a social relationship. This means that "there is no authority
except from God," who has established the norms
that hold for human life. Moreover, authority
must be exercised for the welfare of those subject to it. Paul sums the matter up very succinct-
ly: the person in authority is "God's servant for

your good" (Rom. 13:3f).

In the way Paul rejects the political absolutism that took on concrete shape in the Roman Empire of his time, when Nero reigned. Political absolutism, ancient or modern, proceeds from the notion that the citizen exists for the good of the state. Paul argues the exact opposite: the state and its authorities exist for the good of the citizenry. This, in a nutshell, is the evangelical, the Gospel's message for politics, also in our time of unprecedented corruption in democratic regimes. Politicians are office-bearers. They are to execute their executive, legislative, judicial, or administrative offices only for the good of the citizenry. That good is public justice.

Moreover, it should be noted that Paul does not arrive at this conclusion of the basis of conceptions that underlie modern democracies: the notion of popular sovereignty, government by the consent of the governed, government of and by and for the people. For these conceptions make the government the servant of the people. It is indeed 'for the people,' but it is not 'of the people.' The notion of popular sovereignty in essence develops into the tyranny of the majority, or the tyranny of an elite that can effectively manipulate the electorate at the ballot box. Paul's position points to the possibility of an open political system. But he can do this because he rejects the two major options in western political theory and practice: political absolutism and popular sovereignty. Paul can point to an open political system because he can point to a norm (justice) which the government is called upon to realize in all its undertakings. Earlier I stated that creatureliness is service. Further, that human creatures are to be servants-of-love, both to God and fellow man. Thirdly, that all specific divine norms - like justice and stewardship - are to be looked upon as expressions of

200

love. We now see, fourthly, that the expressions of specific norms may well require certain organizations, like the state. Such organizations, fifthly, require a measure of power to achieve their task and office.

What we should now clearly understand is that the use of power in society belongs to the realm of creatureliness, that is, the realm of service. In the light of the Gospel we can safely conclude that no human organization may escape the realm. If it does, it places itself on a divine pedestal, claiming the kind of power and authority that only belongs to Jesus Christ (Matt. 28:18). The power and authority of the state is subject to the power and authority of Jesus Christ. That means it must establish a social order where love between human beings is given a political shape. Such a social order is one which can still be described in the traditional terms of public justice. Let us briefly outline the contours of what that means for the kind of world we live in today.

Society:

The modern state as we know it is a community of citizens whose government is responsible for the administration of public justice within the state's territory, on the basis of political power, in cooperation with other states for the administration of public justice in inter-state relations. In this article I do not want to focus on the internal building blocks that go into the makings of a state. We would then have to pay attention to the various organs of government (executive, legislative, judicial, and administrative), to the relationship between the state as a whole and its parts ('states' in the United States, provinces, countries, cities, etc.), to the place of the army, and the electoral system with a wide variety of representational links, etc.

Instead, I would like to say a few things about

201

the relation between the state and the non-state
elements within society. The use of the word
'society' is somewhat dangerous, because it can
be defined in a variety of ways. A measure of
clarity is essential here. Some thinkers define
society as the sum total of human individuals
living within a particular territory, along with
the social groups that such individuals have vol-
untarily formed to pursue certain goals. This
is the conception of individualism which holds
that the individual person is the basic social
entity. The opposite conception is universalism,
which holds that society itself is the primary
and basic and all-embracing unit, of which everything else is but a part. Some traditional
socialists adhere to a kind of universalism, in
which the entire human race is viewed as the
total social whole (civitas maxima) with the
state as its primary organization.

Both of these conceptions find the final
source of authority and reference within society
itself. In the Biblical setting, the final
point of reference and source of authority lies
beyond society, in the Creator Whose will for
men is revealed in Jesus Christ. Adherence to
this Biblical vision will entail an alternative
conception of society, such as the one developed
in line with Abraham Kuyper's notion of sphere-
sovereignty. For when we take a look at a
particular society, what do we see? First of
all, we notice human beings who do not owe final
allegiance to any social structuee, nor to
society as a whole. When we are confronted with
a social order which demand's a person's entire
allegiance, we condemn that social order. Hence
we sympathize with the current Russian dissenters
like the novelist Solzhenitsyn who rightly claim
that the communist regime does not have the right
to control their conscience and the literary
expression of their convictions. But in a society
we also notice more than human beings. We are
confronted with a vast variety of institutions
(marriage, family, state), associations (church,
stores, factories, clubs, schools), and inter-

personal relations (which occur in market situations, airplanes, museums, street corners, highways, etc.). Quite clearly, individual human beings are not the only social entities. Nor are all of these elements parts of an all-embracing social whole.

In view of this I provisionally describe society as the horizontal complex of all of these human relationships inter-connecting with each other in a particular culture. The many cross-currents between human beings and social structures in a modern metropolis is a good example of what I mean by society. A metropolis is a 'mini-society.'

The state in society

The state occupies a place in society, in this horizontal complex of inter-connecting human relationships. The place that the state legitimately occupies in society is to be the integrator of public justice. I have to add the word 'public' to justice here since there are also instances of private justice in society where the state does not - or should not - establish the content of rights. Examples of private legal rights can be found in the relations between private persons, such as the terms of a contract to sell and buy a house. Further, the relations among members within a non-state social structure are to be regulated by private law. Concretely, the relations among members of a family, of a local church congregation, of an industrial work community, of a university, are to be regulated by private communal law. Private communal law is indeed subject to the norm of justice, but it is structurally different from the public legal order which the state is called upon to establish. For private communal law (a) pertains to the members of the specific social structure (this specificity is non-public), and (b) it is dependent upon the 'qualifying function' of the respective non-state social structure. The church order of an ecclesiastical denomination belongs to the category of private communal law: it regulates the relations

between members of the denomination and it stip-
ulates the specifically ecclesiastical rights
and duties and responsibilities of these members.
The same is true of industrial law: it regulates
the economically qualified relations between
members of the industrial work community.

The state, however, is concerned with public
justice. It must establish a public legal order.
The word "public" requires brief definition here.
I do not use it in the sense that a worship service is open to the public or that a department
store invites the public to buy its goods. When
I use the word 'public' with reference to the
state I mean that no person or institution that
exists within its territorial boundaries can
escape the state's legal order - both with respect
to the rights and the duties that such a legal
order organizes. To put it more positively,
the state's divine office is to be the adminis-
trator of public justice for every person and
institution living or domiciled within its
territory. The state is the Lord's servant for
our good. The content of that good is a regime
of public justice.

IV. Public Justice in Society

The dispensation of public justice in the
kind of society we live in requires, I think,
that the state ought to pay attention to the
following matters. I mention these only as
illustrations of a larger thesis.

1. Human rights

Earlier I said that the norm of justice
requires social space for human creatureliness.
A just social order involves the creation of
social space of individual persons and their
social structures. It is in connection with
'social space' that a Christian conception of
rights ought to be developed. For a right is
that measure of social space that a person or
a social structure occupies in society guaranteed

204

by the public legal order of the state. Let us first turn to the rights of persons or to 'human rights' as they have been traditionally called.

A Christian conception of human rights finds its foundation in man's creation by God and Christ's work of redemption. The redemptive work of Christ implies the restoration of men to their creaturely status as servants of God. Outside of Christ's redemptive work men have no rights. Because of Christ's redemptive work we are called to fight for the rights of men, of all men, irrespective of whether they are Christians or not.

When I say that rights are founded in man's creation by God I am in effect saying that man is created as the image of God. Human rights are not founded in an inherent dignity of human personality, as humanism claims. Human rights are founded in a dignity with which man is endowed by the Creator. This dignity, first and foremost, is to be God's imager on earth. This divinely endowed dignity requires a recognition of man's unique place and responsibility in society. In the light of this dignity as God's imager we can say that man transcends all social structures. He may not be enclosed in or enslaved by any institution.

On this basis we can say that a Christian conception of society is a conception of an open society, in which men and women have the right to reach out to God or to what they consider to be their final transcendent 'value' to which they desire to render allegiance. Man's divinely endowed dignity requires an invincible sphere of freedom for human personality. This 'sphere of freedom' is what I call the first range of social space to which men have a right. The state does not grant rights in this sphere. It acknowledges them. It must protect them. It must enhance them in accordance with the expansion of cultural and social resources in the historical process.

A single right is never absolute. Rights must be correlative to duties; the realization of rights is the avenue for the expression of responsibilities. The rights of one person may not violate the rights of others. And the pursuit of one right should not occur at the expense of other rights. There must be a kind of simultaneity in the realization of human rights.

The realization of rights is always influenced by the dominant ideals of a cultural epoch. It cannot be denied that western individualistic liberalism has made a distinct contribution to the realization of rights in modern society: freedom of speech, freedom of association, of contract, etc. However, liberalism looked upon one right as supreme to all others, and that supremacy was found in the "right to property." John Locke, who exercised a great influence especially in the English speaking world, singled out "the preservation of property" as the chief end of government, of civil society (Second Treatise, par. 85). The supremacy of the right to property implied the neglect of the realization of other rights; it implied the wijling acceptance of a class-society in which the class of property owners were given the protection of the state while the class of have-nots were left to their own devices. In our time the defense of liberalism and the pursuit of justice are distinctly at odds. This conflict is one of the contributing factors to the disintegration of our society.

How wide is the scope of human rights? Does it include the right on the part of women 'not to have children'? I think so. For even if the exercise of that right would violate the moral conscience of a segment of the population, it does not violate the public-legal order. Hence, there should be no legal varriers to the sale of contraceptives to adults. But does the scope of human rights include an unlimited right to abortions? I think not. For the issue of abortion involves a distinctly new element: the pre-

206

sence of the life of the fetus. That life too
is worthy of protection, by the mother, by the
family, by the medical doctor, and by the state.
I can think of no legal ground for the argument
that the state's protection of human life and
its rights begins at birth. As a matter of fact,
unborn human life has been given a legally protected status in the matter of bequests and the
provision of medical care for pregnant women out
of public funds. The only legal ground for an
abortion, it seems to me, lies in authoritatively
ascertained conflict of interest between one
human life (the mother's) and another human life
(that of the getus). It is peculiarly the state's
calling to provide legal channels for an appropriate weighing of especially conflicting human
interests. If it is the state's calling to
protect the needs of the unprotected, its shield
of justice should encompass the life of the unborn. In other words, unborn human life - in
its distinct stages of growth - also has human
rights that cannot be privately dispensed with,
even if the private persons involved have a
morality that would allow such dispensation.
Abortion is not a matter of laissez faire liberalism.

2. The rights of communities and associations

The rights of human beings ought to be acknowledged, protected, and enhanced by the state
in its dispensation of justice. But rights are
not limited to human beings. The institutions
which men and women have formed in society -
like the church and marriage and the family -
and the associations which they have organized -
in the industrial sector, the media, and the
educational world - also have rights which the
state must acknowledge.

The protection of these rights of communities
and associations will often require that the
state is called upon to prevent the destruction
of one 'sphere' by another. To put the matter
a bit more technically, the state as the inte-

grator of public justice must prevent the violation of the internal sphere of one societal structure by another; it must prevent the development of one sector at the expense of another. We can formulate this a bit more positively: The state must create and maintain conditions that lead to the meaningful and 'open' development of all non-state social structures that contribute to human life in a particular culture. Here, too, the state must prevent friction, oppression, and enslavement.

It is at this point that a Biblically sensitive conception of the normative task of the state can make a distinct contribution to the maladjustments that we are confronted with in our society. Implicit in our conception is the freedom of industrial enterprise. However, that freedom is never absolute. When the exercise of that freedom endangers other relations in society, the state must intervene, and so so if necessary with drastic measures.

What do we now see in our culture? Its chief characteristic is the prominence of industrial production, made possible by scientific advance, technological invention, and gigantic corporations. The expansion of the production of material goods, and their consumption, is the highest good, the summum bonum of twentieth century civilization in western Europe and north America. The increase in the gross national product (GNP) is man's chief end, in comparison with which every other cultural purpose is secondary. The religion of production and consumption is the main cause of social disarray. For it permits the corporate industrial sector to encroach upon the legitimate social space of the family, marriage, education, the arts, and the media. As a matter of fact, the very integrity of the state itself is endangered by the nearly uninhibited growth of the economic sector. For, as John Kenneth Galbraith has rightly pointed out in his books The New Industrial State (1967) and Economics and the Public

208

Purpose (1973), there is a symbiosis and alliance between the world of the large corporations and political institutions which makes the proper functioning of the state itself very difficult. The state functions in the first place for the benefit of the corporate sector to the detriment of the rest of society.

The origin of this extremely one-sided cultural development must be found in a specific notion of human progress that gained preeminence since the days of the eighteenth century Enlightenment. Simply put, that notion holds that progress consists in the unlimited fulfillment of man's material needs. That notion has the character of religious conviction and, since it has become the dominant force in our society, it is not readily dislodged. Especially not if the great majority of politicians of all leading political parties adhere to this conviction.

Nevertheless, I believe that precisely at this point of disarray in our society a revived consciousness of justice and stewardship as presented in the Biblical frame of reference can contribute to the alleviation of the ills of which we are all aware but for which a cure is hard to come by.

IV. Christians and Liberal Democracy

The political-economic order under which North American Christians live goes by the technical title of liberal democracy. Most people, however, are not concerned with the precision of its name or its complex origins and painful historical evolution. It is enough to celebrate its triumph and its considerable benefits: open, competitive selection of rulers by most adult citizens, constitutionally protected rights to write, speak, gather, and worship, and a set of economic arrangments which have led to conditions of economic abundance unknown in world history.

All systems, regardless of benefits, impose costs and some Christians are beginning to suggest that the costs of liberal democracy in its present form, which are often hidden, ought to be scrutinized far more critically than they have been in the past. Bob Goudzwaard in "Our Gods Have Failed", puts the matter forthrightly with his comment that "something is rotten in Western society". This something is the elevation to a point of unquestioned acceptance, bordering on a religious faith, of economic growth and technology, hence our "false gods". If Goudzwaard is correct, this poses a serious problem for liberal democracy which has come to justify itself over its rivals by the very way it facilitates growth and technical development. Indeed, some critics now speculate that the apparently deep-seated popularity of liberal democracy may evaporate quickly if economic growth and technology turn out to be liabilities in the face of energy shortages and ecological constraints.

How could false gods come to dominate the public life of a society which, at least until recently, has prided itself on the title of "Christian"? Earlier articles by Hatfield and Zylstra made passing reference to an explanation which Rockne McCarthy develops in some detail: the existence of a civil religion. This religion,

210

far from pointing to the Creator, calls citizens
to a worship of the nation state and its ideals,
whatever they happen to be. Biblical religion
is simultaneously relegated to the private side
of life and pressed into service to certify the
goodness of the existing order of things. With
such a certification comes respectability and
obedience; indeed, despite provisions for freedom
of religion, opposition to the civil religion
and its cardinal tenets, as identified in part
by Goudzwaard, brings strong pressures to conform
including enforced irrelevance and physical
coercion.

Stanley Carlson's "Interest Group Liberalism"
brings the critique of liberal democracy to more
familiar ground for most people: the increasingly
dominant role of the pressure group in our political life. His concern is that this problem
be seen within the context of our failure to
define both the nature and task of government in
an adequate way.

Confronted with problems of the sort described above, how should a Christian respond?
Jan Dengerink, though alert to some of the
shortcomings of liberal democracy mentioned by
the other writers, is anxious to prevent Christians from succumbing to a feeling that "nothing
can be done" or that problems must be left to
technical experts. He evokes instead the notion
that all of the creation must ultimately heed
its creator and that the Christian community
has a responsibility, subject to a variety of
local circumstances, to work together to make
such a condition a reality.

OUR GODS HAVE FAILED US

By Bob Goudzwaard

Something is rotten in our western society.
We know it, we see it all around us, yet we
don't know what to do about it. Instead of
activating us, the situation seems to para-
lyze us. A society that has chosen to live
an autonomous (i.e. self-governing) life is
now staggering toward its autonomous death.
And such a death can only make us feel quite
helpless.

Am I too gloomy, too pessimistic? I
don't think so. In our cities the garbage
trucks are busily picking up the leftovers of
our consuming society. They are gathering the
remnants of our half-eaten cakes and cream
tarts. And at this very moment the refuse
carts in Bombay and Ethiopia are collecting
the bodies of men, women, and children who
died last night in the streets and fields of
hunger and misery.

In our own "great" society thousands of workers
are forced to perform monotonous, mind-killing
tasks only to serve the prefabricated, dehumanized
needs of our modern leisure activities. We see
the dead fish and the darkening shadows in our
streams and lakes, results of the endless and
meaningless hunt for new detergents and chemicals.
We witness costly preparations for future space
flights, but little if any preparation for the
future of America's black youths. The young make
their hopeless portest against this repressive/
tolerant technocratic society in which nonsense
consumption is a national duty and in which
increased production has become a self-legitimating
issue. At the same time other young people try
to escape the one-dimensional consumer society
by turning themselves into drug-dreaming, zero-
dimensional consuming animals. The riots, campus

212

fights, and demonstrations of the sixties were, I believe, only the partial eruptions of a much greater, more explosive volcano underneath.

How could we have let things go this far? What is at the root of all these destructive developments, these seriously unbalanced situations in our rationally balanced society? And what should our position, our Christian attitude, be in such a world? Isn't everything we do, including all our labour, a confirmation of the very direction of that society, a further establishing of the establishment, a compromise with what we reject? Would it not be better for Christians simply to abandon the whole system and escape from it? These are serious questions, and our answers had better be serious as well.

In attempting to find possible answers we would do well to remember that the challenge of assessing the world's socioeconomic predicament is not a new one. Of course, I realize that this problem today has new dimensions which are characteristic of our time. But it would be foolish to ignore the fact that the Christian church throughout the ages has been wrestling with its assessment of economic life. We can learn from this struggle, for it will help us understand that the communion of saints goes beyond not only the limits of our day and age, but also the borders of our present closed society. In that communion we are not one-dimensional but four-dimensional. We are living before the face of the Almighty God, as well as in front of a cloud of witnesses comprising the saints of all ages.

I will divide this essay into three parts. In the first place I will try to present an overview of the evaluation of socioeconomic life by the early Christian church, the medieval church, and the church of the Reformation. Second, I will lay out three biblical givens and will outline how modern man has responded to them in his socioeconomic life. Third, I will evaluate present socioeconomic life and outline the Christian's attitude in modern industrial society.

"No servant can be the slave of two masters. You cannot serve God and money."
"Sell all that you have, give it to the poor and follow Me."
"You who have great possessions, weep and wail over the miserable fate descending on you. You have lived on earth in wanton luxury, fattening yourselves like cattle, and therefore the day of slaughter has come."
"The love of money is the root of all evil."

These texts from the New Testament refer to the temptations of money and riches. How did the early Christian church read these Scripture passages? Especially during the period between the second and sixth century, the early church adopted a negative attitude toward socioeconomic life. This aspect of life was generally considered to be something sinful in itself. You could not participate in it as producer, consumer, or merchant without defiling yourself one way or another. To be a radical Christian you indeed had to sell all your possessions and give the money to the poor; you had to reject everything beyond the bare necessities of life.

There is undoubtedly a neoplatonic influence behind this attitude. Neo-Platonism holds that sin is somehow closely linked to matter and the human physical body. More importantly, however, that lifestyle led to a dualistic approach to economic life, for economic life had to go on. The common man with a family could not easily withdraw himself from his job and other economic activities. Therefore, according to the clergy, he was obligated to sin; he was delivered to a life of defilement. It is significant that during that period we see the rise of cloisters and monasteries.

These institutions were considered areas of the church where radical Christianity was practical, and as such their inhabitants could do penance for all those other Christians who were forced to defile themselves with economic activities. There simply could be no escapism without dualism; a double morality was inherent in the early church's view of economic life.

This outlook on socioeconomic life, however, underwent a significant change during the Middle Ages. To be sure, no change took place in the church's opinion of the man temptations facing a Christian participating in socioeconomic life. A medieval legend tells us of a traveller who, visiting a cloister, found a host of devils sitting in corners, windows, and staircases. But when he went to the marketplace, he saw only one devil comfortably and lazily perched on a high pillar. The moral of the story was that a cloister needs an army of devils to tempt the monks; in the marketplace, however, there is no need for them since everyone working there is already a devil. The story indicates that medieval Christians had not changed their basic evaluation of economic life. The change occurred in the sense that economic life now could have a useful though minor place in the Kingdom of God, provided that it was sanctified (made holy) by the sacramental means of grace of the church.

The scope of this essay does not allow a detailed elaboration of the medieval scholastic view of society. It is important, however, to point out that the scholastic doctors saw society as a static whole in which everyone had to remain in his "God-given" place. Within this context we can also understand the scholastic regulation of economic life by the doctrines of the just price (justum pretium) and the prohibition of interest. These doctrines served as instruments to maintain the static character of medieval soceity. They prevented the merchant class from obtaining a more important and dominant position than could be admitted in a society of Christians.

In summary, the basic approach of medieval

people to socioeconomic life was not negation but sanctification. There remained, however, a deep distrust of all dynamic tendencies in socioeconomic life.

Finally, we must examine the attitude of the church of the Reformation. And I believe that attitude can be of special importance for us in our far more complex and bewildering society. A first, though minor, aspect in the reformers' assessment of socioeconomic life was their protest against the medieval domination of society by the institutional church, a morality of the prevalence of self-interest in all economic matters. Out of this new morality arose, for instance, the enclosure movement in which the lives of many in rural England were uprooted only because the common land on which they lived could yield greater economic returns to the landlords by turning them into private possessions. That same morality caused the Industrial Revolution to become an industrial dehumanization; any understanding of the social mortgage in the hiring of labour was structurally absent. The goal and destiny of economic life was not Christian solidarity but the realization of human self-interest.

You may have noticed that, in dealing with the important view of the reformers, I referred to only a partial explanation of our problems. I did so because I do not believe that we can rely solely on Calvin's approach in our evaluation of our own social and economic development. Since the Reformation, this development has undergone influences other than the simple desire for economic autonomy.

In order to understand our own times, I should like to draw your attention to three basic biblical rules which together explain man's relation to God and to his theoretical and practical pursuits. Although these rules are more or less well-known to many, I believe that looking at them side by side will provide us with a better understanding of ourselves and our times.

The first basic rule is that every man is
serving god(s) in his life. This rule is known
as Augustine's law of concentration. Augustine
wrote the famous words about the unrest in every
man's life, an unrest which is only removed if
he finds God. The God we have as our resting
point in life can be the living God. But we can
also seek the resting point of our lives (our
happiness and goals) within the creation. We
can seek it in material wealth, in our intellectual capacity, or in progress by means of technique. When, for example, Richard Nixon declared
a few years ago that the spirit of Appollo Eleven
was able to bring peace among all nations, his
words betrayed a belief in the saving power of
technique. To give another example, when we
reject anything that our minds can't comprehend,
then our intellect has become our ultimate
resting point and the origin of our security.
In such a case we indeed choose our god.

The second basic rule is that every man is
transformed into an image of his god. The choice
of a god, of a real resting point in our lives,
is not without consequences. Christians have
the promise to be renewed by the Holy Spirit
according to the image of the living God. But
all those who choose another god - whether they
bear the name "Christian" or not - are transformed into an image of the god of their choice.
The apostle Paul describes this law in the first
chapter of his letter to the Romans. Paul speaks
about those who exchanged the splendour of the
living God for other gods: birds, beasts, and
creeping things. And Paul continues: "For
that reason God has given them up to the vileness
of their own desires and the consequent degrada-
tion of their own bodies; they are now behaving
like animals themselves!" (Rom. 1:24-25) They
have become the image of their god. Likewise,
when we choose progress by means of technique
to be our god (as the foundation of our final
hope and trust in life), we should not be sur-

prised to find ourselves transformed and deformed into an extension of a machine. When
human intellect and our own ratio (reason)
become our deepest source of trust and knowledge,
we will ultimately rationalize ourselves as
well. Then the love for our husbands, our wives,
and our families might well disappear because
it cannot stand the test of rationality. Marriage
and family are, after all, not qualified by reason
but by truth and fidelity.

The third basic rule is that mankind creates
and forms a structure of society in its own
image. In the development of human civilization,
man forms, creates, and changes the structure
of his society, and in doing so he portrays in
his work the intention of his own heart. He
gives to the structure of that society something
of his own image and likeness. In it he betrays
something of his own lifestyle, of his own god.
A biblical reference for this third rule can be
found in the thirteenth chapter of the book of
revelation, where the inhabitants of the world
are commanded by their beast-god to make an
image of him, an image which can speak and is
able to direct their lives.

I sincerely hope that you will be able to see
the direct relevance of these three biblical
laws about the relation between God, man, and
society. In our western civilization, we have
first given our trust to the powers of economic
growth, science, and technique to lead us in all
our ways; we are still following these powers as
our infallible guides. But, correspondingly, we
have turned ourselves into images of these gods,
and we find these traces of ourselves back in
the structures of our present-day, growth-possessed
society. For we cannot deny that our society
displays a powerful belief in the full, self-
sufficient autonomy of economic development as
the source of both private and social happiness.
Of human reason, technical progress, and autonomous economic development we say: "Behold your
gods, who are able to deliver you from any house

of bondage and bring you into the promised land
of welfare!" And now in modern cultures, we are
confronted with the consequences of this religious
choice. This does not mean that western civilization made that choice in all its fullness, denying
any form of Christianity. Our society still knows
some feeling of responsibility, some sense of
freedom, some unrest about the present unbalanced
situations.

Nevertheless, it is true that western man -
and we are all western men and women - has already
made many basic religious compromises, although
he has not rejected the living God in all spheres
of life. Western man has often sought and still
seeks his resting point for his daily life in
his intellectual capacity, in his technical progress, and in the level of his income. To a
large extent he finds the meaning of his life in
a chase after financial gain and luxury.

It is these religious choices which have
scarred western man and his culture. Western man
has been at least partially transformed into the
image of these gods. And the image of these gods
is reflected in the structure of our society.
That structure has in many respects become economistic, rationalistic, and technocratic.

Here, I believe, lie the deep roots of our
present miseries, imbalances, and severe claus-
trophobia. In the area of industrial labour,
for example, our real problem is not that many
workers are treated as dehumanized robots. That
is old hat already. No, the deepest misery lies
in the fact that many of these labourers no
longer experience such a work situation as dehumanizing. Instead, they feel they are quite
happy and reject any possibility of obtaining
real responsibility. Since they often think of
work as simply a means to earn money, they look
on responsibility as a burden. Here we witness
a transformation of man into the image of the
modern gods. This transformation is partially
due to his own choice, but it is also the result

219

of the compelling influence of a culture which worships and adores technique and progress.

We see a parallel development in the structure and direction of the modern business enterprise. There the root problem is not just merciless competition, unethical dealing with workers and consumers, and lack of genuine concern for and solidarity with others. Those are evils that have their origin in a much earlier history and are a direct consequence of the proclamation that economic development is fully self-sufficient and autonomous. No, the root problem is that the modern enterprise in the pursuit of its goals not only tends to captivate men's bodies but also their souls and minds. There is an enormous pressure on every leading person within the corporation to adapt his lifestyle and his life view to that of the corporation and to identify his personal hope for the future with the goals of the enterprise. Love is transformed into loyalty to the enterprise, faith becomes dedication to its goals, harmony turns into a duty to eliminate any conviction which might disturb the development pattern of the enterprise. I believe Galbraith was right when he wrote:

> If we continue to believe that the goals of the industrial system - the expansion of output, the companion increase in consumption, technological advance, the public images that sustain it - are coordinate with life, then all of our lives will be in the service of these goals. What is consistent with these ends we shall have or be allowed; all else will be off limits. Our wants will be managed in accordance with the needs of the industrial system; the policies of the state will be subject to similar influence; education will be adapted to industrial need; the disciplines required by the industrial system will be the conventional morality of the community. All other goals will be

made to seem precious, unimportant or
antisocial. We will be bound to the
ends of the industrial system. The state
will add its moral, and perhaps some of
its legal power to their enforcement.
What will eventuate, on the whole, will be
the benign servitude of the household re-
tainer who is taught to love her mistress
and see her interests as her own, and not
the compelled servitude of the field hand.
But it will not be freedom. (J.K. Galbraith,
The New Industrial State (Boston: Houghton
Mifflin Co., 1967), p. 398.)

However, Galbraith fails to see the religious
roots of that threat to freedom. In other
words, he fails to see that to a large extent
western man has tied his salvation, his deepest
happiness, to what economic growth and technical
progress can give to him. It is this faith that
expresses itself in the structure of our institutions and societies. These gods, in turn, are
now shackling and binding their servants. They
transform their adherents into slaves.

However, there is more. The enterprise also
exercises an increasing spiritual domination over
the consumers. A large enterprise cannot afford
a major insecurity in the level of consumer
demands. Therefore, it has to create a secure
and stable demand. The wishes of the consumer
become more and more prefabricated wishes, made
serviceable to the universally valid progress
of sales and technique. Consumers' sovereignty
is gradually replaced by consumers' dependence.
The master becomes a slave.

Our third and final illustration is the problem of our severely damaged environment. What
constitutes our greatest misery in this vital
aspect of our world? Again, it is not that we
wreaked such havoc on our ecosystem. During the
Industrial Revolution and afterwards, there was
also a severe degree of air and water pollution.
Our most fundamental problem is that our society

221

has a built-in tendency to continue such pollution and waste, a tendency which is often much greater than the will to curb it. To be sure, there is much protest and publicity about the environmental damage. But this protest resembles the portest of the victims of the seven plagues described in Revelation 16. The victims suffered severely but refused to change their lives. For it becomes increasingly clear that a real struggle against further deterioration of the environment will be possible only if western man will be satisfied with a much lower rate of growth of his income and perhaps with a much lower income than he now has.

To quote Galbraith once again, "A rising standard of living has the aspect of a faith in our culture." And faith has great tenacity. I believe that western man will do his utmost to achieve both economic goals. He will try to improve the environment without giving up his attempts to improve his consumption level. In economic terms, however, this mean a structural trend toward continued heavy inflation. For invlation is not a mere defect in the mechanism of our economy, but a consequence of the desire to spend more than is economically possible.

I believe we are now ready to complete our picture. Why are so many young people engaged in a deep and helpless protest against society? It is, I think, because they intuitively feel that their freedom and spiritual independence are at stake when they stay in society. There is an analogy between their protest and the struggle of the existentialists against the domination of positivism in science. Positivism equated human existence with a collection of natural, biological, and physical qualities. Like the existentialists who want to escape the inhuman positivistic fate, modern youth refuses to be put into the box of a closed society which often treats living men as social animals, workhorses, consuming rabbits, and computerized atoms. They no longer believe that man will be saved,

222

made thoroughly happy, by a total dedication to the goals of sales promotion and technical progress.

I would like to conclude with some comments about the Christian's approach to socioeconomic life. What must we do? Flee from it? Compromise with it? Or is there a third way out of the pressing dilemma?

I believe that the basic difficulty lies in the fact that the direction of modern society is indeed a·religious direction. That should be clear when we observe the effect of the three biblical laws mentioned earlier. It becomes clear also when we notice that strange mixture of rationality and irrantionality within our society. Our methods and processes are all very rational and efficient, but they serve goals which are often irrational and unexplainable. We insist on further expansion and growth in the production and consumption of unnecessary and prefabricated luxuries even when the price is a dehumanization of labour, a destruction of the environment, a manipulation of ourselves as consumers, and a woeful neglect of other people who lack the bare necessities of life. Such a strange combination is only understandable after we have enslaved ourselves to these irrational goals and have given them a meaning in themselves, irrespective of their consequences.

Should we escape then, perhaps join the underground movement, and help prepare a coming revolution? I don't believe that is a Christian approach, and I would like to give three reasons.

In the first place, I must remind you of the connection between escapism and a double morality which we already observed in our discussion of the early church's attitude. We cannot take the luxury of an escape when we know that many others have no such possibility. That would be unethical; it would be a flight. It would also be a betrayal, for escapism is always a denial of the solidarity of sinning.

Second, I should like to remind you that evil
is not situated in socioeconomic life itself.
The ultimate horizon of our daily work is not
an unavoidable subjection to the aims of a
closed society. If we believed that, we would
be thinking as one-dimensionally about our daily
life as those who unconditionally love the gods
of our age. For no human endeavour can remove
the creational order of economic life. We cannot
eliminate the fact of God's calling to our daily
work; we cannot neutralize the meaning of vocation as a way to render service to our neighbour.

The third and most fundamental objection to
flight and withdrawal from present society or
to its revolutionary overthrow is that such
courses of action would betray a serious mis-
judgement of the real roots of the crisis. The
decisive question is not how we shall excape
from being put into a box or from being treated
like rabbits or atoms. That may be the decisive
question for an existentialist who loves his
spiritual independence above all, but it can
never be decisive for a Christian. A Christian
should know that the fundamental problem does
not originate from a wrong societal structure
but springs from the hearts of men who made
that structure. It is man himself who chose
his gods and enshrined them in the midst of
society. We may flee from that society but we
can never escape our own hearts. Here we find
the limit of every escapism and therefore the
limit of our hope for other and better societal
structures without a change in the religious
heart direction of western man.

Let me formulate the same answer in a more
positive way. I believe that the living Word
of God is present in our western civilization
as a detecting power. It detects the origins of
the troubles, miseries, and irrationalities in
that civilization. It also discloses that man's
declaration that God is dead must necessarily be

followed by the death of a culture, the death of humanity in man. The Word of God also has its revenging presence. Man cannot choose another god and remain the same.

But the Word of the living God is also present in our society as a liberating power. Wherever that Word is accepted the social mortgage of our own wealth to the hungry and needy will be paid off. The balance between wealth and nature can be found again. Men will no longer allow their deepest convictions to be manipulated simply to attain practical economic goals.

Our western societies have not made an irreversible choice for the gods of wealth and technique. Moreover, some still hesitate, some still have a sense of stewardship in the control of the environment. Some of the young reject an economistic and technocratic way of life and seek a possible alternative. And that alternative is a real one, for there still is a bifurcation, a fork in the road. At the crossroads, however, the right direction is only indicated by the signpost of the living Word of God.

Clearly, I also believe in the directing power of the Word of God. When we follow that Word on its path through our present culture, there is still much that can be done and there are still many possibilities for genuine· Christian witness. This witness is not without promise; for wherever the Word of God is heeded, there is his promise of what Francis Schaeffer calls a "substantial healing" of man and society. This healing begins in our own lives, showing itself in the Shalom that follows our responsible personal choice between obtaining our own luxuries and providing the needs of the hungry, both here and in other countries. But it also expresses itself in society, for the structures of society are a mirror of our own belief, bearing the image of our own hope, trust, and convictions. For instance, every trade union that values the re-

storation of human responsibility in daily
work above the race for more dollars for its
members is working as a power of substantial
healing, making labour meaningful again in
larger enterprises.

The Gospel points men to a more opened-up
society, a better administered environment, at
least a partial redemption of our social mortgage. Last, there is the power of the witness
of the church. Certainly the church can't point
out the way to go by imitating the service of
the gods of this age with luxurious and expen-
sive church buildings. The vocation of the
church is to demonstrate in its own style of
living that the redemption of Christ is also
changing all our socioeconomic relations. In
the Christian community something has to become
visible of the holiness and the harmony of the
economics of the Kingdom of God.

A basic rule of that Kingdom is that happiness
lies more in giving than in receiving, that a
man can become rich in Christ by giving away
his treasures. In that community social, economic, and racial differences, rather than
causing separation, have to intensify genuine
communion and solidarity, transforming that
community into a place of real and substantial
healing for all who are hurt and broken by an
idolatrous culture. Thus we may live today
in the perspective of the great day of our Redeemer, a Redeemer whose distant footsteps
can already be heard amid the noise of our present society.

CIVIL RELIGION IN EARLY AMERICA

By Rockne McCarthy

It is the conviction of the author that all men have beliefs about life that are rooted in their basic religious (heart) commitment. A civil religion exists when one confessional view of life becomes an "obligatory minimum dogma or enforced basic consensus" in a state. This in turn restructs the freedom of dissenting groups or individuals to fully live their lives according to their deepest beliefs.

During the Middle Ages the Church provided spiritual as well as positical unity to Europe. It promoted orthodoxy and sought conformity in a way that was oppressive to those suspected of heresy.

The Renaissance and Reformation meant the breakdown of religious and political unity in Europe, but, although there were more churches and more states, individuals scarcely gained in freedom. The various states adopted official religions, which subjects were expected to accept; deviation from the creed of the established church might well mean death.

When the following age of western revolutions began, political leaders sought a secular basis to maintain public peace. The general assumption of the revolutionary age was that the way to achieve social peace was to subdue the passions that had been engendered by sectarian conflict. Many post-Thomistic political philosophers argued that this could be accomplished by permanently separating the private life of the spirit from the public life of the state. The division of life into two separate spheres meant that in most cases churches were reduced to the status of association and a secular basis was discovered to maintain public peace.

Many Christians shared the secular belief in the division of life into two separate spheres of existence. Although the Christian community was heir to the biblical position that Christ was sovereign over all of life, many individuals and groups had significantly modified this confession by separating life into the realm of grace and the realm of nature - the spiritual and the worldly. This dualism limited the Christian faith to the private aspects of the individual's life while consciously or unconsciously allowing public life to be directed by the other norms. This form of religious individualism took for granted or ignored the structures of society outside the institutional church, and sought rather to build up religious cells of the "saved" within society. By concentrating so heavily on matters of the "soul" a distinctly Christian understanding of societal institutions did not develop. The sphere of nature was soon considered to be religiously neutral.

The grace/nature dualism made possible the development of a civil religion in America. It is the key to understanding the existence of a secular faith in the nation's public life while there continued to be commitment to sectarian beliefs by individuals, families and churches.

There were historical as well as philosophical considerations that help explain the development of an American civil religion. In our early history one of the main problems that faced the country was the establishment of some kind of unity to hold the thieteen separate state together. Having long been a haven for various groups of dissenters, the colonies had been very diverse in religious matters. There was a common cultural heritage, but any attempt to establish one particular church would have immediately destroyed any possibility of political union. The problems with England which had managed to unite the colonies were, to a large degree, political and economic, and in these areas it was possible to arrive at majority opinions. The fact that there was no clear cut denominational majority was an important historical consideration which coincided nicely with the new assumption that the state represented a secular and rational arrangment made by men to govern themselves.

In the ·first half of the nineteenth century Alexis de Tocqueville observed that in Europe religion and liberty had been opposing forces. In America, however, this was not the case. Religious liberty was made possible by the fact that sectarian beliefs were restricted to the private sphere of life, while a secular, ecumenical, civil faith reigned in the public life of the nation. Although the federal government was to establish no churches, this did not mean that there was not a close relationship between the secular civil faith and politics. Commenting about this relationship Conrad Cherry has pointed our that:

...the disestablishment of the church hardly meant that the American political sphere was denied a religious dimension. In fact, that dimension so permeates the political, educational and social life of America that it constitutes a civil religion that cannot be identified with Protestantism, Catholicism or Judaism as such. Americans may be participants in both the religious dimension of their civil life and one of the traditional Western religions.

In a more detailed study it would be possible to indicate how the American civil religion first emerged during the revolutionary era and differentiated, particularly in the Jacksonian period. Given the limitation of space, only some of the outstanding features of the civil religion in its pre-Civil War form will be discussed under

the following headings: Civil Theology, Civil
Peoplehood, Civil Institutions, Civil Ceremonial
Expressions and Symbols and Enforcement of Civil
Religion.

Civil Theology

There were many different concepts which made
up the American civil theology in its pre-Civil
War form: the concept of some supernatural force
(God or a Guiding providence that directed the
affairs of men); the concept of a fundamental
law; the concept of the free and responsible individual. The one central, unique and permanent
belief, however, has been that political sovereignty resides in the people - i.e., the people
are the constituent power. This was proclaimed
to the world at the very birth of the new nation
in the Declaration of Independence and served as
the basic political assumption underlying the
Constitution.

The Declaration presented man as a being who
was by his very nature free, independent and
autonomous. Politically this placed man in the
center of reality from where he governed himself
and nature in accordance with his own reason.
This made the consent of man, "the consent of
the governed," the source of political power.

Making the "People" the creators of the state
made possible a revolutionary concept of government in America. The new belief in the power
of the people was set forth in the Preamble to
the United States Constitution. "We the people
...do ordain and establish," represented fully
the idea of the people as the constituent power.
The people through their reason discerned the
Truth and formed their government. This process
continued in their elected and appointed governing bodies. The simple majority which held
power was not seen as a group imposing its will
upon minorities, but as the possessor of "Truth"
as determined through rationally discovering the
"Laws of Nature and Nature's God."

230

The belief in popular sovereignty flowed
directly from the religious (heart) commitment
that man was the ultimate authority for public
life. The separation of the private/public
spheres of life allowed different individuals
and groups, Baptist, Calvinists, Deists, for
example, who opposed each other in theological -
ecclesiastical matters, (sphere of grace), to join
hands in this common political faith "neutral
sphere of nature). This power of the people
impressed Alexis de Tocqueville more than any
other feature of the American life. He recorded
that...

> The people reign in the American political
> world as the Deity does in the universe.
> They are the cause and the aim of all
> things; everything comes from them, and
> everything is absorbed by them.

At the heart, therefore, of America's civil
religion is a civil theology which proclaims
the sovereignty of man. The commitment of
Americans to this political dogma made the
Declaration of Independence and the Constitution the most sacred documents of the civil
religion.

Civil Peoplehood

For some time scholars have written about
Americans' understanding of themselves as a
chosen people. New England Puritans, following
the Old Testament example, originally believed
that they were God's chosen people, the elect
who were creating a new Israel. Full participation in the covenant community hinged upon the
elect's membership in the covenant of grace, the
church, and the political covenants. The difference between the saved and unsaved disappeared
in the process of secularization. The founding
documents of the nation, the Declaration of Independence and the Constitution with the Bill of
Rights, became the basis of the new democratic
peoplehood. By the end of the eighteenth century

231

the original Puritan covenants had been replaced by these inviolable covenants which not only bound the nation together, but also identified a new peoplehood by explicitly defining the means of participation and, thereby, establish the grounds for membership.

The very meaning of the term "citizen" was unique in the American context. R. R. Palmer in his discussion of the development of constitutionalism in America, has pointed out that the modern concept of "citizen" first appeared in the Massachusetts Constitution of 1780. From there it found its way into the Federal Constitution of 1789. Adams wrote in the Massachusetts preamble: "The body politic is formed by a voluntary association of individuals. It is a social compact, by which the whole people covenants with each citizen and each citizen with the whole people that all shall be governed by certain laws for the common good." Palmer comments that:

> The thought here, and the use of the word "covenant", go back to the Mayflower compact. But whence comes the "social" in social compact? And whence comes the word "citizen"? There were no "citizens" under the British Constitution, except in the sense of freemen of the few towns known as cities. In the English language the word "citizen" in its modern sense is an Americanism, dating from the American Revolution.

Adams was very familiar with Rousseau's Social Contract and the use of the terms suggests Chapter VI, Book I, of that work. It is entirely possible that Rosseau deposited the concept of "citizen" in Adams' mind. Since Rousseau's idea of "citizen" was intimately connected with his concept of "civil religion," it is interesting to conjecture about the possible deeper meaning of the term in the Federal Constitution.

The political controversies that emerged in the early life of the nation were questioning of the principles upon which the peoplehood rested. The controversies represented division within the faithful over the true meaning of the faith.

The debate between political opponents erupted into a bloody Civil War in the 1860's. And yet the war itself was not a conflict of two different world views, but rather a conflict over which side, the North or the South, represented the true "faith of the fathers." Ralph Henry Gabriel shows that both Abraham Lincoln and Jefferson Davis believed their side to be the upholder of the true spirit of the American democratic faith. Jefferson Davis in his inaugural as President of the Provisional Governemtn argued that the Confederates in seceding from the Union illustrated the American belief "...that government rest on the consent of the governed, and that it is the right of the people to alter or abolish them at will whenever they become destructive of the ends for which they were established.

Abraham Lincoln, likewise, drew his inspiration and purpose from the Declaration of Indedependence. At Independence Hall in 1861, on his journey to Washington to be inaugurated President, Lincoln said:

I am filled with deep emotion at finding myself standing here in the place where were collected together the wisdom, the patriotism, the devotion to principle, from which sprang the institutions under which we live. You have kindly suggested to me that in my hands is the task of restoring peace to our distracted country. I can say in return, sir, that all the political sentiments I entertain have been drawn, so far as I have been able to draw them from the sentiments which originated, and were given to the world from his hall in which we stand. I have never had a feeling politically that did not spring from the sentiments embodied in the Declaration of Independence.

The debate between political opponents, the
fighting between brothers on the battle field,
were expressions of commitments to the same democratic faith. The peoplehood was divided, the
South saw itself as the continuation of God's
chosen people and the Confederacy as the fulfillment of the destiny of history. To the
Northerner the situation was just the opposite.
Henry Ward Beecher declared to his congregation:
"I'll thank them (the Confederacy) that they
took another flag to do the Devil's work, and
lift our flag to do the work of God."

The American peoplehood had been born in the
fires of the revolutionary struggle; it was re-
fined by the fires of the Civil War. Instead of
being consumed by the struggle, it grew. For
the first time the black man was a legal member
of the peoplehood. The constitutional questions
of the right of the states to secede from the
Union and slavery were settled by history. The
sectarian controversy ended, and it was possible
once again for the constitution to become the
mass creed for all people. In World War I the
nation would fight another war, but this time
Southerners and Northerners would be fighting
side by side to make the world safe for the
democratic way of life.

Civil Institutions

The American civil religion comprises not
only a civil theology and peoplehood but also
key economic, social, political and ecclesiastical
institutions which embody, interpret and propa-
gate the religion. For the colonist the Revolution proved conclusively that the new Republic
was the primary agent fo God's meaningful activity
in history. It was not surprising, therefore,
that the state emerged as the foremost institution
of the civil religion.

This belief was undergirded by the assumption
that America and Americans were (pre)destined by
a benevolent deity (the biblical God of the Chris-

234

tians or the God of nature of the rationalists) to be freed from England and to spread the gospel of freedom to all men. This understanding is found in the sermons of clergymen as well as the writing of such Deists as John Adams and Jefferson. As early as 1765 Adams penned an entry in his diary which confessed that: "I always consider the settlement of America with reverence and wonder, as the opening of a grand scene and design in Providence for the illumination of the ignorant, and the emancipation of the slavish part of mankind all over the earth."

This vision was also implicit in the Declaration of Independence, where, as Albert Weinberg points out, Jefferson was sufficiently confident of his intuition of divine purposes to present the case for American independence as "indubitable dogmas of truth and destiny." Weinberg concludes that "The Americans...had faith not only in the justice but also the inevitability of independence...Thus the first doctrine which reflected the nationalistic theology of 'manifest destiny' was that of God's decree of independence."

When the Constitution went to the states for debate and ratification, its defenders were quick to describe its significance in terms of American destiny. This was evident in the opening paragraph of the Federalist Papers where Alexander Hamilton argued:

After an unequivocal experience of the inefficiency of the subsisting federal government, you are called upon to deliberate on a new Constitution for the United States of America. The subject speaks its own importance; comprehending in its consequences, nothing less than the existence of the UNION, the safety and welfare of the parts of which it is composed, the fate of an empire, in many respects, the most interesting in the world. It has been frequently remarked that it seems to have been reserved to the people of this country, by their conduct and example, to decide the important question, whether societies of man are really capable or not of establishing good government from reflection and choice, or whether they are forever destined to depend for their political constitutions on accident and force. If there by any truth in the remark, the crisis at which we are arrived may with propriety be regarded as the era in which that decision is to be made; and a wrong election of the part we shall act may, in this view, deserve to be considered as the general misfortune of mankind.

The messianic mission of America, the evangelistic character of the young republic was represented by two different themes. These have alternated in the course of its history.

One theme was "isolationist withdrawal, the conception of innocent nation, wicked world." It was advocated in Washington's "Farewell Adress." America was to be an example to the world, but only a moral example. To intervene actively in world affairs would be to expose the chosen people to the evil forces (entangling alliances etc.) from which they had escaped.

A second theme emerged as the nation became stronger and more confident of itself. If it was not possible to teach the lesson of republicanism by the power of example, the other possibility was to spread it easily and immediately by the use of force - especially to peoples in regions adjacent to the United States. This active messianic mission of America before the Civil War demonstrated itself in the era of Manifest Destiny. America had a mandate to spread the democratic faith and institution over all of North America. It was the destiny (secular form of Providence) of the American people to advance into and to take possession of new lands and territories. The resulting Mexican War (1846-48) was seen by many as a means of regenerating the Mexicans - of spreading the "good news" of a democratic way of life.

As the American state became the primary institution for the external evangelization of those
people outside of the peoplehood, American education and particularly the public school developed
to serve as an institution responsible for the
internal evangelization of the nation's people.

As example of this phenomenon is Thomas Jefferson's announcement that the University of
Virginia "will be based on the illimitable freedom
of the human mind. For here we are not afraid
to follow the truth wherever it may lead, nor to
tolerate any error as long as reason is left free
to combat it." Jefferson believed in reason
and like many other eighteenth century Deists
he rejected the supernatural,
to interpret Christianity as a humanistic code.
He edited the Gospels to produce his own Bible,
cutting the genuine sayings of Christ from the
spurious, "as easily distinguishable as diamonds
in a dunghill." His profound distaste for theology and the church (Anglicanism was the established faith in Virginia) led him to advocate
not only Virginia's Bill for Religious Freedom
(contending "that to compel a man to furnish
contribution of money for the propagation of
opinions which he disbelieves and abhors is
sinful and tyrannical...truth is great and will
prevail if left to herself..."), but·to found the
University of Virginia as a nonsectarian alternative to Virginia's Anglican College of William
and Mary.

In fact nowhere is Jefferson's own sectarian
faith more apparent than in his work as the
founder of the University of Virginia. In the
stipulations for curriculum he did not establish
a chair of divinity, but asserted the separation
of church and state. Because the University was
endowed by public monies and administered by
civil authorities, no sectarianism must be allowed
in the curriculum. (The "neutral" obligation for
developing moral character was in the hands of

237

the professors of ethics.) And yet, when it came time to hire the faculty, he wrote to James Madison about the need to find an orthodox advocate of states-rights republicanism to teach law and declared that:

It is in our seminary that the vestal flame is to be kept alive; from thence it is to spread anew over our own and the sister States. If we are true and vigilant in our trust, within a dozen or twenty years a majority of our own legislature will be from one school, and many disciples will have carried its doctrine home with them to their several states, and will have leavened the whole mass.

David B. Tyack comments: " 'Seminary,' 'vestal flame,' 'disciple,' 'doctrine,' 'leavened thus the whole mass' - what are these terms if not the vocabulary of the sectarian."

Jefferson also prescribed the texts to be used at the University of Virginia "to provide that no ideas shall be inculcated which are incompatable with those on which the Constitution of the state and the United States are generally based."

There is one branch in which we are the best judges, in which heresies may be taught, of so interesting a character to our own State, and to the United States, as to make it a duty in us to lay down the principles which are to be taught. It is that of government ...It is our duty to guard against the dissemination of such Federalist principles among our youth, and the diffusion of the poison by a previous prescription of the texts of be followed in their discourses.

Jefferson's choice of texts was enough to make the Virginia, Federalist, Chief Justice John Marshall complain that he was being forced by the state to support the propagation of opinions which he disbelieved and abhorred.

Religious heresies did not matter; they were in the area of grace - the private sphere of conscience. Political heresy was a different matter. That was the area of nature - the public sphere of the American civil religion. Jefferson's educational ideas were far from being nonsectarian. They were intimately tied to his hope for redeeming society - the republican form of government.

This view was not unique with Jefferson. It was shared by all those who believed that education was not an extraneous issue but interwoven with the democratic faith commitment. It was out of this civil "religious" belief that the public school was born.

During the revolutionary era a common argument was that republican institutions must rest on "virtue" and thus there was a growing need for a universal system of public schools to teach the virtues of republicanism. It was not, however, until the first half of the nineteenth century, and the leadership of such men as Daniel Webster, Edward Everett, Horace Mann, and others, that the common school movement really began to develop.

As early as the eighteen thirties Alexis de Tocqueville commented that politics was "the end and aim of education." This was based on his observation of Whigs and others who, in the wake of the democratization of politics and increased immigration in the Jacksonian Era, attempted to use the public school movement to Americanize new voters and new immigrants. If the "common man" was to have the vote, he had better be educated into the faith of the democratic way of life. If the immigrant was to become a member of the peoplehood, one way to convert him would be through education.

Nervous about their own "Americanism,"

239

natives grew alarmed about assimilating the newcomers. When the teachers of Cincinnati discussed the immigrant problem, Calvin Stowe, and William McGuffey argued that public schools held out the best hope of turning foreign children into Americans. No random education would do; it must be uniform and systematic. Americans must define what it meant to be american and must find ways of inculcating patriotism in the young. In the textbooks of McGuffey and his contemporaries children would find the national pattern.

Governors and Presidents, Whigs and Democrats, Calvinists and Unitarians were soon proclaiming their common faith in public education.

This unity has led Elwyn A. Smith, who recently edited a work entitled The Religion of the Republic, to comment;

The public school were considered from their origin a principal instrument for the moral elevation of the people; and George Washington warned in 1796 that it was perilous to separate morals from religion. The vehemence of the disputes that swirl around public education are largely to be explained by widespread agreement with Washington's judgement, which perhaps justifies the suggestion that the American public school system is the nation's equivalent to the European established church.

After studying the same issue, John F. Wilson, in an essay entitled "The Status of 'Civil Religion' in America," also concluded that "...the public school system certainly must be viewed as a powerful engine for reinforcement of common religion," and the "school systems are in fact the American religious establishment through their state symbolism, civic ceremonial, inculcated values, exemplified virtues and explicit curricula."

As a result of the Americanization process, churches quickly came to serve as still another institutional expression of the civil religion. With the separation of Church and State under the Federal Constitution, all churches lost any political claim to universality and became voluntary associations. According to John Smylie the nation assumed the traditional role of the universal church for most Americans. "Thus the unity which Christian theology localizes in Christ and the Church was actually realized, insofar as it was realized at all in American experience, in the nation."

Although the American churches gave up the functions normally associated with the concept of a national church, they continued to play a very important role in society. American leaders were convinced that the only way to preserve a republican government was by the inculcation of basic morality throughout the new nation. Although there was a continual debate between those who insisted in grounding such morality in revealed truth and others who insisted that it was available through reason and human experience, all agreed that it was essential for the maintenance of the republic.

The observation is substantiated by the fact that churches of many different theological persuasions not only supported the American Revolution but continued to merge religion and patriotism. Examples of the interrelationship between religion and patriotism are so numerous that one is forced to conclude that the American civil religion had found a home in the American churches.

The exceptions before the Civil War were few. One was that of the Mormon Church which regarded itself as the true heir of God's promises, and its own people as chosen by God for his purposes on earth. The Mormons were persecuted more than were the Catholics becuase the former would not

241

assimilate and therefore they were suspected of the ultimate sin, un-Americanism.

Another institutional expression of the American civil religion can be seen in the history and practice of political parties in the United States. The development of political parties was not anticipated by the "founding fathers," for at least two reasons. In the first place, political parties were considered evil by almost every writer in the early eighteenth century. This dislike and distrust of parties was based upon the conviction that they were disruptive of the political process. The second reason was that Americans had developed an ideological attachment to republican government which in a very short time had become a common political creed. Cecelia M. Kenyon has pointed out that while "Americans have regarded themselves, and have been regarded, as an essentially pragmatic people,...the preference for republicanism which crystallized at the time of the Revolution has constituted an ideological, doctrinaire element in their political outlook which has rarely been questioned.

When political parties developed in the United States, they shared the same ideological commitment to republicanism. The commitment to this principle became so sacred that it was never questioned; to have questioned it would have been heresy. In this context the political parties themselves became institutional expressions of the common faith. The failure of the American experience to produce any other kind of party is a manifestation of this common American ideology. Unlike the ideological debates of European politics, American politics have been made up exclusively of functional and pragmatic questions because there is no cause to debate the underlying dogma upon which party politics developed in the United States - the sovereignty of the people.

Civil Ceremonial Expressions and Symbols

The American civil religion, like every religion, has its own unique ceremonies and symbols. They reveal probably as nothing else can, the way in which the civil religion became a central element, not only in the life of the nation but in the lives of its people. The response to these ceremonies and symbols suggests the emotional hold that the civil religion had upon the American citizen.

In the wake of the Declaration of Independence, the meaning allocated to its signing and to the principles embodied in the document, the Fourth of July by the 1780's provided both the occasion and context for one of the annual celebrations of the civil religion. One orator instructed his audience that Independence Day was the "Sabbath of our freedom,...one of the greatest events that has occurred in the history of mankind."

Commenting about the celebration of"the glorious Fourth" in the period following the War of 1812, Professor Ralph H. Gabriel has declared that the Fourth of July was both a "gala day and a national sabbath." After the running of races, celebrating and merrymaking, the participants got down to the serious part of the day. A minister began the ceremony with prayer, in which the blessings of God were customarily assured to Americans because they were His chosen people living in His chosen land. Following the prayer there were the reading of the Declaration of Independence and an oration by a civil leader who traditionally called upon the people to recommit themselves to the founding principles expressed in the Declaration of Independence.

In such an age, the Fourth of July oration became inevitably the principal American ceremonial expression of homage to the nation. It was a ritual performance.

Though the words differed, the pattern was always the same. It was an affirmation of the doctrines of the American democratic faith. It had no sectional variations. Novelty in essential form would have been as unwelcome as a revision of the Bethlehem story. The oration at the center of the Fourth of July celebration was the counterpart in nationalistic ritual of the emphasis in the Protestant service upon the sermon.

In 1821, John Quincy Adams delivered a lengthy Fourth of July Oration which was an exact expression of this type of ritualistic observance. Blending Puritan piety with faith in a virtuous republic founded upon Reason, he declared that the Declaration of Independence (which he read aloud as part of his oration) was a sacred text. The Declaration "proved that the social compact was no figment of the imagination; but a real, solid, and sacred bond of the social union...It stands, and must forever stand alone, a beacon on the summit of the mountain."

Besides the Fourth of July there were other holidays which began to provide an annual ritual calendar for the civil religion. Washington, at the request of Congress during his first year in office, declared that November 26 should be "a day of public thanksgiving and prayer." Although it was not to become an annual national holiday until the presidency of Lincoln, Robert Bellah has argued that it was an important celebration because it served "to integrate the family into the civil religion." In the same way Memorial Day, which grew out of the Civil War, soon became a rite of rededication to the martyred dead, to the spirit of sacrifice, to the American vision, and as such "has acted to integrate the local community into the natural cult."

The first official seal of the United States gave expression to the nation's view of itself and its place in history. On one side an American heraldic eagle holds in his beak a scroll inscribed with the motto, E Pluribus Unum, (from many, one), declaring the establishment of a new peoplehood. The design on the reverse side of the seal is best described by quoting directly from the official "Remarks and Explanation" that was sent by the Secretary of Congress to the Continental Congress in 1782. "The Pyramid signifies strength and duration. The eye over it and the motto allude to the many signal interpositions of providence in favor of the American cause. The date underneath is that of the Declaration of Independence, and the words under it signify the beginning of the new American Era, which commences from that date."

There is no better symbol of the messianic understanding of the American nation. The eye of Providence is a radiant triangle whose glory extends over the shield and beyond the figures; the date of the Declaration of Independence depicts the emergence of the new nation and the motto below (Novus Ordo Selorum) testifies to a new order of the ages. On the reverse side the American Eagle carries arrows in one talon and an olive branch in the other - the symbols of war and peace, and an indication that the future was not expected to be entirely serene.

The colors on the crest of the eagle are red, white and blue which was an obvious reference to the American flag. In no other country was the flag venerated as it was in America. Lacking historic symbols, the country quickly seized upon the flag as the chief representation of the nation.

Religious meaning was also given to the American experience during the Civil War. Julia Ward Howe's "The Battle Hymn of the Republic" stands as a testimony of the religious meaning and destiny of the nation. The last line proclaimed: "As he died to make men holy, let us die to make men free, While God is marching on." The apocalyptic trumpet had sounded and the call went out to the American people to break the bonds

245

of men. From the Revolutionary War to the Civil
War the civil religion was perfected but the
vision remained the same.

Enforcement of Civil Religion

The evidence clearly indicates that in an
American civil religion was deeply entrenched
in the American consciousness and society by
the time of the Civil War. The basic dogma
(civil theology) that the people were the constituent power had been tested by the time and had
matured allowing the civil peoplehood to differentiate significantly. The institutional expressions of the civil religion had developed and
become strong, providing for a high degree of
social integration. The civil ceremonies and
symbols were diversified, and civil leaders,
particularly in times of crisis, had given focus
and direction to the civil religion.

As modern civil religions developed, the means
of enforcement also emerged "indirectly through
mythic evocation of natural rights and institu-
tionalization of the religious toleration." The
former method of enforcement is evident in the
political views of Rousseau, Spinoza, Hobbes,
or in the twentieth century manifestations of
National Socialist and Communist regimes.

The enforcement of a civil religion in some
of the Anglo-Saxon countries is indirect - through
the veil of natural rights and religious toleration. Tocqueville was one of the earliest writers
to detect this coercion. He pointed out that
although Americans enjoyed religious freedom they
were, nevertheless, in danger of losing their
liberty to the authoritarian "voice of the people."
Behind the veil of religious toleration there
was developing in America a "tyranny of the Majority." Tocqueville concluded that faith in
public opinion was becoming "a species of religion," and the majority "its ministering prophet."

The tyranny of the majority is the enforcement

mechanism of the voice of the people. Tocqueville observed that the majority not only made the laws of the new society and formed opinions but also had the power to enforce them. The laws were supported by the police power as in any state, but in America, opinions were brought under the control of the will of the majority through more subtle pressures.

The master no longer says, "You shall think as I do or you shall die"; but the says "You are free to think differently from me, and to retain your life, your property and all that you possess; but you are henceforth a stranger among your people. You may retain your civil rights, but they will be useless to you, for you will never be chosen by your fellow-citizens, if you solicit their votes; and they will affect to scorn you, if you ask for their esteem. You will remain among men, but you will be deprived of the rights of mankind. Your fellow creatures will shun you like an impure being; and even those who believe in your innocence will abandon you, lest they should be shunned in their turn. Go in peace! I have given you your life, but it is an existence worse than death."

The majority represented the community of believers in the American civil religion and the dissenters became the heretics. In order to be politically heard or supported, one had to believe in the will of the majority and stay within bounds prescribed by the majority. (One of the bounds, for example, was to keep sectarian beliefs out of politics.) One who challenged the faith of the faithful was not physically punished but was isolated and ignored by the community. He was labeled un-American and "excommunicated."

The supreme irony of the Western liberal tradition is that, whereas the division between the private and public aspects of life was occasioned

247

by the concern to protect individual freedom
from the authoritarian control of the state, it
has led, as in the case of America, to authoritarian control by the people.

The founders of the Constitution were concerned
with creating a structure that would protect
individual freedom, but their solution, giving
ultimate political power to the majority, created
what in time became a new type of tyranny - a
tyranny of unanimity and uniformity, that is, a
tyranny of democratic society itself.

Few Americans in the eighteenth century saw
popular sovereignty as a license to violate the
"higher law." Given the continued secularization of American society, however, it was only
a matter of time before the people were to
emerge as politically omnipotent. The concept
of "higher law" began to wane as the Christian
influence declined in the United States. During
the latter half of the nineteenth century, as
a relegation of Christian values to an innocuous
private sphere of life continued, the antithesis
between the Christian view of life and that of
the secular civil religion became clearer.

The features of the American civil religion
outlined in this paper must not obscure the fact
that this is just one of the forms that civil
religion has taken in the modern world. Possibly this analysis of America's civil religion
in terms such as civil theology, civil peoplehood, etc., can provide a meaningful tool, not
only for the continued study of American culture
but also for future comparative studies of other
modern civil religions.

Academic interest in the subject is not, however, the most important reason why continued
study is needed. Although the presence of a
civil religion has been largely invisible to
the academic world until recently, its oppression
has been real for a long time to those individuals and groups who have rejected the faith.
This oppression is not because the religion has

not lived up to its highest ideals but rather
the coercion stems from the very structure
(identification of the civil order with a particular world and life view) which allows one confessional group to dominate other men.

All civil religions, regardless of form, lead
to oppression. Civil religion, by its very
nature, denies the possibility of a truly, con-
fessionally, pluralistic society. The only hope
that the future will bring a more just order is
that more peoples and groups will realize the
true character of civil religion. Only once this
occurs will there be a willingness to explore
other political alternatives - one that will
allow all citizens of a nation to live our their
lives completely in a free society under law.

"INTEREST GROUP LIBERALISM"

By Stanley W. Carlson

While most of us have had our backs turned,
somthing new has developed in American government and society. To say it is new may be
slightly misleading, because the outlines of
what has now become obvious to most viewers were
noticed by those with eyes to see years ago, and,
indeed, what is now rather well developed has
grown out of tendencies long within our political
system and tradition. In any case, it is appro-
priat for us to turn our attention to this matter
now, in these pages, for seeing the new shape
of things should help us to put into (tentative)
place many of the facts with which we are continually bombarded, and because if we are truly
to develop a "Christian political mind" and to
grow in Christian political obedience, this new
context must be taken into account.

This new reality in the United States (and
elsewhere) has been called "pressure group" or
"interest group" government, and the public
philosophy that undergirds and justifies it has
been called "interest-group liberalims." (See,
especially, Lowi, The End of Liberalism.) Stories
of political scandals (using public office for
private financial gain) go far back into the past,
as Russell Kirk has recently reminded us ("The
Persistence of Political Corruption," in The
Center Magazine, Jan.-Feb., 1974); what we now
have is more subtle, though not of an entirely
different order, nor, I wish to argue, are its
effects less harmful to the proper task of government and to the well-being of society.

For interest-group government and its philosophy accept as necessary and promote as desirable
that government policy be formed primarily by
the interaction of private groups concerned with
the issue at hand from their limited viewpoints.
That is to say, rather.than government officials

250

seeking first to discover what the various organized groups have to say, attempt to reconcile
these, and expect and assume that "justice" will
be a by-product. Often even the initiative for
any government action comes through the pressures
of interest groups.

PRIVATE VICE AND PUBLIC VIRTUE

In old economic theory, private vice was to
be public virtue through the automatic operation
of the marketplace with its "invisible hand."
Now, while that concept has lost some of its
allure, the same principle has been institutionalized governmentally. Thus the public
interest is thought to consist (primarily) in
maintaining a framework within which private
groups can fight for as large a piece of the
action or initiative in setting policy as they
have the power to do. And government sees its
task as one of reconciliation at this level,
not first of all as one of seeking out the injustice operating in society and the setting of
political and legal priorities for action.

We need to look, necessarily briefly, at the
development of this system, the justifications
given for it, its weaknesses and its effects;
and then we will know better where we stand as
we begin to try to formulate some ways to act
and think that might help steer government and
public officials to a healthier way of governing.
The following example should help in this task.

It is common knowledge that the Penn Central
Railroad lurches from crisis to crisis, saved
mainly by last-minute intervention of the Federal
Government. This railroad performs a needed
public service for large parts of the northeast
and northern mid-west; it has thus seemed clear
to most people that it should not be allowed to
collapse. But in considering just what needs to
be done with the Penn Central, there has not
been careful and independent government study of
the transportation needs of the area, considering

251

the proper mix of air, sea, road, and rail transportation; the needs of small towns and large
cities, varied businesses and industries, and
commuters; the long-term growth patterns of the
area; and so on. After such a study, conducted
in an open way with representatives of all sorts
of views on real and presumed "needs" and proper
solutions, one could hope and expect that some
good beginnings could be made, that governmental
power and authority could be brought to bear
honestly, fairly, and firmly on the problems and
possibilities of this area. But instead, in
time of crisis the government has left the interested parties themselves to come up with "just"
solutions.

One reporter, summarizing the story of the
passage of the bill to rescue the Penn Central
and several other bankrupt railroads, put it
this way:

It is no wonder that the legislative history
of the Northeast railroad bill is confusing,
in that it was designed and pushed through
Congress almost entirely by officers of
special-interest groups that stand to benefit
from its provisions. The original draft of
the act was written not by some inter-agency
task force but by the general counsel of the
Union Pacific Railroad. Once the Union Pacific draft was introduced under the name of
Representative Shoup, it hurtled through
Congress with only minor changes in approach,
save for the addition of a $250-million "labor
protection" clause that was written, down to
the last comma, by a group of railroad and
union presidents. When it came time to set
the final price tag for the bill, Congress
did not get its financial assumptions from
the Department of Transportation or the
Library of Congress but from the First
National City Bank, which will probably get
$300-million in Penn Central prebankruptcy
loans repaid because of the legislation.
(Joseph Albright, "The Penn Central," New

252

York Times Magazine, November 3, 1974)

Examples could be multiplied - they are in the pages of the newspapers and magazines daily - but perhaps the point is clear already. Public policy is increasingly set by private interest groups not restrained by the overview of public servants with a drive towards long-term justice and the whole public interest (which is not limited merely to catering to the majority's demands, or even just to the perceived interests of the United State's citizenry, but must be in response tq all of God's directives and thus with regard to all human and other creatures of the Lord). Rather, restraint, if any, comes through the resources and ingenuity of other groups also wanting some protection of their "interest" - whether it be narrowly selfish (extra material benefits), important in the short-run (higher wages or lower taxes, to maintain, within the existing pattern, a certain level of comfort or provision of necessities), or more altruistic (pollution control, easing of racial injustice, protection of the oppressed overseas). What can be seen as justice is sometimes the result, but not first the aim of all involved. In this style of government and politics, public officials are not directly confronted by the call of the Lord to them to do justice, nor do they grow much in their ability to help provide it for those most needy. The actual public interest is rarely seen as a fundamental necessity or basis for decision-making.

"INTEREST GROUP LIBERALISM"

Theodore J. Lowi, in his excellent book on the philosophy undergirding this kind of govern-ment, has called it "interest-group liberalism" and lays much of the blame, rightly so, at the feet of the liberals (The End of Liberalism; cf. Irving Kristol, "Thoughts on Reading About a Summer-Camp Cabin Covered with Garbage," New York Times Magazine, November 17, 1974). But

our liberalism and conservatism come essentially
from outside of the governmental arena; government is to be feared and kept underdeveloped
since it is the source of all tyranny, and that
the market place is the important sphere of
life after all. One can see how easily these
beliefs, still held to somewhat by present-day
conservatives, could, under the impact of developing big business and labor unions, the apparent
need for government intervention to cope with
the Great Depression, and the imperatives of
the Cold War period, could easily turn into their
mirror image. Thus many liberals and conservatives now defend big government as the focus of
much private action - government which still
takes its initiative from private individuals
and groups and whose own task (as possibly distinct from just acceding to the demands of groups)
has never been adequately considered. And the
form of government set up in the Constitution,
with its checks and balances, separation of
powers, separate constituencies for President
and legislators, and so on, has almost dictated
that if much is to be done at all, it will have
to be by stimulus from outside. Thus it seems
that we have a form of government whose action
almost necessarily becomes piecemeal, short
term, and oriented to log-rolling (trading of
favors).

But even as the form of government, and the
public philosophy that supports such a means of
governmental policy-making, have certain consequences, so also the kinds of political parties
that have resulted, the public attitudes that
have developed, and the style of election campaigns we now see, all partake of the same flaws
and the same style.

Consider the reaction of the groups consulted
in last fall's round of discussions on economic
policy that the Ford Administration called. A
summary report in the New York Times noted:
"Instead of offering President Ford the new and
imaginative remedies for inflation he sought when

he set up his economic conferences, special interest groups have called for policies that altogether would probably add to the price indexes more than they would take away.... Interest groups, representing various sectors of the economy, have said not what they would do for their country but instead what their country should do for them." (Soma Golden, "Self-Interest Stymies Inflation Fight," Sept. 22, 1974, Section 3, p. 1.) The "public" appears to be increasingly adept at looking out for its various "interests"!

In terms of governmental action about the economy, it is impossible to predict now just what will be the outcome of the tug-of-war between the President and his economic plan as set forth in the State of the Union address and the counterproposals put forth by the Democratic Congress, but certainly one prediction can be safely made: virtually no one, either in Congress or the Executive branch (or, the party organizations, the media, the interest groups), will ask any searching questions. Few questions will be asked about the whole economy; about the continuing faith in material abundance as the road to the good life. Few questions about the present pattern of high levels of natural resources extraction from other nations to fulfill our own economic "needs"; or the spiral of energy demand, fostered by energy-wasteful design of buildings, cities, and transportation networks. Few will question the heartfelt desire to continue to see our responsibilities to other peoples and their life-and-death struggles with hunger as needing to be fulfilled only by skimming off the top of our food abundance a bit of aid; or the hope and belief that all will be well with our economy if only we will pump it up again to full production, in spite of all the apparent diseconomies built into it. There will be jockeying over whose ox will get gored, whose "interest" will not be fulfilled at this time; there will be all kinds of proposed mixes of burdens and benefits. But there will be few, if any, deep questions or attempts to use this present distress as an opportunity for readjustment in our self-interest and our wasteful ways.

PARTIES, PRESSURES, AND PERSPECTIVES

In some nations, the political parties serve as proponents and representatives of differing visions, differing whole views of what is significant, what must be done, what is vital for national health - conceptions of the whole within which "interests," details, and policies take shape and find a place; but in the United States, this is less and less so. Thus, though one can say that Democrats are more concerned with helping the poor and other disadvantaged people through direct government action, and Republicans tend to think that the disadvantaged will be aided best by non-interference of government with the operations of societal forces, both parties appear to have accepted the framework of our present social and economic systems, and differentiate themselves mostly by the kinds of interest groups with which they are identified. Thus Lockard remarks, "Party competition may produce a responsiveness to certain dominent interests - the medical profession, oil companies, certain labor unions, or corporate agriculture - but it does not induce the parties to exert themselves for those whose need may be great but whose power to produce official responses is small" (The Perverted Priorities of American Politics, p. 75). Those who are organized can find some response in the parties; those who are not are left our in the cold, whatever their needs may be. Goals, or policies resulting from goals not presently enjoying a high degree of public support are rarely brought to light, even though such rethinking may, in fact, be just what the parties need to assist in if there is to be service and justice by the government.

All of these trends are obvious too in the changing style of election compaigns, as the Ripon

256

Society (in Jaws of Victory) and others have noted. Election campaigns, even - or especially - for the Presidency, are increasingly designed to appeal to the very short-term interests and prejudices of potential voters. In the 1972 campaigns, both the Nixon and McGovern organizations included a great diversity of sub-groups designed to get the support of finely divided "target groups": The National Maritime Committee to Re-elect the President, the Labor Committee for McGovern-Shriver, groups to capture the "youth vote," groups designed to capture the votes of the various "ethnic blocs" and so on. But such tailored appeals, politicians are finding out to their great sorrow, are perverse in their results: the immediate goal may be reached - election or re-election - but the ability of any politician then to lead and not merely give in to such groups, is diminished. The bond of trust needed between representatives and the people, which must be built up over time and withoug excessive regard for the balance of costs and benefits to the "groups" in existence, is destroyed. Having stimulated the creation of such "fluid voters," the problems of governing just get worse, and demands begin to come in for fulfillment of campaign pledges of "goodies" of all varieties to each group, fulfillment which often can come only at the expense of the over-all public interest.

Thus campaigns, rather than opening up new options or helping to measure the existence in the public of differing goals, help to further break down the reservoir of trust needed if public servants are to serve the whole public and not merely the most powerful groups who assisted in their election victory. The public increasingly sees government as a target from which to extract favors or an arena in which to counter the extraction of favors by others. Public officials increasingly see the public as objects to be manipulated if any continuity of action is to be maintained and if any hard decisions are to be carried out. The whole

257

governing task, in which power is needed in order to bring about public justice, degenerates, with the focus on power plays and the powerful, and less and less consideration of what the power is to be used for. A downward spiral is established; power is utilized to gain more power; governing becomes incidental.

For all of these reasons, government is increasingly seen as non-legitimate (we all sense that it is being used by the more powerful in their favor), and it is accurate to talk of the rise of statism (no one seems really to mind an all-powerful state if it also parcels out to them what they demand). But while our government becomes swollen in size, it also becomes less and less effective.

Policies "happen" in a piecemeal way. Laws are passed mandating only that an agency be set up to "end poverty," for one example, leaving the way open for all the interested parties to capture the ear of the direction less agency and bend its path in their direction and favor. As there is less basic trust in government, and more public "brittleness", government almost has to turn to talk of impending crisis to get any action at all - but then gets action that rebounds when citizens discover that there was no crisis of such proportions, that things would have gone well if officials had been looking further ahead than just the next election, that they have been manipulated. The President is forced to govern by Gallup Poll measures of "popularity" and with decline in popularity, citizens turn further away from the policies formulated - and in response, the strategists, managers, and PR people crank up a media spectacular to ease the popularity ratings a few points higher so that something might get done. And in the midst of this, or more precisely, below all this furious and almost self-defeating action, the crying needs of the oppressed, discriminated against, and poverty-striken ones go unnoticed and the course of the lumbering and

258

creaking structure is not moved toward health.

PLURALISM WITHOUT OPTIONS

This is what has been called the "pluralism" of American government, but it is obviously not a pluralism of different conceptions of the way to go, but rather squabbling and log-rolling within the outlines of a virtually unquestioned framework. It is a pluralism without options, policies, or public space for those whose needs or visions fall outside the sphere of the majority culture. With no consideration of ends - except as by-products - the whole degenerates into power plays and "strategic politics", a politics of winning and losing, not of service. A monolithic society, which this pluralism was to guard against, is no solution (but indeed appears to be the unintended result); but also not a solution is the emphasis on the adversary or competitive process without consideration of why or what for: "When attorneys in court use 'every trick in the book,' justice does not necessarily result....When the electioneer uses every trick in the book, leadership does not necessarily result; and when the presidency uses every trick in the book, freedom and good government do not necessarily result" (Jaws of Victory, p. 350). When government is so structured and run as to put the premium on those knowing how to use "every trick in the book" (organized interest groups?), justice does not necessarily result. Condemning this competition to win government support for privately-defined ends does not mean that determing "the public interest" or seeking "justice" are easy; but to think that they will be a by-product of a process geared to other priorities is hardly the way to proceed governmentally! The difficulty of the task should cause all to focus on it, not ignore it and do those things virtually guaranteeing its subversion. Justice and the public interest - both as distinct from a mere mechanistic balancing of powerful private forces with little regard for the powerless - will never be found if not even sought!

IMPLICATIONS FOR US

What does all of this imply for us, as
Christians interested in government that lives
up to its calling as God's servant for the
good of the people? For one thing, we should
hear again through the Bible that government is
there for the service of the whole public, not
for self-indulgence. We should hear again all
the prophetic calls for justice recorded in the
pages of the Old and New Testaments. And we
need, each of us, to think about our own relationships to government and government policy.
When we discuss public questions, do we do so in
terms of service and justice, or in terms of
cynicism, selfishness, short-run advantage for
ourselves? When we vote, are we concerned only
with what politician will help us get a tax cut,
will protect the status quo, will not ask up-
setting questions about the shape of the economy,
our relations to the poor within our nation and
in other nations? Or are we interested in the
candidate who will be the best servant for all
the people and who is the most sensitive to
questions of injustice, poverty, discrimination?
When we contact our congressmen, are we most
interested in getting them to do us favors,
to bend to our wishes on this or that, or to
call them to their office of doing justice?

Albert Camus, in The Fall, has his main
character observe: "We no longer say as in
simple times: 'This is the way I think. What
are your objections?' We have become lucid.
For the dialogue we have substituted the com-
munique: 'This is the truth,' we say. 'You can
discuss it as much as you want; we aren't interested. But in a few years there'll be the
police who will show you we are right.'" Surely
not much can be expected until we turn from that
posture. Prophetic statements are needed, but
we don't need false assurance or unyielding
determination to work the public process in our
own favor.

In the words of Senator Mark Hatfield:

260

Any politician's life is full of those trying to pressure him, argue with him, or extract some promise or favor from him. Most people treat a politician like one who is to be lobbied and won over to their side. However, a politician confronts within himself deep questions about the issues and decisions he must make. He needs to find people with whom he can honestly share and confide his thoughts in order to think through the troubling choices he must make. Further, as one in political life faces such decisions, he often must confront deep moral issues and questions of fundamental values and ethics. In the midst of those dilemmas he can profit from those who will think through these questions with him from the perspective of faith, and even with the support of prayer. Because of this need, I believe churchmen should not view politicians merely as someone who has to be "lobbied." Rather, their aim should be to build honest personal relationships with politicians, based on true concern, love and understanding ("Pastors and Prophets," Post-American, October, 1974).

One the organizational level, then, rather than becoming only another lobby or pressure group, pushing our own projects, we need to find a new way of acting. In Christ, we have a new vision of the whole, not just additional or substitute projects, interests, and issues. In Christ, we are interested in service, not just "our needs." In Christ, we are concerned with justice and healing for all - which may require some fundamental reorientations of our national life - not just benefits for ourselves. If this is correct, then not only the content of our relations with public officials needs to be distinct, but also the way we go about this, a way of turning government back to its calling, not just further reducing it to the sum of external demands.

All of which is a tall order. "Results" are

not immediate. But we are, first of all, called to "do justice," to "love kindness," to "let justice roll down like waters and righteousness like an ever-flowing stream." In so doing, and in supporting those public officials (elected or not) who are similarly oriented, we can assist in the healing process, in sowing "the seed whose fruit is righteousness," the seek which is "sown in peace by those who make peace" (James 3:18).

THE CHRISTIAN AND MODERN DEMOCRACY

By Jan Dengerink

The problem of democracy, especially when one is concerned with the modern democracy, is not an easy one. This is a result of the fact that the concept of democracy has attained an ever braoder meaning in the course of history and that is has even received an ideological connotation. With this it has lost much of its clarity. In the Western World all well-intentioned people and parties are highly concerned about democracy. The adjective "un-democractic" implies a   qualification. But a closer analysis of the concept of democracy will reveal that there are a host of definitions involved in this term. And this becomes even more complex when we notice that the communist states in central and eastern Europe, where in our view not even the shadow of democracy is present, still present themselves explicitly as people's democracies. Similary, an Asiantic leader like Sukarno refers to Indonesia, the state which he rules in a rather dictatoral manner, as a democracy, even if he prefers to describe it as a "guided democracy."

In our view this confusion is a result of the fact that the concept of democracy has been closely lined to the ideas of freedom and equality, whereby the emphasis fell at times on freedom, then again on equality, while it must be recalled that even these terms allow a variety of definitions. Confusion, more than clarity, thus marks the history of the concept of democracy.

This confusion, however, should not disconcert us. Rather, as Christians in the tradition of the Reformation we will have to find our own way in this jungle of ideas in the hope that

thus we can make a valuable contribution to the
political thought of our times.

1. The Origin of Modern Democracy

In the first place we will examine the origin
of modern democracy, as it has developed in
several countries in the western world but also
in other continents. It is not my intention to
present a phase of political or legal history
but, instead, to discover which spiritual forces
have led to the rise of modern democracies.
These forces are the ones of Reformation and
Humanism as they were first embodied in Renaiss-
ance-man.

It is no surprise that the Reformation of
the sixteenth century greatly contributed to
the development of the democratic idea. Contrary
to the hierarchic idea which dominated the Middle
Ages, the Reformation clearly stressed the
general office of believers and the personal
responsibility of every member of the church.
This naturally affected the view of the relation
between government and citizen within the framework of the emerging unified state characterized
by its public-legal nature.

However, in the arena of Western European
culture the Reformation surrendered an ever
increasing area of human life to the forces of
Humanism, affecting even the life of the church
itself. This process already began in the
second half of the seventeenth century and continued with forceful impetus in the following
century. Modern democracy, as we know it in a
variety of Western countries, must therefore be
seen especially in connection with the rationalistic humanism of the seventeenth and eighteenth
centuries. Our attention will first of all be
focused on this phase.

A careful analysis of Humanism will reveal
that is is driven by two central motives. On
the one hand we detect the ideal of autonomous

personality, bound in no way except by an order constituted by itself. On the other hand we discover the ideal of science, viz. the attempt to control the cosmos and human life in every respect by means of science, which, if consistently carried out, would destroy every form of autonomous self-determination. In Humanism, the ideal of personality and the ideal of science are thus ultimately in diametric opposition.

It is especially the idea of autonomous self-determination which has been the inspiration for modern democracy and the philosophies which have defended it. However, even then one must distinguish between two clearly different trends: the first of a more individualistic and liberal type (John Locke), the second tending more to political absolutism (Rousseau).

2. Democracy as a Universal Principle

In distinction from contemporary trends it must be clearly understood that the democracy defended by Locke and Rousseau was seen mainly in connection with the state and political life. This in itself is not surprising. For in the first phases of humanistic thought the state and the individual were the two poles determining the scope of human life. In all this there is a marked reaction to all sorts of privileges and guilds which greatly characterized the Middle Ages, and which could exist as more or less independent forces between the individual and the state. As a result of this reaction, for example, there was practically no recognition of the need for organizations of employers and employees in the last century. Labor unions, especially, were often contraband.

However, in due time this changed. There came an increasing recognition of the particular significance of diverse social relations and communities alongside of or at least apart from the state. And the idea took hold that the democratic principle should also be realized in these

265

non-political relationships and communities. Terms such as industrial democracy, educational democracy and even family democracy came into vogue. In this connection one can think of the endeavor to grant employees a greater share in industrial life ("co-determination") and that not merely by means of trade-unions in general industrial relations but also in specific industries by means of industrial councils and company directors appointed by the trade-unions. This idea of industrial democracy has been systematically elaborated by the famous Russian sociologist Georges Gurvitch, who claims that a political democracy cannot remain in existence without a "economic democracy." Gurvitch defends an all-embracing anti-centralistic and anti-statist democratization of human life in its various expressions. Only in this manner can the most profound elements of the various communities find expression and only in this way can we arrive at a true synthesis between individualism and universalism. For Gurvitch the principle of democracy is not specifically political. It can serve as a principle of organization for both the state and society.

But this development did not stop with democracy viewed as only a principle or organization. In certain political circles democracy was connected with a striving for social reform. This implies that the idea of equality received greater stress in the definition of democracy. Dr. W.P. Berghuis, Chairman of the Central Committee of the Christian Anti-Revolutionary Party in the Netherlands and one of the Vice-Presidents of the International Union of Christian Democrats, in a publication about the nature of democracy, has made the observation that "democracy" was no longer in the first place confined to the administration and institution of the state with respect to the proper execution of the government's task but that "democracy" was also related to the material content and purposes of the state's administrative bodies. Democracy and the "law-state" (Rechtsstaat) are thus identified and, at

a later stage, democracy and socialism are
viewed as one and the same. Berghuis shows how
the socialists were averse to democracy in their
first marxistic phase since they viewed democracy
as opposed to the revolutionary character of
socialistic ideology but that they accepted the
democratic form of the state in the first decades
of our century and even made democracy one of
their political slogans. And contemporary
socialism, drifting away from its early marxistic
foundations, has proclaimed democracy as its new
basis, as its creed, as the sum-total, in form
and content, of everything implied in a socialistic order of state and society. "Democracy"
has thus become at once a view of life, a Weltanschauung, and a political program. As a fundamental political principle democracy has been
absolutized. It has become a myth, says Berghuis,
for many of our contemporaries, the indication
of the highest political and social ideal. And
as such democracy is no longer susceptible to
rational description but is rendered absolute
as a faith, as a creed only acceptable to those
who accept the content of this political and
social outlook. And thereby the idea of democracy has attained that vagueness which we have
already referred to.

3. Authority and Freedom

Contrary to the development of the idea of
democracy in modern times, we would prefer to
maintain this idea as a principle of organization and, within the scope of this study, specifically as a principle of political organization, with reference to the relation between
government and subjects.

It is undeniable that life confronts us constantly with relations of authority and subjection. The Bible presents a fundamental perspective here when, in several passages, it calls
the believer to subject himself to those who are
placed over him and to obey the rules, the ordinances instituted by those in authority. One
can mention as an example the Fifth Commandment

of the Decalogue and the explanation of this commandment in Lord's Day 39 of the Heidelberg Catechism.

In the community of the state one can also distinguish between rulers and subjects, between government and people. Romans 13 speaks of this relation in lucid language. The government is clothed with authority which is not based on or derived from the people (the doctrine of popular sovereignty). The government's authority is derived from God, and for this reason this authority must be exercised in accordance with His will, His law. The governmental authorities have a "right of their own," a right peculiar to themselves. Over against this it must be seen that the people also, as subjects, possess "rights" in a specific political democratic states in the right to free formation of political opinion, both active and passive; further, the right to establish political parties; right to franchise; right to petition, etc. By means of these rights the citizens, the subjects of the state, can effectuate their co-responsibility for the decisions to be made in the political process.

In all of this we are concerned with the central problem of authority and freedom with which, for that matter, we are confronted in every human community. The stress must lie on the proper balance between these two. Freedom without authority ends in chaos and licentiousness. Authority without freedom spells tyranny and ends, as if by a natural law, in totalitarian dictatorship, embracing the whole of human life. History presents ample evidence of this. A true balance between authority and freedom can only then be attained when government and people accept their respective responsibilities, each in its own way and in accordance with its specific place in the community of the state.

It is of utmost importance here to distinguish between the above-mentioned political

rights of liberty (whose nature and breadth
wholly regulated by and dependent upon the legal
order of the state itself) and the socalled non-
political rights of liberty (which can be regulated in one way or another by the state's
legislature, but which because of their very
nature and essence escape the competence of the
state government). One can mention here the
freedom of worship, the freedom of education,
the freedom of association and private meeting,
the freedom of the press, of speech, of vocation.
These rights and liberties can be limited by
the legislature in a certain way. As such, however, they are independent of the state. And
as soon as the government infringes upon these
rights and liberties and attempts to control
them in their totality, by means of legislation
or its executive power, it exceeds its proper
competence.

4. The Meaning of Democracy from a Reformational Standpoint

How are we, in the light of the preceding,
to view and evaluate democracy?

We have already seen that, within the state,
government and people each occupies its own position, but they do so in an unbreakable correla-
tion. As in the human body the head cannot say
that it does not need the foot or hand, and the
latter also cannot function properly without
the head, so also government and people are
dependent upon each other. For a sound development of political life close cooperation is
essential. Although government and people each
has its respective rights (and obligations!),
they are jointly responsible for the course of
political life. For this reason the government
may never without ground declare the people
politically immature. This joint responsibility
of government and people is one of the fundamentals of democracy as J.P. Mekkes has correctly taught us.

But this does not exhaust the meaning of

modern democracy. Berghuis has brought to light another aspect of this question in the study mentioned above. In concurrence with Dooyeweerd he shows that the idea of law, which must become valid in its own way also in the community of the state, is an "idea on the march," and the path for this "march" in the fulfillment of the idea of law is bound step by step to the historical development. And this idea, we may add, finds its ultimate realization only in the direction towards the Kingdom of God. The application or positivization of legal principles not possible without taking due account of the historical development of culture, including the ideas and convictions of the people. The government, in the fulfillment of its task, is also dependent upon the situation of the people. An example of the religious conditions is the hardness of hearts of which Christ speaks in Matt. 19:8 and Mark 10: 5. The degree of knowledge of and obedience to God's law on the part of the people co-determines the degree to which the idea of law can be approached in political life. And in this connection it is important, Berghuis claims, to achieve that form of government in which the stage of cultural development can immediately be deteched as it were right in the very constellation of the organs and administration of the government. And that form of government is present in a well-functioning democracy. Democracy implies that form of government in which in the most simple and direct manner the policy of the government can be attuned to the social, economic, cultural, moral and religious situation of the people. The democratic method of government, so to say, has a built-in thermometer.

The foregoing implies that democracy is not universal as a political principle of organization in this sense that it can and must be applied everywhere under all curcumstances.

A democratic system of government can only function properly where the people have attained a certain measure of political maturity, i.e., where they have been able to grasp and articulate definite political convictions. Democracy can flourish only where the people, by and large, have become conscious of their co-responsibility for the course of events and the decisions in the community of the state. Democracy presupposes a people possessed of a sense of citizenship. Without these conditions democracy cannot exist. The political development of various countries in South-America and Africa gives clear evidence of this.

5. Democracy and Spiritual Relativism

All of this confronts the Christian with this highly important problem: Does the Assumption, that a democratic system of government can only function properly if its policy is at least in part attuned to the religious and political convictions of the people, not automatically lead to spiritual relativism? Or - to phrase the problem a bit differently - do we not, by accepting democracy in this sense, directly come into conflict with the absolute nature of the Christian faith, with the unconditional requisities of God's Word and His law which also pertain to the life of politics?

Hans Kelsen, the well-known Austrian-American legal philosopher, stresses the close affinity between democracy and relativism as a life- and world-view. Since democracy respects the political desires of each citizen equally, Kelsen asserts, it must also respect equally every political creed, every political opinion, of which the political desire is only the expression. The opposite opinion must also be considered a possibility when absolute values are abandoned. In Kelsen's view the democratic idea presupposes the Weltanschauung, the outlook of relativism. For this reason democracy allows the expression of every political conviction. The principle of majority-rule, so characteristic of democracy, distinguishes it from every other principle, and this logically does not merely imply the opposition of the minority, but in a democracy this minority is constitutionally recognized and protected by means of the fundamental rights of liberty and the principle of proportional representation. The relativity of every political creed and the impossibility of claiming absolute validity for a political program or a political ideal clearly requires the rejection of political absolutism.

One cannot escape the impression that in this viewpoint of Kelsen truth and error are mixed in a critical fashion. We can agree with Kelsen when he states that no political principle has absolute validity in this sense that every practical political policy in a democratic regime more or less has the character of a compromise insofar as in such a policy the different convictions of the people and even the rights of minority-groups must be reckoned with. We are, however, radically opposed to Kelsen when he, on the basis of the limited possibility of the application of certain political principles, assumes the relativity and the relative value not merely of certain political convictions but of every political principle. For such a view involves the implicit denial of the radical and universal nature of the spiritual conflict which, according to the Word of God (cf. e.g. Gen. 3:17 and Eph. 6), is constantly waged between the Kingdom of God and that of satan. And the life of politics certainly does not escape this spiritual conflict.

Dr. A. M. Donner, formerly professor of political theory and constitutional law at the Free University of Amsterdam and currently President of the Court of European Communities, has observed that the indication of relativism as the foundation of democracy has not failed to make an impression. The "fin-de-siecle" mentality, typical of this, has become common property in our day. But, Donner writes, as soon as man becomes fully conscious of this relativism and accepts it consistently, human life becomes a bare, monotonous desert and the human spirit becomes dull. For indeed, this relativism is miles apart from that spirit of toleration which arises out of respect for the convictions of one's fellows. This relativism is not a fruit of spiritual richness but of decadence and disillusion. And a democracy founded on such a relativism cannot recognize the continuity in the life of the state. There is no value which embraces the whole and authority is no longer acknowledged. Government no longer derives its authority from generally accepted legal norms but only from its origin: the people. And authority derived from that source, Donner claims, knows no bounds and limitations.

In our view, the recognition of the "specific rights" of the various views of life in the political order is indeed dependent upon the recognition of the limited competences and possibilities of the government in its relation to the people of the lånd and the balance of authority and freedom inherent in the community of the state. For we may not forget that the political activities of the citizens do not merely have an external character. These activities are a matter of the heart, and the government is given neither the competence nor the power to force the conscience of its subjects. Such a compulsion of conscience, even if executed by a Christian government, would not enhance the cause of the Kingdom of God. Still, it is precisely in democracy that Christians may find an acceptable form of government because this form makes it possible to effectuate divine ordinances for the life of the state in the activities of government and subjects without compulsion of conscience. The task of the Christian with respect to the state concerns the redirection of the political conviction of both government and people through the power of the Word of God. But the execution of this task presupposes the existence of spiritual liberty in political life, also for those who do not want to subject themselves to this Word of God.

In the spiritual struggle which unfolds itself also in the political arena the victory is not decided by the sword of the state but by the Sword of the Spirit.

We are fully conscious of the fact that this view entails the possibility that a governmental policy, directed in a Christian sense by means of democratic procedure, can also again be changed to another direction by means of the same demo-cratic procedure. This, however, is a "risk" which the Christian must accept according to his own starting-point.

6. The Christian and Modern Democracy.

It should be evident by now that in our view politics is not a matter of impersonal, neutral, or purely technical affairs, that politics is not merely concerned with the striving for "practical ends." The battle of spirits (Gen. 3:17; Eph. 6:12) is also waged in the realm of the state, even if we are not always conscious of this and even if this does not constnatly and expressly come to the foregound. The Christian community may not withdraw itself from this struggle because of Him Who tells us, "All authority in heaven and on earth has been given to Me" (Matt. 28:18). In politics, no less than in any other domain of human life, we are ulti-mately involved in religious decisions, confronted as we are with the question whether we will serve the Lord, the God of the Covenant, or call upon the idols of our time (Josh. 24:15). The poli-tical arena is also subject to the Word of God as a two-edged sword (Hebr. 4:12). The Christian community may not be passive in these matters, but must actively assume its responsibility.

This responsibility begins with the prayer of faith. The Apostle Paul urges us, first of all, that supplications, prayers, intercessions, and thanksgiving be made for all men, for kings and all who are in high positions, that we may lead a quiet and peaceable life, godly and respect-

274

ful in every way. For this is good, and it is
acceptable in the sight of God our Savior, who
desires all men to be saved and to come to the
knowledge of the truth (I Tim. 2:1-4).

However, the Christian community may not
limit its activity to the inner room. It must
engage the world, it must enter the political
arena itself, to be a salting salt and to let
its light shine (Matt. 5:13-16). This already
is implied in the cultural mandate which the
Creator gave to mankind (Gen. 1:28), for modern
culture is not possible without a well-organized
state-life. It is also implied in Christ's
commission to make disciples of all nations,
teaching them to observe all that He has commanded (Matt. 28:19,20). Also in political life
men must live in accordance with the divine man-
dates. Here lies a dimension of that spiritual
service of which Paul speaks in Romans 12.

The question remains how the Christian community, wherever it is still given the freedom
for this end, can make its influence felt on the
specific policy of the state.

Here one must first point to the official
proclamation of the church. As soon as the
Word of God is proclaimed in the church with
conviction in an integral, radical sense, it
will make its power felt immediately as a two-
edged sword to the world outside, and thus also
in public life. The Spirit of God is our
guarantee here.

This does not mean that the church in its
official, institutional organization is clothed
with a certain political authority. Nor does
this imply that the church must orient its proclamation in a special way to political life.
The highest authority for the state lies in the
Word of God itself, regarding which the ecclesiastical offices only have a function of service.
The proclamation of the Word of God is intended
to equip the believer in a spiritual, centrally

directive way so that the Christian can be
molded to maturity. With this the general
offices of all believers comes into view.

It was precisely the Protestant Reformation
which posited with great emphasis the maturity
of the regular, non-ordained member of the
church, and that not only in the church but also
for life outside of it. This had the consequence
that wherever the Reformation made itself felt
in the populace, a "democratic" form of government arose as it were automatically both in the
church and in public life.

By means of the proclamation of the Word, as
well as by personal and communal study of the
Scriptures, the believer becomes a bearer of
that Word, which directs him in his vocation, in
his family and in his civic responsibilities.
In all of these areas he will have to fight the
battle with the Sword of the Spirit.

In the realm of political endeavor this implies that the Christian must renew and reform
his view of the state and its life by the Word
of God. And this does not imply merely incidental
corrections or a limited number of special topics
(such as, e.g., the relation between church and
state, marriage-legislation or the consecration
of the Lord's Day), no matter how important these
may be in themselves. Instead, this renewal and
reformation demands a radically altered view of
the state itself. With less we cannot be satisfied. It is only too true, as Harry **Blamires**
observes in his stimulating book, The Christian
Mind (1963), that twentieth-century Christianity
has chosen the way of compromise by making religion a private affair. It is exactly against
this spiritual dualism, which permits "religion"
the control of private life while public life
is dominated by socalled commonly accepted "norms,"
that we must wage the battle.

It is clear that the task which this implies
is not only one for Christians individually but

for them communally. The initial step to be taken will involve the creation of study-centers where these problems can systematically be subjected to serious reflection.

But this study and reflection is not the end. For politics may indeed be determined by spiritual motives; it is nonetheless an extremely practical activity. Our purpose must be the reformation of political life itself. For this reason Christians, standing in the tradition of the Reformation, who have the capacity and the opportunity to do so, should not be afraid to accept public offices, especially because of their scriptural convictions. The possible influence of this may not be underestimated.

Furthermore, in a democratic state Christians can employ the opportunity to express their political opinions in freedom by means of the press and other available methods. Here especially one must point to the importance of the formation of a political party in which evangelical Christians can unite in order to influence political life in a reformational sense by means of cooperative effort. Such an influence ought to be exerted not to dominate but to serve, according to the Word of God.

Herman Dooyeweerd points out, in the third volume of his A New Critique of Theoretical Thought, that a political party is precisely an organization in which the uniting force of a political conviction is expressed with respect to the principles which to guide political life, the state and its administrative organs. One can right say that even those parties which claim to find a basis only in a "common goal for practical action" are not devoid of certain principles or spiritual motives. For such political parties are controlled by the forces of modern pragmatism - a philosophy of life which is hardly in agreement with the fundamentals of the Christian life and which can spiritually affect political and social life in a disastrous manner.

We are conscious of the fact that the possibility for Christian political party-formation will depend to a great extent on the potentialities of reformational Christians in the respective countries. But we must not, with an eye to tradition and present fact, immediately think that this is impossible. There are situations in which even a small minority can exert great power. This also depends upon the power of faith, of conviction, and the competence of those involved.

One can also point to new opportunities which possibly may develop in the not too distant future. Here I am thinking of the voices of those Protestants, lost until now in largely Roman Catholic or non-Christian nations, which can become of fundamental importance if placed in a larger whole, for example, through the election of a European parliament. Our principle obliges us to follow such developments with great care.

However, no matter what the situation may be, the Lord calls us in Christ to be His witnesses and co-laborers also in the realm of the state. And for this reason Christians may not withdraw to the trenches and catacombs as long as He gives us the opportunity to fight as His soldiers in public, and that in steadfast faith in the Lordship and victory of Jesus Christ.

Chapter V. A Response to Marxism

When Karl Marx penned his now famous dictum in The Communist Manifesto that "the history of all hitherto existing society is the history of class struggles", most Christians either shurgged it off as nonsense or failed to listen. That was over a hundred years ago, and now Marxism, in one variety or another, is the way of life in increasingly many countries around the globe. More manifestos are published today than Bibles; what has happened in this century?

The attraction and power of Marxism is a fact to consider. Do Christians have a response? How can we understand the appeal of Marx's gospel? Is this post-Christian, humanist, prophet profoundly at odds with the Christian God? Is Marxism an insidious enemy of the church or a secularized descendant? What would "spiritual warfare" against Marxism amount to?

In "Promethean Faith" Theodore Malloch looks at the religious character of Marxism-Leninism. Marx included the abolition of religion in his program; he was a devout atheist. But if Marx wanted to get free of religion, why is this apocalyptic messenger so dependent on theological baggage from the past? This article points the way toward an answer to that root question.

Johan van der Hoeven allows us to see inside "Some Key Notions of Marx". For years people have "hated" communism without knowing at exactly what they vented their anger. This exegesis of the holy books of Marxism gives insight into Marx's philosophy of "critical", "historical", "materialistic" dialectic. Many commentators think that Christians must know an enemy, or a heresy, as well as they do their own faith. Recent history demonstrates that there is no reason to neglect or ignore Marxism any longer.

Understanding Marx on his own terms will not

suffice. A thoroughgoing Christian critique of
Marxism demands that we size up its "Strengths
and Weaknesses". S.U. Zuidema, in the next
selection does precisely that. His conclusion
is worth noting: "The strength of Communism is
its weakness. The weakness of Christianity is
its strength."

To conclude this section, Rene Padilla looks
at the core of Marxist doctrine - "Revolution",
and compares it to the Christian core doctine
of "Revelation". Noting that revolutionary
theory idealizes man, converting the gospel
into a utopian ideology which is foreign to
the eschatological message of the Bible, Padilla
calls the disciple of Christ, an anti-revolutionary but "reforming" attitude, to take up
the cross and follow the true master. Christians
are to be disciples of Christ, not zealots in
a political army ready to violently overthrow
the State.

PROMETHEAN FAITH

By Theodore Malloch

Marxism has always placed itself in opposition to religion, has always cursed the opiate of the people, yet its faith has helped create some of history's greatest moral monsters: the Soviet Union and its satellites. The materialist and historical determinist presuppositions underlying Marxism can be considered "a faith" in the most deeply religious sense: a faith that rules individual and society and one that claims to reveal ultimate truth.

Two thoughts stand out about the enigmatic partner of the USA in detente: the Soviets believe in something and that faith is tied to a particular reading and understanding of political history.

A western Christian studying Marxism-Leninism is first struck by the believer's naive faith in the facts they have been taught. A history book refuses to believe there are 50 states, not 51, and declares such to be the case. A literary magazine relates an interest in Faulkner, and is surprised that so few Americans had even heard of him? Even tourist guides believe much of what they say: that Solzhenitsyn was a terrible writer, a hack who had made millions from lying about the Soviet Union and lived in luxury in the United States; that Stalin's purges never happened; even that the plaster cast reclining in Lenin's tomb is Lenin.

But there is a deeper, ideological faith underlying and supporting the "factual": the subjugation of history to a Marxian dialectic, casting contemporary problems as struggles between the (advanced) socialist nations and the (decadent) capitalist/imperialist ones. And that layer of faith is covered by an almost mythic faith in "the revolution." Marxists for sixty years have argued that regardless of the problems of their theory, all will work out in the Communist end. The problems do not call their theoretical position into question; they must simply be accepted until they are worked out.

It is this which leads one to conclude that Marxism, far from working towards the elimination of religion, practices a rather rigorous and stifling secular faith. The party, the vanguard of the proletariat, functions as the priesthood, enforcing a devious, undeclared faith - the ideology of Marxism - which is a form of idolatry.

Lenin provides a good illustration in his later work Imperialism: The Highest Stage of Capitalism. The revolutionary overthrow of capitalism forecasted by Marx had not happened (an empirical difficulty, since Marxism is primarily a theory of history, and thus may be historically proved or disproved); and Lenin himself had led a distinctly non-dialectical revolution in a pre-industrial country. Lenin's essay explained both anomalies away. Contemporary history - and the Soviet socialist state - remained within the overarching dialectic. The collapse of capitalism had merely been postponed by the creation of markets in colonial possessions, and colonization along justified the revolution in Russia.

A Marxist dialectical understanding of history, supported by its claim to be scientific and empirical, thus provable and beyond question, was accepted on faith by Lenin, who bequeathed it to the state he founded. When anomalies arose in Marxist analysis, one did not question faith in the direction of history, but sought a way to explain events, however anomalous, as "history." The science of Marx is that of an unrepentant economic positivist.

Marxist faith is in that way both similar and dissimilar to Christian faith. Both live under a view of directed history moving towards

282

a vague but utopian end; both argue that the
individual must orient life within it, especially as there is nothing one can do about its
progress or end. Both keep the time of history's
end (whether the Communist utopia or Christ's
second coming) unknown, making the theories
nearly impossible to disprove, and keep the agent
of direction (whether the forces of history or
God) invisible. The immediate difference is
that Christianity believes in a personal,
transcendent God, not some secular, immanentized
eschaton.

The ways of examining history, especially
with the modern profusion of disciplines and the
paradigms within them, allow one to prove or
disprove nearly any theory one wants. Christianity is, however, more difficult to disprove
than Marxism (if not impossible), because its
historical vision is actually ahistorical, arguing for something transcendent (God), which
begins and ends history at will and whose control over history is not evident in observable
thesis, antithesis, and synthesis. God could
have begun history, for instance, gone to
sleep - as a deist would argue - and then arisen
and ended it. And if one accepts the orthodox
description of God intervening vertically in
horizontal history, intervening as wholly other
from outside, one can see, if one wants to, God's
hand in everything or nothing.

But the nature of Marxist faith - or the nature
of any faith that claims to see one's nation as
having passed beyond the current thesis into
the next - is unique in that it is a two-step
faith: one must first believe that history is
indeed dialectical (and in the Marxian sche-
matic) and then one must belive that the Soviet
Union for instance, fits into the post-capital-
ist, post-revolutionary, socialist thesis. This
two-step faith is integral to Marxism-Leninism,
since unlike Christianity its view of history
is a national one. Revolution occurs and the
socialist thesis developed (Stalin's "socialism

283

in one country") in a nation, which generally
maintains its pre-revolutionary geographic and
cultural boundaries (unless, of course, trying
to expand them). There is no way of knowing,
as Lenin's coup d'etat in 1917 shows, whether
the events in one's country are a part of the
great historical synthesis, whether the revolution is indeed "the revolution," the cathartic
moment when one thesis ends and the next begins,
or whether it is a power struggle among capi-
talists or even an accidental rehearsal for the
revolution that succeeded. One is then faced
with the problem of a Communist government
coming to power, taking over rather than riding
the crest of revolution, before the inherent
collapse of capitalism, a problem aggravated
by the vague relationship between the necessity
for action and the inevitability of history
found in Marxist thought.

Some western and even certain Chinese thinkers
have in fact argued that the Soviet Union, by
skipping over a great deal of development, must
still, because of the requirements of history,
go through a captialist stage, evidences of
which they find today. Capitalist economists
and philosophers see the same things as evidences
of the pragmatic truth of market economics,
again an act of faith. However explained, .that
problem is a central problem of Marxism, because it brings dialectical materialism as a
rational faith, as a vision of history, as truth,
into question.

One quickly realizes in the Soviet Union and
other Marxist states that Marx has secured a
haunting place in history throught the Bolshe-
viks' creation of an avowedly Marxist state
which sacrifices human needs while the dictatorship of the proletariat goes on and on: the dialectic goes unresolved.

Marx often quoted Rousseau: "We are not our
true selves." Man is a victim. The new victims
are in fact the citizens of Marxist states, for

state capitalism and the unwithering away of
the state have simply replaced the earlier
feudal autocracy of the Czars and Princes.
Marx left no blueprint for Communist society,
believing that by definition, by its place in
a progressive history, it would be free, cooperative, non-alienating; the state would disappear and authority would be noncoercive if not
nonexistent. If Marx returned today, one can
ask would he be pleased with the USSR?

In Marxist states there are many churches
and cathedrals which have been made into museums, one into a hall of the history of religion and atheism. While traveling in the USSR
one passes many churches that are slowly crumb-
ling, decayed by sixty years of conscious neglect. So proud of their heritage, their architecture, their great writers, their history,
the Soviet Marxists have maintained cultural
monuments to their past, but they have let many
churches decay, no matter what their beauty
or significance, perhaps symbolic of a hatred
of religion even greater than their hatred of
capitalism.

Marxist states find religion undesirable, a
symptom of what man had become because of the
logical necessities of capitalism, no longer
necessary as a sedative. But the secular religion of Marxism-Leninism (or more correctly
Leninist-Marxism) emerges today triumphant
and preeminent - a faith of the promethean God-
builders.

Marxist totalitarianism attempts a final,
total domination of a society while proclaiming
final and absolute truth. Leninist-Marxism thus
wants to be "as a god," to proclaim the truth
of a secular faith.

SOME KEY NOTIONS OF MARX

By Johan van der Hoeven

1. Marx's New Conception of Philosophy

In order to understand Marx's enterprise as a whole and the reason for its influence, it is necessary to notice that he is developing a new conception of philosophy. We have already referred to Marcuse's continuation of this theme. Marcuse distinguishes between philosophy in the traditional sense and a critical theory of society. The term society used here includes the sciences. Marcuse wants to unmask the involvement of the so-called empirical sciences in this society. He reveals the empirical character of these sciences to be largely pseudo-empirical; for they include little or no awareness of how their basic concepts and their general framework are predetermined by the current ideas of this society. Scientists-duped, unsuspecting victims unaware - promote the establishment in their empirical work. The philosophies whose basic tenets are oriented to these sciences, especially neo-positivism and analytic philosophy, are even worse in this respect than these sciences themselves. Although Marcuse cannot be said to set forth an altogether orthodox Marxism, he is right in emphasizing Marx's awareness of himself as standing at a critical and crucial point in the historical development of philosophy. Marx felt that although philosophy had been striving to be critical for a long time, its method of criticism had been too general, too abstract, and far too aloof from the real issues of society. Philosophy had to become more directly relevant to these issues. It is this same awareness that Marcuse picks up in his distinction between philosophy in the traditional sense and as a critical theory of society.

Marx rightly felt that the relationship of philosophy to the fullness of experience had become obscured. The fullness of our experience

286

is first of all non-scientific and continues to be so even after the appearance of science. Non-scientific is not to be confused with unscientific; the latter would mean in contradiction to the standards of science; whereas, non-scientific intends to point to the fact that experience is much broader than just scientific knowledge. Marx saw that philosophy had become more and more irrelevant to life's concreteness and fullness. This insight was heightened all the more through his acquaintance with the philosophy of Hegel, which claimed to be critical and, at the same time, all-encompassing. Marx reasoned that if Hegel's philosophy is the logical outcome of traditional philosophy and if it presumes to be the final, comprehensive word about man, his world and his society, then the time had come for a new interpretation of the task of philosophy. The inadequacy, abstractness and irrelevancy of Hegel's philosophy to life was felt all too keenly by Marx.

2. Marx's Notion of "Critical"

The society that Marx lived in was torn apart by and suffered under traumatic changes not only of the Industrial Revolution but also of the French Revolution and the resulting conservative reactions. The grand system of Hegel was supposed to encompass even the miseries and sufferings of contemporary family and factory life in its negations. In Hegel's philosophical showroom, negativity or evil is located among the essential truths or undeniable states of affairs that philosophy objectively describes or interprets. Marx saw this as an estrangement of philosophy from its proper critical function. For the historical role of philosophy is the intensification of man's critical self-consciousness. Thus, philosophy unmasks religion as just such an attempt to escape from self-consciousness. However, when negativity, conflict, suffering evil get its own ascribed niche in the objective showroom of philosophy so that it becomes something to be contemplated, then philosophy serves to affirm the status quo. As such, it becomes another form of estrangement, like religion, for it does everything but intensify man's critical self-consciousness.

Genuinely critical thought is directly relevant to our human existence and to our being human (human being); it is thought directed towards the service of humanity; it is a "demonstration ad hominem". An often quoted statement of Marx - one of his "Theses on Feuerbach" - is: "Philosophers have only interpreted the world in different ways; the point is to change it". Philosophy itself becomes involved in the practical struggle for the change, in fact, the revolution of society. It becomes a means in this struggle. The question that remains is: does it function as an expedient or as a mean of power?

3. Marx's Notion of "Historical"

Another concept that we encounter frequently in Marx's writings is the notion of the "historical". Actually the notion already recurred very often in Hegel's writings. To both Hegel and Marx it indicates that man and his society are not fixed: man produces himself. This process is called history. For Marx this process of self-production is further characterized by dynamic needs and drives or forces. Especially in his later works, Marx further qualified these needs and drives as economically determined. The development of these needs and drives or forces evidence a certain continuity. For example, it is possible to trace the development from feudal society to civil or bourgeois society. However, there are always antagonistic forces present that oppose development. Here the necessity for or the call to revolution enters in. The existing conditions of production can no longer accommodate the new drives or forces of production which history has created. This situation forces a choice between either suppressing these new drives or forces, or employing

them to break through the existing conditions.
The former reactionary alternative is, of course,
not a viable one for Marx: stopping these new
drives or forces is impossible.

When the term "historical" becomes prefixed
to "philosophy", we can detect a connection with
our earlier concept of "critical". When Marx
says that it is important to philosophize historically, he means that it is the duty of philosophy to recognize and point out critical historical situations and reveal their ripeness
for revolution. In this unmasking, philosophy
itself becomes a historical power, for it contradicts (i.e., speaks against) the existing situation in its positive, established character. By
deliberately compromising that situation, philosophy opens possibilities for change.

Inevitably Marx must face the question whether
his view of society and historical development
is just a description of bare facts or whether
it is itself an interpretation. In the light
of this question we ask: what happens to the
earlier contrast we saw Marx set up between an
abstract, detached, intellectual philosophy
and one that is engaged and critical, a protest
What does Marx mean when he calls for philosophy
to stop appealing to or presenting universal
interpretations of established or given states
of affairs? Does not such a philosophy, that
foregoes an appeal to some state of affairs,
become purely eschatological, that is, a prophecy
and advertisement for a preconceived future?
Then, in its theoretical aspect such a philosophy
becomes utopian, while in its practical aspect
it becomes an incitement to violence. Utopia
and violence are usually siblings.

But Marx does appeal to historical reality.
That historical reality gives obvious evidence
of human self-estrangement; in fact, that self-
estrangement is total; it affects man as a
species being. Both capitalist and proletariat
share in it. But it is especially in the pro-

letariat that the absolute and radical suffering that comprises the negativity of history embodies itself. The radical character of this suffering forms a limiting situation in its dehumanization of human existence so that a genuine possibility for radical self-recognition and self-redemption arises. This suffering involves a rediscovery by the proletariat of the fundamental trait of human existence, for it refers not to a merely external state of affairs, but to a state of affairs that is experienced immediately, radically and concretely. This fundamental human trait Marx calls Leidenschaft, which may, like the Latin passio, be translated as either passion or suffering. In this rediscovery man finds himself to be a being with real needs, a being who wants something other outside of himself and also other people. Nevertheless, he finds these needs within himself, so that his striving to satisfy these needs is really a striving for self-realization. Therefore, Marx can speak of self-redemption even while pointing to our need for the other. It is only when a universal class of men, the proletariat, appeared on the historical scene - a class that experienced this suffering, this dehumanization, this negativity - only then could the philosophy of Marxism appear. Thus, Marx wants to make his philosophy credible by appealing to this given: concrete human suffering. He does not wish merely to be a prophet or to spin out utopias.

In our discussion of the first essay, we discovered insurmountable tensions and polarities in Marx's views on the position and the role of philosophy with respect to both the existence of the proletariat and their struggle for practical emancipation. In this connection, we discussed the "arm of criticism" and the "criticism of arms". These tensions and discords persist throughout Marx's writings; they are basic, ultimate elements in his thought which he could not overcome. As a result, he is unable to provide a truly radical and integral view for the redemption of man in his society.

Although our critique of Marx issues from a
Christian commitment, we cannot, in contradiction to the Marxists, pretend that we, on the
other hand, do possess such a view. Or that we,
in contradistinction to the Marxists, are capable
of redeeming and reforming man in his society.
We must confess that we are no longer able to
establish out of ourselves the nature of the
given, not by means of an autonomous philosophy
nor by means of the experience of suffering.
We must learn to accept the given as it is revealed to us and then it can direct our philosophy and even our suffering accordingly. Mankind,
society and history are in even worse straits
than Marx felt them to be. The suffering and
cross of Christ tell us how much worse. Moreover, all our desperate attempts at self-recognition and self-redemption are deceptions and
illusions. Even a small community like a family,
which is based more on a bond of moral love
rather than a power relationship, cannot maintain itself on the basis of these notions of
self-recognition and self-redemption. Self-
denial is the reverse side of radical belief
in and radical surrender to Jesus Christ. That
self-denial involves the radical denial of our
own power of self-recognition and self-redemption
and also of our own ability to establish what
is given, whether through thought or suffering.
By such self-surrender we become part of the
power, the grace and the redemption of Jesus
Christ; for he desires to include us in a new
mankind, with a new hope. Out of this surrender
a new activity arises which cannot be circumscribed by any of our current descriptions of
"activity".

4. Marx's Notion of "Dialectic"

The concept of dialectical has to be under-
stook in close relation to the concept of historical. We have seen that history, according
to Marx and Hegel, is the process of man's
self-production. Man and his society are not
fixed but developing entities; they are in a

process of becoming, in a process of self-production that proceeds in and via polar opposi-
tions. It is essential to this process that a
certain position or a realized, established
state of affairs does not merely continue in a
pure identity with itself, but that it provoke
a negation. This negation reveals the limitations of the first position, of the first
established state of affairs. In this way, new
possibilities are also revealed which are open
to realization. However, this position and its
negation, taken in themselves, stand over against
each other and continue in a polar tension over
toward each other. This tension demonstrates
their need for each other in the sense that the
first position itself provokes its own negation,
but that negation is still a negation of that
position. Thus, the two refer to each other.
However, at the same time, they repel each other.
As long as the polarity continues there is the
possibility of something new, but not yet the
realization of the new. The possibility of something new is evidenced by the appearance of the
negation, but since it is only a negation, it
is not yet a new reality. This new reality
first appears in the synthesis, which is the
formation of a more comprehensive whole that in-
corporates both the original position and the
negation as limited parts of the greater whole.
Marx also calls this incorporation "appropria-
tion". The earlier polar tension called for this
solution or synthesis; but in due time this new
snythesis will reveal its unique limitations and
the process will begin all over again. This
synthesis, thus, becomes another positive starting point that evokes a new negation and then a
new and even more comprehensive synthesis.

The terms "position" and "negation" give the
impression of being neutral logical terms that
can be applied objectively without relying on
value judgements. However, they usually carry
definite connotations of such judgements. As
the original or established position, capitalist
society is called positive, but in another sense

it is also called negative; whereas, the proletariat and the revolution is the destructive
negation of capitalist society, yet it is also
called positive. There is another level of
ambiguity contained in the term "negation" or
"negativity". It refers not only to the conflicts and competition involved in achieving
certain unattained goals, but also includes in
the power struggle the brokenness and disharmony
that the Christian recognizes as the fruit of
sin. Thus, their usage is constantly ambiguous.
Marx seems to wish to maintain the impression
that he is just using a neutral instrument to
supply an objective interpretation of history,
but at the same time the terms exhibit a definite
evaluative viewpoint.

The tension or polar opposition that Marx
posits between the original position and its
negation is conceived of as arising out of
given conditions of production and the forces
of production. The conditions of production
and the forces of production need each other;
but at the same time they are continually at
odds. This tension is necessary for the progress of the historical process, otherwise it
would stagnate. Without the presence of this
tension history would resemble Nietzsche's eternal recurrence of the same. Thus, dialectic,
in attempting to combine logic and history,
caused confusion and distortion in both areas.
The struggle for power in history had to be
explained in such traditional logical terms as
thesis, negation, affirmation and the principle
of contradiction. This yielded a rigid and
meager explanation of history. Logic, on the
other hand, had to be reinterpreted so that it
could account for the appearance of something
new in history.

However, a dialectic exists in Marx's thought
that is more basic and deeper than this polarity
between the conditions and the forces of production. This basic dialectic is that between
man himself as he exists in his own individual

sphere and that which is external to man, including other men. To put it differently, a dialectic exists between the needs and possibilities possessed (really "owned") by the self and those things and persons necessary for the realization of those needs and possibilities. We discussed this bifurcation of man according to a subject-object scheme in connection with Marx's definition of man as a species-being. The idea of self-alienation is largely determined by this basic dialectic. Because everyone is so structured that his positive awareness of his needs and possibilities reveals his need of something and someone outside of himself, self-alienation is not just a chance occurrence in history or something alien that can be eliminated, but an indispensible element in the progressive development of history, i.e., in the process of man's self-production in society.

In this notion of self-alienation we once again encounter the ambivalence that we pointed out in his use of the terms "positive" and "negative". As an indispensable element of history self-alienation cannot be gotten rid of. Yet, it is also something that ought not to be, something antinormative, which should ultimately be overcome in the goal of a completely human and positive socialism. Marx tries to eliminate or tone down this ambivalence in several ways.

1) First, he projects the ultimate goal, or as he calls it in Das Kapital the realm of freedom, into a transcendent sphere, a utopian "beyond" that functions as a beckoning ideal. But then it can no longer serve as a real directive principle for his philosophical thought.

2) Another way that Marx tries to remove the ambivalence in the dialectical tension is his shifting the center of gravity from man to his natural world. He emphasizes the role of the material substructure in historical development; material conditions such as the availability of natural means and resources become primary.

However, Marx never attempts to give the natural world an independent status, i.e. a role separate from man and his labor. It involves no more than a shift in emphasis.

Third, he placed more and more emphasis on the class struggle and on the urgent demands for practical involvement in that struggle. In this connection, philosophy is seen more as a practical instrument; gets a more pragmatic function in conceiving strategy for and agitation in favor of the class struggle.

5. Marx's Notion of "Materialistic"

This category was referred to above under Marx's second method for toning down the ambivalence in the concept of self-alienation, namely, by emphasizing the material substructure. We also encountered this same element much earlier when Marx stated that revolution needed a passive element or a material basis. As we pointed out, this element plays an ever increasing role in the development of his thought. He qualifies it economically in terms of conditions of production. These conditions of production, in turn, are dependent upon available natural energy sources. The technical exploitation and control of these resources is of cardinal importance to the development of society. Despite this opposition to it as an establishment philosophy, Marx shares this emphasis with positivism.

Included in this material basis are man's needs, i.e., immediately experienced needs such as hunger, thirst, shelter, etc. Also included are the means immediately available to satisfy those needs, the first of which is the bodily apparatus of the laborer. In this connection Marx especially stresses the function of hand labor; true manu-facturing, as the Latin root implies, is done by hand.

A tension exists within the material substructure: between the given conditions of production on the one hand and the experienced needs and means for satisfying those needs on the other hand. The real motivating force for the forward movement of society resides, not in the given conditions of production, but in the acute experience of needs (suffering) and in the bodily force and drive of the laborer to satisfy these needs. In the first essay that we dealt with, Marx stated that material force can only be overthrown by material force. Thus, the motivating power of society appears as a destructive power over against the established conditions of production; for the latter are characterized by the private ownership of both the material resources and the immediate means for satisfying needs. Even the bodily force and drive of the laborer is owned by the captialist. Private ownership of these resources and means has made itself to at home in the established conditions of production that a complicated superstructure has come to be built upon it which, at the same time, serves to justify this economic situation. Thus, this superstructure serves to veil or camouflage the material economic establishment that produced it. Included in this superstructure or second floor are the established systems of right and law, but also politics and traditional morals and philosophy. The establishment deceptively tries to concentrate the attention of culture on the latter level in order to misleadingly divert attention away from the importance of the first floor, the floor of private property.

However, according to Marx, the floor of private property and possession of bodily forces already involves alienation or estrangment from man's direct relationship to nature. Nature or matter is, to use a metaphor, the soil from which we all must live; everything that we manufacture with our practical labor is drawn from there. Therefore, if nature becomes private property, i.e., if its possession is limited to a certain group, then man as a whole no longer retains a direct relationship to nature: in other words, he is, to a certain extent, estranged from it.

The establishment of the ideological superstructure means an even further estrangement
from that fundamental relationship to nature;
in the first place, because it camouflages that
estrangement; and secondly, because it provides
a new means for the dominant class to oppress
the suffering labor class, the proletariat.
Although the acute experience of needs and the
bodily drive of the laborer to satisfy these
needs may appear as a destructive or negative
force when it evidences itself as the total
revolution of society, it, nevertheless, has
its roots in a positive experience, namely,
the experience of that direct relationship with
nature. The ultimate aim of the total revolution
of society is also supposed to be positive: a
society without property, without oppression,
without class struggle, a society without
those camouflaging superstructures, a society
with a real, direct, common, socialist life.
Thus, the ultimate goal is a restoration or
recovery of that positive relationship to nature.
However, as we have pointed out before, this is
not developed beyond scattered hints in Marx's
writings.

Using these hints, let us try to compose
a picture of what this societal development of
mankind might be. In his later development, Marx
emphasizes more and more the material basis for
the development of society; thus, although some
of this is present already in his early writings,
most of it is drawn from his later writings. In
the material basis a tension exists between the
forces of production and the conditions of production. This tension results in the formation
of social groups or classes which stand opposed
to each other. Thus, the proletariat "class"
stands over against the capitalist class: as the
oppressed over against the oppressor. This
results, according to Marx, in the class struggle,
which in turn generates total revolution, on the
one hand, and the building of superstructures
and forms of private property, on the other. The
ultimate aim of the class struggle and total re-

297

volution is to overthrow the oppressive side
of the tension. We can picture the process as
follows:

SOCIETAL DEVELOPMENT

"Material Basis"

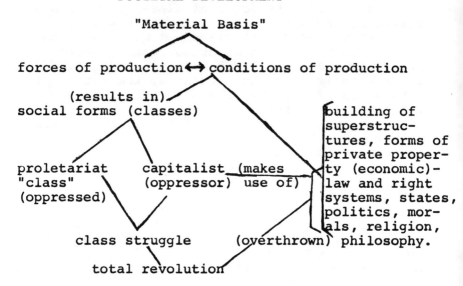

forces of production⟷ conditions of production

(results in)
social forms (classes)   building of
                                                superstruc-
                                                tures, forms of
                                                private proper-
proletariat   capitalist (makes   ty (economic)-
"class"   (oppressor) use of)   law and right
(oppressed)   systems, states,
                                               politics, mor-
                                               als, religion,
       class struggle   (overthrown) philosophy.

       total revolution

This diagram does not mean to suggest that Marx
wishes to advocate a full-fledged materialism;
even in his later development, when he emphasizes the material basis more and more, he never
slips into a rigid deterministic or mechanical
materialism. Marx stresses that his is a historical or dialectical materialsim. To him,
matter is never pure matter, by which he means
to say that the availability and structure of
matter never completely determine human existence.
Marx's emphasis on the material basis is ultimately made to serve his summons directed to man
to intervene practically, to revolt. Such an
appeal to man as an active, responsible being
would not make sense under a full-fledged
materialism.

    As long as the dialectic of self-alienation
is located primarily in man himself, in the

human subject, there is little or no basis for Marx's appeal. For then the alienation is radical: that's just the way man is as a human being. One must then resign himself to the situation. Or at best, one might long for a utopia in which man's inborn alienation has been overcome. But such a utopia could never be accounted for; it remains a mere fiction. However, matter can be manipulated; it is pliable to human purposes; man can change matter and use it to bring about changes. This is why Marx shifts his emphasis to the material basis. Marx's dialectical materialism makes materialism a function of his appeal to man's activity. In thus making this shift in emphasis, however, the place and significance of Marx's own philosophical theory becomes more precarious. Granting for the sake of argument that philosophical theory could be traced back to a material basis, the problem arises when we try to do so with Marx's own theory. Even though it claims to be an ultimate, "revealing" interpretation of the material basis and the tension there extant between the forces and the conditions of production, Marx's philosophy cannot be traced back to that material basis. As we have seen, Marx's attempt to solve this difficulty by pointing to material evidence for the claims of his philosophy in the undeniable existence of the proletariat also falls short. The important thing to notice here, however, is that as Marx becomes more of a materialist in his thinking, his philosophical theory becomes more and more a pragmatic instrument; in fact, it begins to sound like a battle cry.

Our discussion of Marx's philosophy has been rather sketchy throughout. However, so is Marx's philosophy itself. But this is no reason to neglect or ignore it. Nor is it a reason to concentrate only on his specifically economic theories. Often his philosophy is so sketchy that interpreting it becomes a difficult and unsatisfying task. Frequently, we would wish for a more elaborate explanation of some of his main concepts and statements. Frequently, too, his arguments are poor. But for all its sketchiness and its inherent problems, his philosophy is undeniably the background to his economic and social theory. The importance of these early manuscripts is that they are the basis and source of his economic and social theory.

Moreover, for all its sketchiness, it is a radical philosophy. It tries to account for its ultimate commitment. And it also tries to express philosophically concerns which are highly relevant to the concreteness and fullness of life. In other words, it attempted to be an universal, integral approach, instead of just a specialistic analysis of certain aspects of life. It is this radicalism which is so instructive and challenging; it challenges us to a serious confrontation, especially in our day.

We have confronted Marx by examining first of all, the (conservative) nature of his expectations with regard to philosophical theory and the precariousness of these expectations. And, then we have shown how, in becoming aware of the precariousness of his expectations, Marx turns into an agitator for the practical, violent overthrow of the existing order; in short, how Marx became the prophet of world revolution.

THE STRENGTH AND WEAKNESS OF COMMUNISM AND CHRISTIANITY

By S.U. Zuidema

I. The Strength of Communism

1. Communism is a movement that moves mountains and is also bent on moving mountains. Communism is conscious of being called and predestined to do so, and is aware of its responsibility to do so. Communism stands for its case and in its cause, being a movement of people who know themselves to be gripped by their creed; a movement of people who not only believe their confession, but also confess their faith; who think to have found the firm foundation, the "totality" of Truth which sets them free, and who keep every trace of doubt far from their "Truth," their firm foundation.

A movement is as strong as its faith, and as strong as its faith in itself as a movement. Thus Communism stands or falls with Communist faith; with the assurance by which it knows itself to be rooted in this faith. The strength of Communism is the strength of its believed "Truth" and the strength of its faith in this believed truth. In Christian terms: the strength of Communism is that of her religious ground-motive as motive, i.e., as loco-motive, as driving force.

Guins' final conclusion in his Communism on the Decline: "The weakness of the West was and is one of the main sources of communist strength," expresses a half-truth, and a dangerous one inasmuch as it directs our attention to the wrong side, at any rate the less important, inessential side of the matter. Certainly, the West is also part of the situation in which Communism appears, but let no one forget that Communism intends to master the situation, and believes to be master of the situation. Whether this be a true faith is another story, but it is certain that for

301

Communism this faith is essential, and unassail-
able too, it is beyond discussion, it is the
"dos-moi-pou-sto," the Archimedean point of Communism, whence derive its thought, acts, loves,
hates, negotiations and direction.

2. Communist faith is faith in se, faith in
self-credibility and self-dignity. In an expanded sense it is faith in man and man's humanity, it is faith in humanity. The first, middle,
and last article of this universal undoubted
Communist·faith reads: "I belive in man and
humanity, creator of heaven on earth. I believe
in man from whom all blessings flow, beyond whom
there is none greater. For of man, and through
man, and to man are all things and all mankind:
to whom be the glory for ever, world without
end."

3. In the eyes of the Communist this faith
in se is so imcomparably superior that it cannot,
absolute as it is, be characterized, let alone
branded, as "atheistic." When Karl Barth
designates Communism as being "god-less," he
contradicts and underestimates the Communist.
To the Communist "godlessness" is a meaningless
word, and a meaningless distinction. Since
there is no God, there is no godlessness either.
According to the Communist the concept 'godlessness' is a description of nothing by means
of nothing; just as is 'Christian faith-in-God,'
which is an illusion, an escape from humanity,
an attack upon humanity, unbelief. That is why,
for the Communist, there is no common rule of
thumb by which to judge of both Communist faith
and "Christian" faith-in-God; the former is
superior to the latter. Since Marx and Feuerbach
the Communist "understands" the Christian religion; in their footsteps he sees right through
it and reveals it for what it is: an inferior
and pernicious illusion. On the other hand the
Communist does not consider Christians ever to
be able to understand his faith in humanity,
not to mention the possibility that they should
be able to unmask his faith. Stated in Biblical

302

terms: "But the unhumanistic man receiveth not the things of the spirit of man: for they are foolishness unto him; neither can he know them, because they are humanistically discerned. But he that is a humanist judgeth all things, yet he himself is judged of no man." (Cf. I Corinthians 2:14,15.)

This humanist-communist sense of superiority, rooted as it is in Feuerbach's anti-theological theology which constitutes the reverse side of his radical faith in humanity, is a basic ingredient of Communism's strength. In its own eyes Communism is unparalleled and unequalled. It is the choicest and ripest fruit of centuries of man's self-reflection and self-redemption and the beginning of the end of man's "self-estrangement." It is the dawn of that day in which man shall be nigh and sufficient unto himself. The communist-humanist faith in self is the most natural thing in the world, and is self-evident in its self-evidency. It is the Ground of grounds and Alpha and Omega of truth and reality.

4. Communist humanism considers itself blessed, and, when it compares itself with "faith in God" or naturalistic primitive religion, it considers its own faith alone to be an enlightened faith, the faith of emancipated humanity. As such the movement finds itself to be in step with the times, while all belief in God must needs be old-fashioned, antiquated, reactionary, old-hat, childish, stubbornly stupid compared to its own progressive character in heeding the call of the hour as it, Communism, believes it is doing. Communism is progressive!

And indeed, it is a fruit of "progress"-- of the progress of that Western thought which, since the Renaissance, has constituted the dominant cultural force within the West. The bourgeoisie of the nineteenth century, made infamous by Marx and the Communists, at least

carried the process of secularization to hitherto
unknown proportions (though it had been in the
making for centuries) by casting away even the
dead branches of faith which Kant had still
tried to rescue: "God, virtue, and immortality,"
the postulates of practical reason. The bourgeoisie made both reason and morality absolute,
by definition, i.e., it servered them from any
man-God relation. This "bourgeois philosophy,"
which, led in particular by theologians, undermined the foundations of the Christian religion
in the thirties and forties of the previous
century, has created a situation eminently fit
for the belief in autonomous, enlightened,
rational-moral man, a belief which became the
cultural dominant of the West. Communist-humanist faith in self accepts this heritage as its
patrimony, thus taking itself to be the only
historically justifiable, enlightened faith.
The Communist knows himself to be in harmony
with "History" - the power which has filled the
empty place formerly occupied by the providential rule of God - and consequently knows
himself to be progressive, enlightened, autonomous, moral and fully human. This new "idea of
man" - containing within it the new Mitmenschlich-
keit-idea as well - replaces every trace of
"divinity" in man's mode of being on earth.
Then heaven, one of the Communist leaders has
suggested, is for God and the birds. Communism
knows itself to be up-to-date, hence does not
distinguish itself from bygone religions by
calling itself irreligious or secular; rather,
it stands out as the Light, Truth, and Life in
contrast to the Darkness, Error, and Ruin of
times past. Communism believes that Communism
is the fulfillment, the perfection, the enlightenment, the emancipation of man and humanity, as
the very meaning of history. That is its
strength.

5. In the relational context of human forces
this strength of Communism is considerably
buttressed by the non-Communist world, in particular by Western European culture, moved as it

has from historicism to relativism which a priori condemns all faith in a meaning of world history. In line with its inner dynamics such relativism prepares the way for nihilism: the final confession of meaning, viz. that of the meaninglessness of human life.

The "discovery" of the meaninglessness of man and of mankind's history lives as a parasite upon the bygone faith in the meaningfulness of mankind's history and of human life. It lives upon the remnants of bygone strength, upon tradition. It is eating into the inherited capital of earlier generations. It is self-corruption: the putrid smell of it is over-taking us already.

In addition there is positivism, which also rejects a world-historical idea of meaning, reducing history to a strictly rational-methodical search for the "facts." The resulting no man's land separating an ideological philosophy of history - which, in time, with Hegel, will parry the objection that its vision does not square with the facts, with the haughty and self-devastating comment: "so much the worse for the facts!" - and a positivistic science of history practiced by technical historians - who, so to speak, consider a semi-colon in history to be as important as a Homeric ipic - this no man's land threatens to become scorched earth; a scorched earth smiting its environment on both sides with barrenness: with the nonsense of the philosophical idea of meaning in history, and with the senselessness of a meaning-less historical search for facts.

In this milieu Communism is facile princeps, winning hands down. For Communism firmly be-lieves in a meaning of man and his history and can even see the suffering, the expropriation of rights and goods from the proletarians under captialism's reign of terror, in the light of some reason: it is "the cunning of history," after all, which creates the joy of the future out of present suffering and so gives the suffering proletariat, precisely as suffering proletariat, a substitutionary and redemptive messianic task, and therein a meaning.

The Communist martyr and Communist martyrology constitute the strength of Communism. Communism has its saints!

6. Communism believes in history as redemptive history and in the present as the axis of history. Our age is decisive for the redemption of all mankind. According to Communist faith, men today not only control their own fate and future, but they stand in the crucial present of the entire course of history. Communism considers the fate of mankind to be once and for all in the custody of the Communist and his movement today. Since Lenin especially, Communism has explained and redirected Marxism in irrationalistic fashion, and considers itself it be the bearer of all responsibility, the agency of decisive importance, in a "now-or-never" way, for all ages. This sense of destiny - that all of man's history up to the rise of Communism is really only "pre-history," a prelude to the very essential historic event that is to create the conditions indispensable for the establishment of man's salvation, heaven on earth, world-paradise - gives the Communist that powerful sense of calling in which he ascribes more to himself than Herder's "dasz Ich etwas bedeute." After all, he, and his activity, as well as his movement, not only signify "etwas," but the end-all and be-all, the one thing needful, the universal salvation once and for all time. After he was created the conditions of the kingdom of freedom - in which paradisial welfare and co-operative labor go hand in hand, and each produces according to his ability but receives according to his need - there is really no further sequel to the story save this: and mankind lives and works happily ever after. Communism believes in itself as savior of the world, the Savior of the world, and allows nothing to distract it from

following its own, the Savior's call. Thus in 1956, the "salvation army" of Russian Communism entered Hungary as liberator, to free that country from its doom-pregnant predicament.

The Communist knows no vacuum between principles-for-practice and practice-according-to-principle: practice affirms principle, principle justifies practice.

The Communist practice of life is not arbitrary, not whimsical, not just to pass the time, not just pastime. It is not spare-time activity, but principled, purposive, goal-directed behavior. It is task-completion, redemptive action. The Communist's view of life, his ideology, his dogmas and his Communist catechism are to him not some game of "Pure Reason" speculating noncommittally about the possibility of the ground of knowability et cetera - or to use another (I think Windelband's) image: no whetting of the blades without ever slaughtering the pig - but his political catechism, his science, his philosophy, his dogmas and his ideologies all march in the front lines of the Communist movement; they are Light and Life, the controlling foundation and first principle guiding the activity that brings salvation.

That is the strength of Communism. Neither in thought nor in action can the Communist choose to act or not, to be engaged or not, to invest his time or not. In both thought and action the Communist redeems the time, converting it into a time of salvation and redemption. He knows what he lives for, suffers for, fights for; and he knows why he thinks, philosophizes, dogmatizes, catechizes. There is nothing that reveals Communist strength quite as plainly as a Communist catechism. The Communist sets practice to his doctrine, and examines practice for his doctrine; simultaneously he focuses his doctrine on practice and checks his doctrine in practice. Doctrine and practice are in permanent revision. In fact, the Communist personally undergoes permanent

307

revision - the revision of "critique and self-critique." It is the revision of "daily repentance."

7. The Communist faith is exclusive and intolerant. It does not consider itself to be "a" way, "a" truth, "a" way of life, but it believes in itself as "the" Way, "the" Truth, and "the" Way of life. Where the Communist takes a stand, there he stands and cannot do otherwise. He does not need God to help him in this: that sign of "weakness" is not his. The Communist "amen" is the amen of self-assuredness and self-assurance, thus going it one better than any kind of conceitedness. The Communist as Communist, as member of the movement, is his own dos-moi-pou-sto right along with the movement. He takes Fichte's humanist credo, "Das Ich setzt sich selbst und das Nicht-Ich," and applies it to himself and his movement: "The Communist I posits itself and all non-I." The Communist is his own competence, and the competence of others as well; as truth he is the criterion of truth as well; in his light will he see light - and so, necessarily, as he sees it, must everyone else. He is the via salutis also for and of everyone else. He is "the life," he has put on the "new man" who truly loves his neighbor, he believes in his own unlimited power: shortly he will even be able to make all men come to repentance and cause them to be born again: his movement is the true Pentecostal movement of all mankind. He believes, particularly if he resides beyond the borders of Soviet Russia, that socialism has been well established in Soviet Russia these twenty years now: the construction of a cooperative society of the new mankind where each man is his brother's keeper has there been achieved for a good part already: yet a little while, and the blessed Communist realm will appear on the horizon there. Hence the Communist's parole is: "He that is not for me, is against me." He exiles, excommunicates, damns, anathematizes, and brooks no compromises except as a means of tactics necessary to achieve

308

dominion; he does not discuss, he dictates; he does not negotiate, he proclaims; he knows not dialogue, or even monologue, but only infallible revelation, books of revelation, the good books - the holy scriptures of the doctores revelationis "ecclesiae" - Marx, Engels, Lenin, Stalin, and the Party, i.e., the Scriptures plus Tradition - the living Tradition of today's Party decisions included. The Communist demands of everyone as a matter of course that he surrender himself captive in faithful obedience to the Movement, to its doctrines and ordinances.

Tertium non datur.

That is the strength of Communism. The Communist, so to speak, coincides with himself; and so he also coincides with the Party, and therefore the Party with him; and the Party leaders coincide with the Party and with the Communists, since the Communists coincide with the Party, and the Party with the leaders.

Stalin is a "Stalinist," and beyond Stalin there is none else. Stalin is the "Ego Sum," and in Stalin the Party and the Communist partake of his "Ego Sum," of absolute "Esse": beyond the pale is wailing and gnashing of teeth. The earth is the Communist's; and as for the rest: the "godless" - to wit, the non-Communist - he should and shall be banished from the earth. Hallelujah! - i.e., praise be the Communist, the Party, Stalin, and his successors, "of whom, through whom, and to whom..."

The strength of Communism is the Communist "Ego Sum"!

II.   The Weakness of Communism

1. Communism's strength is Communism's weakness, in fact is its downfall. Its strength is self-consuming. Communism's faith in itself as the movement that is to bring the world its long awaited state of blessedness is being continually

309

controverted and contradicted by reality. Thus belied, this faith in the long run manages to maintain itself only as a dictate, as a dictatorship of man over himself, as a strait-jacket. Only by command and as "blind faith" - the very opposite of "enlightened faith" - can it yet stand.

One may properly describe the development of Communist faith from Marx to Khrushchev as a process of self-consumption, of self-liquidation. Engels already found himself compelled to accommodate Marxism, to "reform" it, to explain it in an essentially un-marxistic manner. Marx's materialism had taught that the crux of man's history was to be found in the labor process and in the development of tools; Engels destroyed this doctrine by teaching that there is a "dialectical" relation of mutual interaction between "being," i.e., being laborer, and "consciousness," i.e., being political movement among other things. The process of dissolution was furthered by Lenin, who shifted the main emphasis of the Communist movement away from the trade-unions and the sphere of labor, in favor of the political party organization and its revolution: the laborer, receded into the background.

But this movement too failed to meet the demands of the times: only Russia experienced the outbreak and breakthrough of revolution; not even faintly did it resemble the world-wide revolution that had been announced. Faith in the coming of the Communist realm was sorely tried, and for the time being its arrival was postponed and deferred to the future.

Stalin found himself forced to prolong the delay by means of a self-revision of the Communist faith: not the world-wide revolution, but "socialism-in-one-country" became the first objective of the program. After that we will see again! Marx's "tomorrow" became a thing of the past; Lenin's "tomorrow" was shelved; Stalin's "tomorrow" too has had its day: only the word "tomorrow" remains - it is prolonged. This hope deferred can only make the heart sick. A Communist disease develops, and Communism becomes its own case-history. Marx's "tomorrow" proved to be Lenin's reign of terror; Stalin's "tomorrow" proved to be Khrushchev's terrorization of the workers - the workers, mind you - of Hungary. The world's salvation appears to be a euphemism for the terror of the Russion state Moloch. Only by command is this terror still called bliss, while in fact the bliss consists of terror.

Mankind's emancipation ultimately appears to be the emancipation of the few, who mercilessly dispose of the millions by means of the prison state, factory slavery, and forced labor camps.

Not a mankind which assumes control of the situation by means of Communism, but a dictator who by means of Communism assumes control over mankind, is the result.

Communism digs its own grave, and refuses itself. Not recognizing any limits to human emancipation, it cannot but prevent the emancipation of men, making them superfluous. Instead of the history of humanity and of emancipation, Communism becomes a history of human guilt. Without penitence! But not without penalty. Communism becomes ever more unreal, ever more... an illusion, ever more a demonstration of its "Truth" as...fiction!

2. The belief in man's ability to work out his own salvation realizes itself as the practice of tyrants who injure their fellows. Not only does the existence of emancipated emancipators prevent emancipation, but neighborly love in fact proves to be not love of the neighbor close by, but a professed love of the stranger far away - who will not benefit by it one bit. But in addition, Communism's acknowledged pledge of concrete love of men anywhere and everywhere,

unfulfilled as it is, implies a Communist debt;
and the payment of this debt is exacted from the
nearest neighbor - from, of all people, the
worker. Under Communism it is the worker who
experiences the terror of arbitrary rule and
who finds himself in every state except the promised blessed one: at night he isn't safe, in
the morning he is anything but master of his
situation, and after tomorrow he may not be
around to see the Light. The practice of this
faith in man's own efficacy unto salvation
proves to be injurious to man as man, i.e., as
child of God. When man, who after all does not
possess the power to bless, reaches for this
power, he becomes a curse. The blessing exists
only on paper, sola fide, by faith along, while
the curse is reality.

3. The self-evidence of Communism as a redemptive movement for the world begins to look
more and more like the conclusion to a ficti-
tious argument. It is comparable to the following syllogism: "All the dead are alive. Socrates is dead. Therefore Socrates is alive."
When Russian psychologists began to conduct
tests among the population in the nineteen-
thirties, the results included anything but the
conviction that Russia was the land of the first
fruits of the blessed kingdom coming, the first-
born of the promised land. Immediately Pravda
castigated these psychologists and the testing
was forbidden. After all - it was said - everyone knows that in Russia the blessed socialist
state has been established, and such is everyone's experience too. To enquire after it is
maliciously to sow the seeds of uncertainty and
unrest. Henceforward the following decree is
effective: "All people in Russia fare well.
Socrates lives in Russia. Therefore Socrates
fares well." To know this, no one need ask
Socrates, for it follows, by force of logic,
that Socrates thinks of it the same way. It
cannot be that he thinks differently, ergo...
In fact this "ergo" means: "He wouldn't dare
think otherwise."

The self-evidence of this faith in humanity
begins to look more and more like the self-
evidence of this faith as a delusion: the
corollary of the truth that whosoever makes
God superfluous makes man superfluous as well.
He who stands by such faith, will fall it as
well.

4. Self-confident Communism, confident of
its historic rights as the most progressive
phenomenon yet to appear in the progression of
history, hence confident of its place in the
forefront of the march of history, is nevertheless as such overtaken by history. To the
extent that this faith is produced by time, to
that extent it is destined to disappear with
time. To remain in touch with the times,
therefore, the only means still available is
resorted to: brute force. This "might-is-
right" imperialism is proclaimed to be "in
tune with the times," and liberating. It is
said to be the beginning of the consummation of
history. And such it is - by decree! By any
other name it is contrary to the times, out of
step with the times, illiberal. Its progressive
sense of time and history reverts to regressive
tyrannic action, while the messianic character
of the movement continues to assume more and
more the forms of a self-refutation. In its
race against time Communism increasingly falls
behind. It can only keep up the pace of time
by becoming less and less Communistic, i.e.,
less and less redemptive, and more and more
like brute force, naked power politics.

5. Accordingly, Communism's strength increasingly comes to consist exclusively of
Western weakness. In this respect Guins
appears to be more correct all the time. To
our shame, Western weakness has been demonstrated anew, and that clearly, in November,
1956. And ever since those days. The final
statement of the final broadcast of Hungary's
free radio was the appeal: "Help!" As yet it
appears that the appeal may as well have been

addressed to the fish in the ocean. That would at least have spared them the illusion that the appeal might be heard and acted upon. The Communist calendar commemorates its martyrs and its saints. The West? It has a welfare program, period. With or without days of prayer and thanksgiving - as long as there is a welfare program!

6. The permanent vision of the Communist and his Communism implies internal Communist revolution. Marx would hardly recognize himself in today's Communism. Daily repentance increasingly becomes daily revision, i.e., apostasy from original Communism and acceptance of what now remains: the terror of brute force! The blessedness of man, already revised, is being progressively reduced to the blessedness of the Communist movement and its leaders, in casu to the raison d'etat. Only posthumously do the workers receive the good life. The good of the state devours men: worker, intellectual, and party member. What is called voluntary service on the labor front is becoming little more than a euphemism for enforced discipline, and the personal right to self-determination - emancipation! - is becoming an impersonal right to the duty of allowing oneself to be exploited as worker. For the good of the state. Tomorrow will be different. But the Communist "tomorrow" does not differ much from ad calendas Graecas: "tomorrow come never"; all it means in fact is: "not today anyway."

7. Exclusivism and intolerance cause Communism to become increasingly a closed enclave in the history of mankind, an erratic bloc, a sectarianism devoid of all catholicity, patent narrow-mindedness. This is particularly evidenced by the Communist catechism. Materially it now consists of little else than banalities and pseudo-scientific simplicities. The "Ego Sum" of the Communist is becoming more of an "ego" and by the same token less of a "sum," an "esse." So it shrivels up and turns into the

314

naked force of self-assertion, of a self-adoration increasingly lacking in all ratio, even the ratio sufficiens that to some extent still supported it in the middle of the previous century; whereas the grounds for establishing the superfluity, impropriety even, of the movement are becoming more than sufficient. Ever since it degraded authority to mere force, Communism has worked only deeds of violence, and has invested these with authority; what is left is raison d'etat, the cannon (of the militia) and the gun (of the police, the secret police). The secret police becomes Communism's only real secret: its self-refutation, its self-destruction - as Communism!

III. The Strength and Weakness of Christianity

1. For a good part the strength and weakness of Communism is also the strength and weakness of Christianity. In the foregoing there was nothing that we cannot recognize and call forth in ourselves. All of it is applicable to ourselves. Let me leave it at that. I would advise you, however, to re-read what has been said about Communism and not to rest till you discover its analogies in Christendom, yourself included. Discover - it won't be necessary to invent. Let me note just one thing: this self-examination will become especially difficult when you set yourself to discover a-theism in our own way of thinking and practice of life - the a-theism that we refuse to call atheism precisely because we have, as the most ordinary thing in the world, shut God out of certain areas of life, eliminating there God's relation to us and our relation to God, and considering it to be downright nonsense if anyone should there call us to God's holy order.

2. Only formally, structurally analogous to Communism is the Christian faith which the Apostle has in mind when he writes: "...this is the victory that overcometh the world, even our faith. Who is he that overcometh the world,

but he taht believeth that Jesus is the Son of God?" (I John 5:4,5).

In content, direction, and origin, this faith is from, through, and unto God. It is the antipode and breakdown of the self-assertion of man and humanity, because it is of, through, and to the glory of God; not abstractly, and not a pious afterthought, or as a bandwagon-slogan, but in the intertwinement of "oremus et laboremus," let us pray and also work, in concrete reality; so that it is the motive, the ground-motive, the locomotive of ourselves in our everyday living. To that extent and in this way it is valid to say: "Deo servire libertas": To serve God is liberty. Or again, to quote another Apostle (since we cannot improve on the Scriptures): "In Christ Jesus faith availeth, which worketh by love" (Galatians 5:6).

He that has the audacity to set this faith "on its own," to shut it up within man's immanent horizon, does not know what it is he speaks of. For this faith lives by the grace of God, and is, before it moves mountains, itself first driven to move. "For it is God which worketh in you both to will and to do of his good pleasure" (Philippians 2:13). Not without reason does Paul expressly say that "it is God...": or again: "when I am weak, then am I strong" (II Corinthians 12:10). Just as he testifies too that he desires to know - certainly not in an intellectualistic sense but as a living reality - "the power of Christ's resurrection" (Philippians 3:10).

That is by no means the conclusion to an argument, nor is it deductive proof; but that is the well-spring, the source, the fount and origin of our entire being, our action and our thought: "the God of Israel is he that giveth strength and power unto his people. Blessed be God!" (Psalm 68:35). He is "the glory of their strength" (Psalm 89:17). Here, if God grant, our silence will be telling. That is the language of silent adoration.

The strength of Communism is its weakness.

The weakness of Christianity is its strength.

REVOLUTION AND REVELATION

By Rene Padilla

There is a whole range of possible definitions of the term 'revolution'. The one consecrated by general use in school textbooks is
that which makes reference to social and
political events 'clearly different from all
other phenomena because they suddenly cause
a violent and far-reaching change in the whole
pattern of society and especially in the traditional political structure that is being
transformed and replaced by a new order'.

For the Christian as an individual and for
the church as a community, such events create
an ethical problem that demands an answer.
What position should they take?   Isolation?
Participation?

The position that we take obviously depends,
among other factors, on our political ideas.
We must not deceive ourselves about our ob-
jectivity; it is even possible to use theology
to justify attitudes whose roots are not in
revelation, as we would like to think, but in
purely human premises. If we reject revolution,
it may be that our rejection is due, more than
anything else, to a compromise with the status
quo and a fear that change might affect our own
economic position. If we support revolution,
on the other hand, it may be that our support
is due to the fact that we have been conditioned
by the myth of man's ability to build a new
world order. For this reason it is urgent that
we place our motive under the judgment of the
revelation of God in His Word.

This must be the starting-point of our theological consideration of revolution. Its purpose must be to clarify the significance of our
commitment to Jesus Christ in relation to today's
revolutionary ferment, to understand the mission
that Christian discipleship involves in the midst

of the conflicts and the political, social and
economic changes that surround us. All this
should result in a fuller, more integrated
Christian life.

Revolutionary ferment in the Bible

Every revolution is characterized by a certain ambiguity which makes it difficult to
evaluate from a Christian point of view. It
would be much easier to decide for or against
a revolution if all the factors involved were
always perfectly clear and definable. The
problem is that usually they are not. In every
revolution there is a mixture of good and evil,
light and darkness, white and black.

On the positive side, revolution presupposes
the recognition that life in society is not what
it ought to be, that it is deformed by evils
that demand a radical change in the social
structures. The revolutionary is, at least on
the surface, a nonconformist par excellence. His
very existence depends on the premise that something is wrong with the world - so wrong that
whatever action taken to remedy the situation
cannot be limited to mere reformation of the
present order. What is required is a new
order, a world purged of all the weeds, the
abuses and the imperfections that alienate man.
This is the world that he seeks to bring in by
means of revolution.

The Christian cannot close his eyes to the
injustices that surround him. To do so would be
to deny an important aspect of the Hebrew-Chris-
tian tradition. Seven centuries before Jesus
Christ, Amos, the shepherd from Tekoa, proclaimed
the judgment of God against those who exploit the
poor:

O you who turn justice to wormwood,
    and cast down righteousness to the earth!...
They hate him who reproves in the gate,
    and they abhor him who speaks the truth.

319

Therefore because you trample upon the poor
and take from him exactions of wheat,
you have built hourses of hewn stone,
but you shall not dwell in them;
you have planted pleasant vineyards,
but you shall not drink their wine.
For I know how many are your transgressions,
and how great are your sins -
you who afflict the righteous, who take a
bribe,
and turn aside the needy in the gate.
Therefore he who is prudent will keep silent
in such a time;
for it is an evil time.

The same courageous denunciation of the abuses
of the rich is found in the messages of other
prophets of Israel: Isaiah, Micah, Jeremiah,
and Ezekiel. One of the greatest glories of
the Jewish people is that from them arose the
first champions of social justice.

This prophetic note breaks into the world
of the first century in the preaching of John
the Baptist.

You brood of vipers! Who warned you to flee
from the wrath to come? Bear fruits that
befit repentance, and do not begin to say
to yourselves, "We have Abraham as our
father"; for I tell you, God is able from
these stones to raise up children to Abraham.
Even now the axe is laid to the root of the
trees; every tree therefore that does not
bear good fruit is cut down and thrown into
the fire.

Asked about what conduct is fitting in the light
of the judgment of God, John answers, "He who
has two coats, let him share with him who has
none; and he who has food, let him do likewise';
tax collectors ought not to charge 'more than
is appointed' and soldiers should not take
advantage of their position to become rich by
extortion.

Jesus Christ Himself defines His mission in
words of profound social significance when He
says,

'The Spirit of the Lord is upon me,
because he has anointed me to preach good
news to the poor.
He has sent me to proclaim release
to the captives
and recovering of sight to the blind,
to set at liberty those who are oppressed,
to proclaim the acceptable year of the Lord.'

His whole ministry is marked by a constant
identification with the destitute - an identification that won Him the title "Friend of tax
collectors and sinners'. The crowds move Him
to compassion because they are 'like sheep
without a shepherd'. He chooses His disciples
from among the common people, the am-ba-arets,
scorned for their ignorance of the law. He
teaches that no-one can serve God and wealth,
He cautions against the deceitfulness of riches,
He warns the rich that their comfort in this
world will be limited to their material possessions,
and He accuses those who in the name of religion
exploit widows.

In the actions and words of Jesus there is a
revolutionary ferment that, apparently at least,
corroborates the Jewish leaders' accusations
against Him before the Roman authorities -
that He is subverting the order. Although the
thesis that Jesus was a Zealot cannot be sustained on the basis of biblical data, it must
be recognized that there is a grain of truth in
it - that Jesus shares with the Zealots their
dissatisfaction with the established powers and
their hope for the coming of the kingdom of God.

This prophetic tradition finds echo later in
the teaching of James:

'Come now, you rich, weep and howl for the
miseries that are coming upon you. Your

321

riches have rotted and your garments are moth-eaten. Your gold and silver have rusted, and their rust will be evidence against you and will eat your flesh like fire. You have laid up treasure for the last days. Behold, the wates of the labourers who mowed your fields, which you kept back by fraud, cry out; and the cries of the harvesters have reached the ears of the Lord of hosts. You have lived on the earth in luxury and in pleasure; you have fattened your hearts in a day of slaughter. You have condemned, you have killed that righteous man; he does not resist you.'

Revolution and human nature

So the Christian stands in a prophetic tradition. He agrees with the revolutionary in his desire for a better world where justice and liberty reign. Biblical faith does not permit the Christian to be resigned to the status quo nor to align himself with the oppressor. However, this same faith demands that he has reservations about the dynamic of the change proposed by the revolution.

Every revolutionary ideology presupposes a faith in man's ability to create a new world. It sees the historical process as the result of factors over which man has control. Obviously, not any man, but only the revolutionary. In a sick society, plagued by the evils of misery and exploitation, the revolutionary represents the only hope for a new order, because he, and only he, is free of contamination by the regime in power. 'Because of the historic possibility that it glimpses ahead of it, the revolutionary group (class or nation) considers itself a messianic group, the principal protagonist of history, for the period that its action initiates, and which is the final period.' Underlying this messianic sense is the conviction that man is good by nature, that evil is not inherent in man, but only in the social structures that con-

322

dition him. The immediate objective of the
revolutionary, therefore, is orientated toward
changing these structures. And it is in order
to accomplish this objective that he resorts
to violence. Violence thus becomes the moving
force of history, the way to usher in the perfect society.

The Christian agrees with the revolutionary
in his dissatisfaction with the state of things
as they are and the desire for a change in the
situation. He admits with the revolutionary
that what is needed is not only technological
and industrial development, but a complete change,
a transformation of the whole system. He dis-
agrees with the revolutionary, nevertheless, in
that he does not believe in violence as the solution for social problems, the road that leads
to the perfect society. He may perhaps recognize with Reinhold Niebuhr that there may be
occasions when the balance of power, necessary
for justice, demands violence as the compara-
tively lesser evil. That would be the case in
a 'borderline situation' in which the Christian
would accept violence and at the same time the
blame and the necessity of God's forgiveness
which violence implies. What simply does not
fit into the mental system of the Christian is
violence as the norm of history.

The Christian's rejection of violence is con-
sistent with his understanding of man and society.
The unjust conditions that prevail in society
are not brought about primarily by causes outside
man. They are, rather, the result of the inclination toward evil that is inherent in man. This
is basically a moral question. It finds its
centre in the very essence of man. In the words
of Jesus Christ, 'From within, out of the heart
of man', come all these evil things which defile
man. In the final analysis, here is the root
of all social evils. This is the centre of the
ills of humanity - the I out of place,' says E.
Stanley Jones. And he adds, 'Everything else is ·
a symptom - this is the disease.' Quacks try to

cure the symptoms; doctors cure the disease.

All human history corroborates this analysis.
There has always been an element that has eluded
the examinations of politicians, sociologists
and economists, but which has determined to a
large extent the course of historical events –
the moral corruption of man, human depravity,
what theology calls sin. Every interpretation
of history that ignores this element will necessarily be idealistic. If there is anything
that history teaches us, says Herbert Butterfield,
it is that human nature cannot be trusted: 'It
is essential not to have faith in human nature.
Such faith is a recent heresy and a very disastrous one.'

Like the revolutionary, the Christian desires
the destruction of all the patterns of the established order that enslave man. He echoes
the words of the prophet, "Let justice roll
down like waters, and righteousness like an
ever-flowing stream." But, following Jesus
Christ, he knows what is in man. Furthermore,
he sees in history the judgment that falls upon
those who try to transform society before
transforming the individual, that 'law of gravity'
which pulls down to earth man's dreams of building a new world for himself. For this reason,
he discounts 'the' revolutionary solution and
looks for a revolution that is still more radical,
more complete, a revolution that will overcome
the estrangement between man and God and between
man and his neighbour. As Nicholas Berdyaeff
has said, 'The Christian is the eternal revolutionary who is not satisfied with any way of
life, because he seeks the kingdom of God and
his righteousness, because he aspires to a
more radical transfromation of man, of society
and of the world.'

The problem with violence is not that it is
radical, but rather that it is not radical enough.
It attempts to eliminate the symptoms without
curing the illness. It prescribes pep pills

324

when what is needed is a surgical operation.
Its error stems from an erroneous concept of
man. The revolutionary closes his eyes to the
moral deformity of human nature - this evil
whose depth even the idealist Kant was forced
to admit - and thus trusts in the adequacy of
his ideology to establish a new order. He
assumes that social evils are a question of
political, social and economic organization, and
that they will disappear through changes external to man. Sooner or later his ideal of a
perfect society will be shipwrecked on the reef
of the human ego. From this not even the revolutionary is exempt. No political party nor
social class, neither the bourgeois nor the
proletarian, is immune to the desire to convert
itself into a god and appeal to force to achieve
its own ends. Revolution does not change man;
it does not touch the root of social evils. For
this reason, as soon as the revolutionary regime
is established the injustices of the old order
reappear and the revolutionary class becomes a
new oligarchy. The revolutionary becomes the
defender of the status quo and his ideology of
change becomes the instrumentum regni, the means
of power that is transmitted to the masses on
the basis of authority, thanks to a monopoly on
education, literature and the mass media. As
Romano Guardini has warned, man has power over
many things - and today more than ever! - but
he does not have power over his own power.

The gospel of revolution

Every revolution sets before the Christian
faith the question of the relation between the
kingdom of God and the kingdoms of men, between
eschatology and history. In the final analysis,
every revolution is a human attempt to create
here and now the perfect society that God has
promised to created at the end of the present
age. The problem is to know to what extent the
new order introduced by the revolution is the
fulfilment or (at least) the beginning of the
fulfilment of the purpose of God in history.

We must begin by recognizing that nothing in
the world lies outside the control of God. God
rules over all the nations of the earth and He
executes His government through Jesus Christ.
Jesus Christ is Lord not only of the church but
also of the whole creation. This is the con-
sistent teaching of the New Testament. Furthermore, according to the biblical record, God uses
'secular' powers that remain outside the sphere
of redemption to work out his purposes for the
world. In Isaiah, for example, Cyrus is described as God's anointed one, raised up 'to
subdue nations before him and ungird the loins
of kings'. In Romans Paul refers to the authorities as 'ministers of God'. In the presence
of Pilate Jesus Christ Himself admits that the
judgment being passed on Him is based on an
authority that comes from God Himself. Are we
then to say that God is the author of violent
revolutions?

This, in effect, is the thesis sustained by
some contemporary theologians. To them, revolutions are nothing less than the means through
which God is carrying out His purpose in history.
God's action is of a political nature - it is
orientated toward the transformation of social
structures. Harvey Cox says that God is present
above all in political events, in revolutions,
in revolts, in invasions, in defeats. God not
only permits or desires change, but He carries
it out, and He does this through revolutions.
Richard Shaull, in agreement with Paul Lehmann,
maintains that 'revolution must be understood
theologically, for it is set firmly in the context of God's humanizing activity in history.
As a political form of change, revolution represents the cutting edge of humanization.' He
believes that the presence and power of God in
the renovation of life are manifested above all
wherever there is a struggle to make human life
more human, 'on the frontiers of change where
the old order is passing away and the new order
is coming into being in the world'. In the light
of this concept of revolution, the responsibility

of the Christian is obvious - to be present in
the revolution, involved in the struggle for
'humanization', though always aware of the
possibility of 'dehumanization' and ready to
admit the limitations of the new revolutionary
order. Cox concludes, "God is acting; if we
want to relate ourselves to Him, it is impera-
tive, then, that we also should act." Shaull
says, 'Our task is not to impose certain values,
but rather to recognize and live according to
those that hold sway in the world; it is not
to give meaning to life, but rather to discover
the meaning that life has in the world that
participates in redemption; not to establish
order in the universe, but rather to share in
the new order of things that is taking shape
through social transformation.'

This position, which the Conference on Church
and Society held in Geneva in 1966 adopted as
its platform, represents above all a way of
thinking characteristic of our time, particularly
in underdeveloped countries - the position
according to which violence offers the masses
the only hope of change. Salvador de Madariaga,
the Spanish writer, has observed that the West
today lives in the disillusionment that belongs
to a post-revolutionary stage in which it has
lost faith in violence and has chosen to submit
to dictatorial governments. Whatever the validity
of this thesis may be in regard to the West, in
the rest of the world the hope generally prevails that, on the basis of a supposed dialectic
of history, revolution will create the new society
that the majority desires. The 'theology of
revolution' takes upon itself to provide theological justification for this hope. All its errors
stem from the fact that it takes as its starting-
point the revolutionary situation and interprets
Scripture on the basis of presuppositions derived
from leftist ideologies. Instead of showing the ·
relevance of revelation to revolution, it makes
revolution its source of revelation. The result
is a secular gospel whose dominant emphasis parallel those of Marxism.

The 'theology of revolution' is in essence
a new version of the 'other gospel' that Paul
combatted so vigorously in the first century.
Like it, it holds that man can attain the kingdom of God by means of his own works. It is
basically a negation of the gospel of grace.
It puts man in the place of God; and not even
man as he actually exists in history, with the
limitations that his sinful state place on him,
but an idealized man, a mere projection of an
optimism devoid of biblical content. It ignores the Bible's diagnosis of human nature and
takes as its basis the simplistic thesis that
evil is external to man and consequently can be
eradicated through change in the social structures. Its concept of man coincides with that
of Marxism, not with the Christian concept,
although it pretends to be an expression of
Christianity.

In the final analysis, what the 'theology of
revolution' challenges is the Christian's future
hope. As Michael Schmaus says, the worldly
optimism reflected in utopian concepts of history is the death of the Christian hope. In
the New Testament, the only hope that has validity is that which is based in Jesus Christ -
He is 'our hope'. In this other gospel, the
hope is epitomized in revolution. In the New
Testament the action of God is orientated toward
the creation of a new humanity in which the moral
image of Jesus Christ, the New Man, will be
reflected; in this other gospel, the purpose of
God in history is a 'humanization' to be understood in economic terms, a 'salvation' of the
social structures within history. The fact is
completely ignored that the ultimate cause of
the injustice that prevails in the world and
creates disorder in the whole of society is in
man; that this is a power that cannot be purged
from the present order by means of any programme
contrived by man. Because they believed this,
the Old Testament prophets 'set all their hope
on a new creation of the world through the power
of God, and rejected, as a radical delusion, the

idea that a new humanity and new conditions could be created through human reforms'. Their hope is carried over into the New Testament because Jesus Christ and His apostles agree with the prophets in their diagnosis of the human situation. The 'theology of revolution' idealizes man and consequently converts the gospel into a utopian ideology that employs theological terminology but has little relation to the eschatological message of the Bible.

It must not be denied, of course, that the supporters of this type of theology see revolution not as an exclusively human effort, but as the result of 'the humanizing activity of God' in history. From this point of view Shaull, for example, argues that revolution is not an inevitable process, determined by a law of history, but rather a reciprocal action involving a challenge for change from God's side and the response of obedience from man's side. Instead of solving the problem of the man-centredness that is found at the very root of this other gospel, this reference to God as the ultimate author of revolution aggravates the problems, for it assumes that a human programme has God's approval. In other words, there is a 'sanctification' of revolution, which puts God at man's service. It may well be asked if this identification of revolution with 'what God is doing in the world to humanize man' is not a fulfilment of Jesus Christ's prophetic warning regarding the proclamation of false Christs in the last days.

What allows the theologians of revolution to think that revolutions are the place where the action of God intervenes in history is what Paul Ramsey has aptly called 'a mutilated Barthianism'. Taking as their starting-point Karl Barth's objectification of the work of Jesus Christ, they assume that the world has been reconciled and that all that now is asked of men is to recognize that they are in effect living under the sovereign rule of Jesus Christ. But they neglect Barth's 'christocentric' ethic and interpret

social transformation indiscriminately as the
expression of the will of God to place all things
under the feet of Christ. The net result is to
make violence sacred, which eliminates any possibility of discerning the elements of evil involved in all revolutions. Furthermore, if one's
starting-point is the principle that, since God
has reconciled the world, revolution cannot be
understood except as the expression of His redemptive purpose, it is difficult to understand
why the conservative should not defend the status
quo in the name of the same universal reconciliation. When revolution is understood as an event
that originates in the will of God, the Christian
becomes, as in the conservative position, a slave
to the social order. In spite of all the apparent differences between the revolutionary and
the conservative there is basically one essential agreement - both identify the purpose of
God with the present historical situation. In
the one there is a conformity with the status
quo; in the other a conformity with the revolution. 'In the final analysis, both positions
identify the will of God with the so-called permanent necessities of history.'

The attitude of Jesus Christ toward the
revolutionary programme of the Zealots should
suffice to define a Christian attitude toward
revolutionary movements today. The modern idea
of creating a perfect society through revolution is no less evil than the Zealot's conception
of the messiah as a political leader called to
establish the kingdom of God by the power of
the sword. And the attitude that the disciple
of Christ should take toward it cannot differ
from that of his Master: "He who does not take
up his cross and follow me cannot be my disciple."

VI. Toward A Biblical Politics

The readings to this point have concerned
themselves with what might be called the more
substantive aspects of a Christian politics,
i.e., its basic foundations and direction, stance
vis a vis the primary alternatives, and a consideration of the political milieu which
it must address and within which it will
develop. This final section takes up a more
tactical consideration: How can we get from
where we are to where we think we should be? To
put it more pointedly, if the Body of Christ
wants to discharge its political responsibilities
in a communal, biblically faithful way, what
should our course of action be? Such questions
are seldom asked in North America and we offer
the following selections as a mere hint of the
rich and continuing discussion which must begin
among all those Christians who take seriously
the biblical word for politics.

Writing here under a provocative title, Bernard Zylstra provides us with a rare example
of systemtic and comprehensive political strate-
gizing by a contemporary North American Christian.
His answer to his own question, though in the
affirmative, should leave no one with any illusions about the difficulties of rallying the
Christian community, most of which has yet to
grasp its own unique existence and political
responsibilities. The heart of his deceptively
simple prescriptive analysis confronts our present
amorphous fragmentation directly: we must have a
common way of looking at politics -- a Christian
political mind -- before common political action
can begin.

The next selection develops some of the themes
announced by Bernard Zylstra. Building on his
insights, William Harper's concern is to pre-
clude the "ghettoizing" of Christian politics,
whether by ill-advised pre-occupation with building a Christian political party or the self-
righteous neglect of Christians already active in

politics. He suggests forging strong links between Christians in public office by election or appointment and Christian political organizations operating outside the constraints of conventional politics. Both groups could benefit, the former through an infusion of new hope and fresh idea and the latter through first-hand exposure to what it is they are trying to change.

While Zylstra and Harper are concerned primarily with politics in its more conventional forms, Clark Pinnock's field of vision is wider. Drawing on the "liberation theology" of Latin America, he issues both a reminder and warning about what social, economic, and political changes ought to come about if the Apostle Paul's metaphor of our lives as a "living sacrifice" is to be realized. In particular he points out that typical North American lifestyle, put in the context of the way most people in the world must live, shows insensitivity and contributes to growing inequity. Echoing Goudzwaard in an earlier chapter, he calls on Christians to liberate themselves from bondage to Mammon not only in their personal lives but also in the pursuit of a distinctive political style that will reflect the biblical principles of stewardship, neighborliness, and justice.

Where will Christian politics lead its practitioners? Our final selection is a somber reminder, well documented in the history of the church, that forthright Christian witness is frequently a costly affair. Will there be a "Christian problem" Plantinga asks, as a result of a distinctive and comprehensive cultural witness? Shouldn't there be?

Are we willing to pay the price--at the very least in terms of psychological strain, career prospects, reputation, and financial well being-- of being so different politically that we are perceived as a threat and hence as a problem? The answer we give will in large measure determine

whether Christian politics remains the private,
exotic passion of a few or the customary way
by which the followers of Christ in North America
give recognition to his Lordship.

DO CHRISTIANS HAVE A POLITICAL FUTURE?

By Bernard Zylstra

Christian citizens are in a political limbo. They have returned to the land of Egypt where the pharaohs rule assisted by their high priests and their chariots. Christians today experience a Babylonian exile: their voice is not heard loud and clear in the places where our lands are given direction. Do we now hear the expected song of lament: "How shall we sing the Lord's song in a foreign land?" Hardly. Instead, we find God's People stumbling along on two opinions, trekking to Jerusalem and to the high places of Baal.

Do Christian citizens have to remain in a political limbo forever? Perhaps, but not necessarily. Today is still the day of repentance, of salvation, and thus of service. I would propose that Christians weld themselves together (on the basis of a new consciousness of the Word of God as the only rule for faith and life) into national Christian political movements. Further, I would propose that these movements become political action fronts first at the local and state/provincial levels, and then at the national political levels.

I will attempt to clarify this proposal in two articles. The first will deal with the scope of politics. The second will suggest concrete steps that can now be taken to move ahead in a practical program for the political emancipation of the Christian citizenry.

Why is it necessary to first focus on the scope of politics? Because the immensity of this scope distinguishes Christian political action from action on other fronts. That vast scope also makes political action frightfully difficult. Christians, with sincere commitment, ingenuity, financial backing, and persistance, can set up a local church, an evangelism campaign, a foreign mission, a Christian school, or a Salvation Army philanthropic project without altogether too much ado. This is possible because the thrust of such actions is usually local.

But that simply isn't the case with politics, even if politics also does have local dimensions. Whenever we properly use the word "politics" we refer to the action of states, of entities like the US, Canada and India. A state is the community of citizens responsible for the administration of justice within the state's territory in cooperation with other states for the administration of justice in inter-state relations. Any movement that is concerned about <u>political</u> action must be aware of what is implied in the word "politics." There are three distince (though interrelated) aspects in the life of a state: (1) the internal components of a state, (2) relations between a state and the non-political sectors of society, (3) and relations between states. In this article we will look at each aspect briefly so that from the beginning we can at least in principle avoid the danger of a one-issue political movement.

1. THE INTERNAL COMPONENTS OF A STATE

What are the minimal components of a state as a state: To answer the parallel question: What makes a family a family? isn't too difficult. For one thing, we know the members of a family: a father, a mother, and children. We like to think of a family living together in a house, which we call a home, related to other families, which we call a neighborhood. A family has something unique about it by which we can distinguish it: we look for a special bond of love and respect between parents and children. We are convinced that parents should provide a home for the children; that they are responsible for bringing up the children to maturity so that they will be able to stand on their own feet in society. A family, we rightly feel, must have a certain identity of its own in society, a certain sovereignty in its own sphere of activities, so that it can ward off the many undue pressures from the outside that might endanger the realization of its God-given tasks.

"Passive Citizenship"

We can approach the state in a similar manner.
To begin with, who are its members? In principle
each permanent resident within a state's territory
has a right to be a member of the state. That
right is recognized in the US and Canada, where each
person born within these territories is a citizen by
birth, and where immigrants, after certain conditions
have been met, can acquire citizenship via naturaliza-
tion. Citizens are the members of the state. Since
the state is a community for the administration of
public justice, the right to citizenship is exceedingly
important. It is really the right to fair and equal
treatment along with all the other members of the
state, with the entire citizenry. For this reason
I will call this right "passive citizenship" to
distinguish it from "active citizenship" which I will
discuss later.

What is the foundation for this right to citizenship, for this right to be treated justly? Is its
origin simply the good will of the state itself? Not
really, for that would make the state the origin of
rights to be enjoyed by its members. The comparison
with the family is again illustrative. Johnny doesn't
become a member of his family because his parents
like him. He is a member for the simple reason that
he is the parents' child. So with citizenship.
I am or can become a citizen of the state within
whose territory I live simply because I am a person.
Citizenship is the state's recognition of my person-
hood. The origin and foundation of the right to
citizenship is a person's place in God's redeemed
creation where each man and woman has a right to be
treated as a creature made in God's image. This implies the right to just and fair treatment.

Here we must linger a moment around the concept of
justice since it is central to all of the state's
activities as the bond of trust is central to the
family. Justice is a Word of the Lord for mankind.
It is one of the expressions of the encompassing Word
of the Lord addressed to man: be my servant by loving
Me above all and your neighbor as yourself. One
of the many ways in which mankind can respond positively
to God's encompassing Word is the path of justice

which requires social space for the development of all of God's human creatures as persons. Since Christ has atoned for the sins of the world on the cross His disciples, as instruments of reconciliation, are mandated to oppose all sin, including injustice, and positively work for the establishment of a just social order. Within the political arena a just social order implies the state's recognition of men as citizens, as recipients of the good that governments as God's ministers are to bring about. That good is justice for every citizen irrespective of race, class, creed, income, ethnic background, etc. For this reason the state (with reference to its norm) must be a re-public, a res publica, a community of ciitzens responsible for the administration of public justice. No discrimination may take place in a state. As a matter of fact, it is especially the oppressed, the alien, the widow, the poor, the orphan, who should look to the state as his protector in time of need. The Bible provides ample evidence for this. The state is the Lord's instrument for the protection of the needy -- His little ones.

The first task of a Christian political movement is to clarify exactly what constitutes public justice for our society. For a new political action movement can make a contribution to the well-being of the state only when it has a lucid conception of justice relevant to the needs of the entire citizenry. Such a conception of justice, based on the biblical view of man, has not been fully developed for the North American scene **because we lack** a mature Christian social consciousness and practice. So developing a lucid conception of justice is our first assignment.

"Active Citizenship"

Let's return to the internal components of the state. Who should be responsible for the administration of public justice? Here we move from passive citizenship to active citizenship. In earlier times this task was often executed by one person (monarchy) or by a few (oligarchy). Since the time of the Renaissance and the Reformation the notion has gained ground that in principle the entire politically mature citizenry is really responsible for the affairs of state. That

337

notion is correct and in harmony with the Biblical
conception of man as the doer of God's Word in this
world. The normed development of states therefore
not only calls for the passive right of citizenship --
the right to receive justice -- but also for the
active participation of an ever-increasing body of
persons co-responsible for the direction of the state.
The criterion for this active participation is political maturity, or insight into the requirements of
justice for the entire citizenry.

A state in which the entire citizenry -- politically mature -- is finally responsible for the direction of the body politic is often called a democracy.
That is still a good word if it is employed in its
originally limited sense: a state whose key officers
are elected by the citizenry.

Government

This brings us to the next component of the state:
government. It is not my plan here to discuss various
conflicting theories of governemtn, such as fascism
(which identifies the state with the government),
anarchism (which denies the necessity of government),
or behavioral systems analysis (which looks upon
government as the body of institutions that make
authoritative decisions allocating values for an entire
society). The government is the total body of officers
and entrusted with the execution of justice within
the state or one of its parts. In the most fundamental sense of the word, the government is the civil
service: the minister of God for the good (justice)
of the entire state. The government is a body of
officers, that is, of persons entrusted with an
office, a divine assignment. This office requires
a measure of power so that its task can indeed be
realized. Only is this way can we speak of authority.
Political authority is power to implement the divine
norm of justice for the good of the entire citizenry.
Nothing more: that would lead to totalitarianism.
Nothing less: that would lead to anarchism.

So far we have detected three central components
of the modern state: passive citizenship (right to

e treated justly), active citizenship (right to co-
etermine the affairs of state), and government (ser-
ant of justice). There are many other elements that
ake up the internal chemistry of state-life: the
elation between governmental organs and departments,
etween the nation as a whole and its parts (states'
ights or provincial rights), taxation, fiscal policy,
olice, metropolitan politics, judiciary, etc. I
on't dwell on these now. My point is: any Christian
olitical movement in the US and Canada has to under-
tand the process of political interplay between the
hree elements mentioned above. For a political
ovement is interested in influencing the political
ecision-making process at the governmental level.
hat influence can be brought to bear upon local
overnment, state or provincial government, and the
ational government. There are indeed three inter-
ocking levels here. This implies that one cannot
se the word "political" meaningfully unless the last
ircle of the national setting is taken into account.

But that is precisely where the real problems
egin. For in Canada and the US there is a well-
established machinery that relates the citizenry to
overnment. The channels by means of which the citi-
ens are allowed to influence government are there,
ainly as a result of the Anglo-Saxon political experience
f more than two hundred years.

Government Interplay

There are three main channels: (1) parliamentary
odies where representatives chosen by the citizenry
an determine the standards for governmental action
y legislation; (2) political parties which present
andidates to the citizenry for representative func-
ions; (3) geographic districts which serve as the
electoral units within which the citizenry chooses
its representatives for state/provincial and national
legislative bodies.

These three existing channels, which converge into
a single stream, make the expression of a new political influence extremely difficult. The problem
begins with the district system of elections. It
is not necessary here to inquire into the origins

339

of the system: whether it is a remnant of feudalism --
linking man closely to the soil -- or a consequence of
the theory of popular sovereignty -- in which just
government was formally defined in terms of individual
consent to governmental authority. This theory
simply requires a majority vote of citizens in a local
district as a basis for legitimate representation.
It is important to know that: (1) the district system
of elections nullifies the votes of those citizens
whose candidates did not receive a majority or plura-
lity in their district or riding. (2) It tends to
promote the development of a two-party system. (3)
It tends to create an unjust imbalance between total
votes cast for a particular party and that party's
actual power in the legislature. Such an imbalance
is often increased by the presence of third parties,
as we see in the present Ontario provincial parliament. On the basis of 44% of the popular vote in
last October's election the Progressive Conservative
party holds 66% of the seats in the Ontario parliament. A goodly number of Ontario voters, 56% to be
exact, are "under-represented." Their votes brought
34% of the representatives of their choice into the
legislature. This example of an unfair imbalance between citizens' votes and the composition of legislative bodies -- a composition which in Great Britain
and Canada also determines who will be the chief
executive -- can be seen again and again.

The district electoral system is partly responsible for another problem as well. Since the results
of national, state or provincial elections are decided by obtaining pluralities in local districts,
election campaigns easily degenerate into popularity
contests between local candidates that often have little
to do with the broader issues at stake. Further, it
often reduces campaigns to survival-of-the-fittest
battles where the opportunistic and well-financed
candidate reaches first-base before his opponent has
a chance to grip the bat. In such battles money
often counts more than principle and political acumen.
The need for money to finance a campaign easily ties
elected officials more to the suppliers of money than
to the public welfare of the nation. The system invites corruption and opportunism, intensified by
brainwashing of the voters via paid political com-
mercials on radio and television. Finally, this

system leads to the potential identification of the national welfare with the welfare of numerous local constituencies on whose support an incumbent relies in the next round. This is notably so with members of the US House of Representatives who are only given a two-year term in Washington. Hence they must coddle their constituencies if they hope to survive for the next round. In this setting pork barrel politics is often the rule rather than the exception, with public funds appropriated for local improvements secured on a political patronage basis to ingratiate legislators with their constituents.

This electoral machinery tends to favor a two-party system because pluralities in local districts are what count, not proportional percentages of votes cast within the entire relevant political unit: the nation, the state or province, and the city. We now see two things. First, because political parties depend on local victories for their very existence, it is almost impossible for them to achieve their true purpose: to act as channels between an entire citizenry and a government. Political parties should be the organized expressions of the different conceptions of justice and authority present in the citizenry. Such conceptions should be clearly articulated in the political platforms and programs of parties, related to the total national welfare for a distinct period of political action. Political parties in the US and Canada cannot afford to be organized expressions of different conceptions of justice and authority. They're really conglomerations of local, state and provincial units loosely federated around pragmatic aims of roughly distinct economic classes and organized to win elections in geographic parts largely devoid of principles and programs for the whole.

In this context it is not surprising that platforms accepted at national party conventions hardly play a role in the actual political campaigns, especially in the US. It is not surprising that different political parties are the umbrella for an immense variety of really similar political **opinions** -- a phenomenon that, for instance, links southern conservatives to northern liberals in the US Democratic

Party. It is not surprising that millions of citizens
have no party affiliation and party commitments since
they do not trust these opportunistic vehicles. It
is not surprising that many citizens do not know how
to vote until the day of election: they cannot distinguish between the tweedledee and the tweedledum
of the options offered. It is not surprising that
millions of citizens don't bother to vote at all.
What difference does it make, anyway?

Finally, this electoral machinery defeats its very
purpose. For citizens whose political convictions
fall outside either party are in effect disenfranchised.
Two parties cannot possible offer enough options to
a citizenry divided among four or five basic political
conceptions. Thus representative legislative bodies
hardly represent the real alignment of political conviction at the grass-root level. And third-party
movements fact obstacles at every step of the way.
Their partial success, as with the socialist New
Democratic Party (NDP) in Canada, is generally based
on a pragmatic adjustment to the struggle for power
instead of principle that characterizes the entire
party-system. Does this system really permit a principled option, whether that be socialist or Christian?
The system effectively smothers the political witness
of minority groups and thus makes "democracy" an empty
word.

In view of all this, it should not come as a surprise that since the first world war parliamentary
government in the western democracies has been subjected to penetrating critique. Legislative bodies,
it is argued, seem to be out of touch both with the
people and with the executive organs of government.
There's a lot of truth in this critique. But I
would reject the solution offered by both fascists
and communists, viz. the elimination of parliamentary
government. Indeed, there are extra-parliamentary
avenues which can be used to influence the political
porcess. It may well be that a Christian political
movement can only use such avenues in the immediate
future. Public opinion and governmental agencies can
be influenced in a variety of ways. Nader's Raiders,
the neo-Marxists, and the Christian Labour Association
of Canada, have shown that. The very avenue of <u>dissent</u>

which belongs to the spiritual arsenal of Christians who have not identified the Kingdom of God with any political kingdom, is the first avenue of Christian political conviction. Nevertheless, a Christian political movement need not bypass the parliamentary system because it's part of the political scene in the US and Canada. Recognizing this makes talk of a new political movement utterly utopian for many. To me it is part of Christian realism. To me, it is also part of political honesty: the parliamentary system is part of politics, cannot be avoided and needs a drastic institutional overhaul to make it serve its authentic representative function for the entire citizenry.

2. THE STATE IN SOCIETY

So far I've focused on the internal operations of the state. We noticed how tough it is today for any group (especially for a new political voice) to influence the political decision-making process. The problem becomes even more complex when we turn from the internal structure of the modern state to its place in the entire societal scene. Society is the horizontal interdependent complex of the totality of human relationship. Within this broader context the state's administration of public justice concerns four main areas: (1) It must protect the individual civil rights of its subjects. (2) It must protect the beneficent development of the non-political spheres in society, such as marriage, family, the church, schools, universities, industry and commerce, the media, and other voluntary activities, without interfering with their internal freedom of operation.

(3) It must prevent the violation of the internal freedom of one societal sphere by the activities of another sphere and the development of one sphere at the expense of another. (4) The state must, finally, advance the interests of its citizenry as a whole in national and international life, in the context of an international legal order. The basis for political action in

these four directions must be legal, legitimate,
that is, it must be a concrete outworking of a
norm that the state itself does not establish but
to which it must subject itself. That is the
divine norm of justice. A state has no other
ground for action. Without that ground it degenerates into nothing or blows itself up into
everything - the all-absorptive totalitarian
state.

I'll briefly illustrate what I mean by these
four areas of state activity.

1. Civil rights.

Since membership in the state in principle is
as broad as the entire population, the state is
normatively bound to recognize, without discrimination, the civil rights of the entire population within its territory. For civil rights are
the political expression of human rights, that
is, of human personality. This entails the progressive elimination of discrimination in both
passive citizenship (right to just treatment) and
active citizenship (right to participate in the
co-determination of the affairs of state). The
state as a community of justice must work towards
removing discriminatory obstacles due to race,
religion, economic status, ethnic background,
etc. If a state cannot politically integrate its
entire population into a single community of
citizens equal before the law, then that state
either disintegrates or maintains itself as a
fascist institution, favoring one segment of the
population at the expense of the other. This is
the problem in the US race question, the place of
Quebec in Canada, the position of the blacks in
South Africa, the relation between Hindu and
Muslim in East Pakistan (now Bangladesh), limitation of citizenship to Jews in Israel, the tensions between Roman Catholics and Protestants in
Northern Ireland, and the one party system in
communist countries. In the measure that governments in these political communities are not
actively engaged in a program of equalizing civil

rights, in that measure these governments pursue a path of injustice preparatory to the modern equivalent of the religious wars of the post-Reformation period.

2. Sphere sovereignty.

The very notion of justice implies the state's protection - instead of absorption - of the internal freedom of the non-political sectors in society. It is the conception of social pluralism or - in Abraham Kuyper's words - sphere sovereignty. Its foundation lies in the biblical teaching of the Lordship of Christ, allegiance to Whom makes impossible total allegiance to any human institution, whether that be church or state or industry. The state-school problem clearly illustrates what is implied in the principle of sphere sovereignty. Allowing for a few (at times notable) exceptions, the US and Canada pursue a policy of educational socialism, that is, a policy in which the spiritual direction and the curriculum content of education from kindergarten through university are determined by the state. Through educational socialism the state can best guarantee assent to the realization of its political ideals. In this way the modern state has effectively eliminated political dissent to the religion of the "democratic way of life" which, in violation of the First Amendment of the US Constitution, is established in the hearts and minds of the great majority of citizens. Contrary to this form of socialism, the principle of sphere sovereignty affirms two basic points: (a) parents have the right to determine the religio-spiritual direction of the education of their children; (b) schools, colleges and universities must be free of state control if they are to perform their tasks meaningfully. Most of us pay lip-service to these basic points. But their realization would, of course, radically restructure what we now know as the public school system in the US and Canada.

3. Justice and capitalism.

The principle of sphere sovereignty implies industrial freedom, but it rejects capitalism. Society can be characterized as capitalistic when the industrial sector, especially of the larger corporate production conglomerates, is (a) given a special status in distinction from other cultural sectors, (b) is advantageously protected by political power at the expense of other cultural sectors, and (c) is given free reign in determining the society's values for its own benefit by means of a co-opted state-dominated education system and through excessive advertising. A capitalist society defines justice (and thus the task of the state) in its own light: it will induce the use of the state's immense power for the protection of productive forces and it will discourage the use of the state's power for "non-productive" elements in society such as the poor, the alien, the widow, and the orphan - and whatever else belongs to the category of these biblically loaded words in today's world. A redirection of the state's administration of justice is necessary in the industrial sector.

4. Metropolis.

A fourth area of the state's presence in society concerns the interests of the citizenry as a whole in national and international life. One can point to numerous examples: cultural development, medical care, education, ecological sanity, etc. One major facet of future politics concerns the growth of cities as the habitat of the greater majority of people during the next one hundred years. Metropoles must be human, not subhuman as they presently often are - especially in the US. Keeping or making them human implies a just interplay between numerous factors: residence, industry, leisure, transportation, mobility, psychical and social health, architecture, cultural facilities, etc. The metropolis, like society itself of which it is a microcosm, is a horizontal complex

weaving together nearly all of the human relations.
In this complex the political bond of munici-
pality is often the only bond which people have
in common. One does not have to argue therefore
that the predominant conception of justice and
political power within a society will color the
contours of future city-life. Will the future
metropolis be a City of Man, a survival-of-the-
fittest habitat, or will it reflect something of
the City of God, where men can live as God's
creatures?

3. THE INTERNATIONAL ORDER

The third major fact of politics deals with
the relations between states, generally referred
to as international relations. I will only
mention it here, though I consider it to be the
most important area of future politics. For in
this realm of politics the issues of war or peace
are to be decided. Whatever I have said above
about the internal components of the state and
about the state's activity in society depends upon
the question of whether peace between states can
be achieved. The history of politics since the
middle ages has been largely the history of
sovereign states doing sovereignly what their
power permitted them to do in the international
setting. Sovereignty did not belong to the Lord
Jesus Christ, the Creator and Recreator of the
universe. Sovereignty instead was the supreme
characteristic of autonomous states. Hence
the tragic history of political life in the West,
the bosom of Christendom, with its wars, its atom
bombs. And alongside of this history haunts us
with the failure of alliances for peace, of the
failure of the League of Nations, of the weakness of the United Nations, of arms races and cold
wars. Yes, all this too belongs to the stuff
of politics.

Conclusion

My reason for spending so much space on the
scope of politics is clear. We must at all costs

347

avoid a narrow conception of what is involved in politics. For that might from the outset imply a basic irrelevance by a confinement of action and reflection to some emergency actions or to some kind of neighborhood social evangelism. Political movements that arose out of concern for some single issue, no matter how important, never lasted long. Such movements, if they are to be of lasting value, must orient themselves to the very structure of state life.

The immensity of the task to be accomplished in the political arena is further complicated by the absence of unity, catholicity, apostolicity and holiness in the Christian Church in Canada and the USA. There is no general biblically-directed social and political consciousness on which one might rely.

What can we say today when we face these two polar realities: the bigness of the job to be done and the utter weakness of true-to-the-Bible Christianity as a cultural force? A few answers suggest themselves. We could say: The world of politics is neutral with respect to the claims of Christ; it can run its own affairs. Or: The world of politics belongs to the devil; let's stay away from it as far as possible. Finally: Let's join up with the best elements of humanism, either in its capitalistic or socialistic form, and see if we can't make this world a bit of a better place to live in. In 1972 most Christians, evangelicals included, give one of these three answers to our question.

These three answers, I think, are not worthy of the gospel of Christ, and for this reason I would propose an alternative: A genuine alternative demands the organization of a Christian political movement in both Canada and the United States. In each country the purpose of the organization would be twofold: (1) the establishment of a center for Christian political reflection where the building blocks for a practical political option would be developed; and (2) the establishment of an action division responsible for the implementation of a political program first in those states and provinces where sufficient support can be found among Christian citizens, and subsequently at the national livel in Ottawa and Washington.

This proposed alternative must be interpreted in an utterly realistic manner. It is not a utopian proposal. The full development and fruits of a Christian political option will not be seen in one generation. Further, the practical realization of such an option at the action front, even in a beginning way, will take considerably more than one generation even if the Lord revives His People. Patience, perseverance, proper priorities, and pain will be the watchwords of a movement for a new Christian politics. But we must start now. The parting words of Joey Smallwood, the former Premier of Newfoundland, are relevant to the position of Christians in politics: "It's not where you are. It's where you're headed that matters."

LAUNCHING A NEW SHIP

By William Harper

What should we do next in politics? That is to say, what should that group of people which holds the confusing mixture of conflicting attitudes, values, and practices to which to we assign the label of "evangelical" find itself doing for the next ten years? A brave question for an editor to pose and perhaps a foolhardy one for anyone to try to answer, but our responsibilities are so great and the biblical imperatives are so clear that an attempt at an answer must be made.

For the most part, evangelicals (and here for special historical reasons I must exclude those in the South) have occupied the center too far right of the ideological spectrum and have held membership in the Republican party. A certain number have been relatively apolitical though it is doubtful many were consistently so; the American culture puts great stress on citizen participation in government and evagelicals have respected the norms of the system with little hesitation.

There is evidence to suggest that some new elements are being stirred into the evangelical political brew. One is a higher level of interest and participation. Some signs of this are the Calvin College conferences on politics beginning in 1973 and a veritable blizzard of books dealing with politics and related issues by evangelical scholars and politicians. Whatever the particular topic under consideration, the underlying message has been unmistakable for the average man or woman in the pew: political activity is at least permissible and perhaps even necessary. Ironically, ten years after the heyday of New Left activism and the general ferment of the post-Kennedy era, when political apathy and cynicism seem to be on the increase in the culture at large, many evangelicals are at long last "getting politics."

Another element of the break with evangelical
politics-as-usual is the recent number of attempts
to make completely fresh starts in the way politics is viewed and practiced in this country.
One interesting effort, the so-called Post-
American group, initially began with a core of
former New Left activists. Feeling keenly that
politics could not be ignored, and appalled by
the unthinking acceptance of American institutional life by most evangelicals, they developed
a political model which drew heavily on the
historic Anabaptist tradition. This model en-
abled them to both participate in politics via
prophetic criticism of the status quo and to
satisfy their lingering fear of being co-opted by
institutional forms, especially political ones.
Another fresh start has been inspired by the
vigorous but previously ignored Christian cultural movement in the Netherlands of the past
eighty-five years. Though as critical of the
existing order as the Post-Americans, this group
has not been marked by the same ambivalence toward
institutional participation in the existing
political system. To date, however, its success
in North America has been in Canada rather than
the United States, where its insistence on a
distinctly Christian cultural witness causes it
to run afoul of our toned down but ever present
nature-grace dichotomy.

Neither of the above-mentioned efforts has
contributed to a decisive change in the character of evangelical politics, though both have
succeeded in breaking its rigid, lock step conformity with the American way of life. Two
elements that bid to be more influential must now
be considered. One aims to substitute ideological liberalism for ideological conservatism.
This has been a development promoted relentlessly
by many evangelical scholars who in some cases
seem determined to prove their authenticity and
legitimacy to their secular colleagues by destroying any hint of a necessary link between
evangelicalism and conservatism. Richard Pierard's
The Unequal Yoke provides a good example. After

being exposed to his devastating critique, one is left with the unmistakable conviction that the only alternative for the evangelical newly liberated from the bonds of political conservatism is political liberalism. Unfortunately for the cause of evangelical respectability, all this comes at a time when many secular scholars are moving away from liberalism, denouncing it as morally and intellectually bankrupt.

Far more important numerically at the present time is the expansion within evangelicalism of the political right, particularly that segment of it which relies on the time-honored formula of hyperpatriotism, individualism, free enterrpise, and law and order. Explicitly evangelical organizations are now being formed which identify true faith with radical conservatism. Republican Congressman John Conlan of Arizona has been especially active in this regard.

A 'Christian' politics

But are those the only options open to us as Christians? And what then of the future? My judgment is that the only course of action worthy of our time and money is one specifically Christian in its inspiration and outworking. Only something which is specifically Christian will be able to compete with the far-right's version of Christian America. What such action is and how to achieve it were laid out in detail by Bernard Zylstra several years ago in two Vanguard articles entitled, "Do Christians Have a Political Future?", but his main points are well worth recapitulating.

Zylstra's central notion is that Christians, whatever their cultural activity, should act "Christianly"; they should, among other things, exhibit unity and holiness, the prime characteristics of the Body of Christ. He proposes four steps to bring about his kind of Christian politics: 1) continue to try to convince evangelicals that politics is a necessary and not

optional expression of their faith commitment;
2) insure that those who go through step one begin
to perceive political reality as Christians and
not, for example, as liberals or conservatives;
3) establish a center of political reflection and
research to produce Christian policy alternatives;
4) have a Christian political movement ready to
promote those alternatives in appropriate ways.

There are three great strenths to these proposals.
One is realism; instead of considering the forty
million odd evangelicals in the country as in-
stantly capable of mobilization, Zylstra envisions
a painful and probably lengthy period during
which they must have their American idolatry
exorcized and transformed. Urging Christians to
"get involved" without such a reformation of
their political selves will merely perpetuate the
existing rot. Second, the proposals are flexible;
the stages can be pushed as rapidly (or as slowly)
as interest and resources permit. Total unity
need not be achieved before anything may be
attempted. Finally, the proposals take culture
and thus politics, seriously; they do not allow
any circumstances under which Christians could
relax in their attempts to see Christ's rule
heeded in this part of his Kingdom. This is
important, for evangelicals, unlike Marxists, have
yet to demonstrate the stamina and patience which
are demanded of serious political movements. It
is relatively easy to hurl prophetic thunderbolts
or withdraw to the company of the saints. What
is needed in politics is the same kind of commitment that evangelicals have historically only been
willing to give to harsh and unrewarding overseas
missions' fields.

The next step

Though what Zylstra recommends is basically
correct, it leaves us with a yawning void: what
do we do between now and the time a Christian
political movement is ready to make its mark?
Should we drop everything, ignore politics in
its present form, and marshal all our resources

for this task? Certainly the needs are great
enough to make such a course of action plausible.
That kind of decision, however, would overlook
the large number of Christians already involved
in politics and public service. Though most of
them are, to be sure, enmeshed in the coils of
existing party and ideological systems, or worse,
improvising without any sense of direction, they
represent valuable stores of electoral and governmental expertise that cannot be duplicated.
They must not be written off by a Christian
politics movement as so many junk cars or incorr-
igible criminals; they should be sought out,
nurtured, and employed as a vital part of any
new politics. The future will be bleaker than
it needs to be if we perceive the choices as
no more than working passively within the existing system with all of its shortcomings or trying
to build a Christian alternative out of thin air.
The course recommended here is to provisionally
endure what we must and use what we can in the
work of Christians presently in public life,
while simultaneously working to change the general
climate and specific contexts within which they
function. We can expect these Christians to
behave in ways significantly different than their
secular counterparts only as the latter two conditions are significantly improved. As a re-
source-poor political community we have no other
choice.

In theory, at least, any existing organization
ought to be able to adapt itself to this kind of
orientation. In this context, two new efforts
might be particularly helpful. One is a caucus
of Christians in Congress similar to the black
caucus which already exists. Such a group would
be bi-partisan in nature and serve many purposes:
a forum to air new ideas, a sourse of mutual
encouragement, and a means whereby the Christian
public could identify and relate to Christians in
office. In short, it could be a first step in
the formation of a sense of political community
among Christians.

The other effort which might be useful is a

political newsletter aimed at the evangelical
community; there are many political newsletters
in existence, serving a wide variety of constituencies with apparently good results. It might
go to a relatively small group of opinion leaders.
They would gain a deeper understanding of current
developments than that normally provided by newspapers or news magazines and would be introduced
to Christian policy alternatives as they become
available. If done well, it would complement
the sense of Christian political community represented by the caucus.

Is the next step possible? Twenty years ago
the answer sould have been an unqualified "No."
Conventional politics then meant Democrats and
Republicans, religion was practiced properly on
Sunday, and minorities were thought to have been
disposed of in the legendary melting pot. Today, under the impact of the civil rights movement,
the New Left, the anti-war protest, women's liberation and assorted other causes fueled in part
by a decaying social order and rampant cultural
relativism, the situation is quite different.
True, we still sail into political battle in
the same old party and ideological ships, but
the captains clearly lack confidence in their
missions and many of the long-suffering crews
are openly mutinous. The risk and folly is in
continuing to sail in these "coffin ships" of
the old order instead of launching our own.

A CALL FOR THE LIBERATION
OF NORTH AMERICAN CHRISTIANS

By Clark H. Pinnock

Because we must hear and obey the Word of
God in a specific context, many Christians are
seriously asking after the divine command for
them in a world largely poor and hungry. A
"theology of liberation" is in the air. Latin
American and Black theologians are pressing for
a radical understanding of what it means to do
the truth in a situation of oppression and
suffering. We dare not, as Hugo Assmann has
warned us, reduce their efforts to a new toy
on the theological playground of the affluent,
Western thinkers. Instead we are summoned to
enter into the same struggle, to hear the Lord
of God ourselves in a world of poverty and dire
distress. Evangelicals have in recent years
been rather more inclined to defend the gospel
than to practice it. Yet a defending of the
gospel which is not matched by a living of it is
hollow and ungenuine. The "theology of liberation" is in reality God's instrument for the
refinement of our own commitment to the gospel,
and has been leading many to reflect on the
need for the liberation of North American Christians.

Theological Groundwork

Before issuing such a call, there is a theological assumption to be stated and accepted.
All believers in Jesus Christ have been summoned
to a life of radical discipleship, oriented to
his cross (Mark 8:34). Although the point is
familiar and obvious, grounded in the most certain and lucid commands of our Lord himself, it
is here that many of us have become stalled. We
do not wish to think that the gospel might have
radical, life-changing implications for the entire
range of our existence. Nevertheless, according
to the New Testament, it most certainly does.
Paul describes the "reasonable" service of the
believer in Jesus in terms of the presenting of

356

believer in Jesus in terms of the presenting of
our bodies to God as a living sacrifice (Rom.
12:1). Such a metaphor can only be termed
"radical," calling as it does for a total, un-
reserved commitment of the whole life to God.
We are invited to respond to Christ on no other
terms than these.

Furthermore, the general shape of our discipleship also is made unmistakably clear as an
orientation to the cross of Jesus, a life
patterned in accordance to the normative event
of the gospel. In the cross, as Peter says,
Christ has left us an example that we should
follow in His steps (I Pet. 2:21). Because He
was among us as one who serves, we are to be
present in the world after the manner of servanthood. The presence of a community following this
rule is, according to Jesus, a primary mark and
sign of the truth of the gospel and the coming
of the kingdom of God, a city on a hill which
cannot be hidden, the pilot project of an entirely new order. The call for the liberation
of North America Christians is based on the
well-founded assumption that radical discipleship in the mode of servanthood is a primary
demand of the gospel. It is so plainly scriptural that it scarcely can be denied in principle.

The Context of Our Obedience

Christian discipleship in this mode does not
take place in a vacuum. It has to be fleshed out
in the particular cultural setting where we are,
in relation to a critical reflection on our
social, political, and personal situation, in
which we are expected to act responsibly before
God. Just as our Lord in the incarnation identified with the needs and condition of people
in His day, so we are sent to shine as lights in
the world of our day, addressing its central
concerns as we proclaim good news.

As soon as anyone undertakes to analyze the

357

worldly context in which we live, personal
assumptions and perceptions rise swiftly to
the surface to influence the mental image.
Nevertheless, such a judgment has to be made,
and on the particulars of which I am thinking
there is already widespread agreement. The
global context of discipleship is simply grim,
and beset with crises, on a colossal scale. We
are being reminded from every quarter of the
awful disparities in wealth between nations, of
the enormous investments in deadly armaments,
and of the frantic consumption and irresponsible
pollution of the earth's limited resources. The
North American context, on the other hand, in
relation to the global one, sees itself as a
safety island, unaffected by these harsh realities, and largely indifferent to cries for help
issuing from the Third World. One need not be
an economist or ecologist to sense the enormity
of the world's crises, nor an ethical philosopher or theologian to feel shame and outrage
at the moral callousness involved in our collective North American behavior. Let us consider
two items.

Item One: No Mercy

    North Americans - and Christians are not an
outstanding exception - are continuing to con-
sume the products of earth at indefensively
high rates and appear to be firmly set on reaching even higher levels, at the very time when
it is a matter of public record that unaccounted
millions are seriously malnourished and even
starving. To put it most mildly, we are insensi-
tive to the cries of the world's poor. Like the
rich man with Lazarus at his gate, we are largely
indifferent to the distress of the needy. Like
ancient Sodom, we "have surfeit of the food and
prosperous ease, but do not aid the poor and
needy" (Ezek. 16:49). Of course humanitarian
aid has not been wholly lacking. Mission and
relief agencies in particular have faithfully
tried to channel funds to needy situations.
Even the U.S. and Canada have been active in aid

to the poor countries. But it should be recognized that, although these gestures are good, the effort hitherto has been meager and half-hearted. A serious attempt to assist the world-s poor has not been made except by a very few, and we stand condemned as pretty largely indifferent to the problem. How then do we suppose we shall escape the wrath of God, we who hold down the truth in unrighteousness? God's Word warns us: "He who closes his ear to the cry of the poor will himself cry out and not be heard" (Prov. 21:13). How can we deny that the attitude of North Americans in general is callous, pleasure seeking, and hardhearted in the face of the world situation? Are we not behaving in a merciless manner that is both globally irresponsible and morally depraved?

Item Two: No Justice

As if that were not enough, to this relative absence of tender-heartedness must be added a shocking lack of justice and fair play. The fact that we control a disproportionately large share of the world's real wealth is partly due to our domination of "world trade," a new economic colonialism by which we have repatriated large profits from countries which have only some basic raw material to sell and a large supply of cheap labor. In every way they are disadvantaged in relation to our superior economic leverage and technical development. We are rather like the fat sheep in Ezekiel's pathetic picture which "push and thrust at the weak until they are scattered abroad" (Ezek. 34:21). We, the wealthy six percent of the earth's population, cluster around the well of the earth's resources and drink deeply from it, while the vast majority of peoples are shunted aside lapping up the trickles that spill from our cups.

Why do we act in this way? What can account for such behavior? Suppose a visitor arrived from outer space and discovered a small group of people feasting on abundance while the majority

was in need; found them pursuing policies which
drove the poor deeper into despair; and saw them
refusing to accept even a slight lowering of
their standard of living out of considerations
of mercy and of justice. What would he think?
Surely he could only conclude that this small
but favored minority was in a condition of
bondage to the godlike power of materialism and
comfort over them, which had closed their hearts
and minds to the most elementary demands of justice and mercy. Although God's Word is unequivo-
cally clear in such matters, it would seem that
"the cares of the world, the delight in riches,
and the desire for other things have entered in,
and choked the Word so that it proves unfruit-
ful" (Mark 4:19). The Word of God is choked
in the churches of North America. Our comfortable
life and culture have blinded our eyes to the
scriptural teaching about tenderheartedness, stewardship, and justice. I see no way to deny,
though I wish it were not so, that the context
in which the Bible is to be responsibly read and
applied today is that of a suffering and poor
world, containing a small pocket of affluence,
in which the privileged, among whom are to be
counted most North American Christians, are
largely indifferent to the hungry millions at
their gate. If the Bible is to be believed,
and if this situation is not changed by the
costly repentance of these favored few, all we
can expect is the wrath and indignation of the
God who regards the needy and hears their cry.
Where is there mercy and justice amongst us?

Liberation from Bondage to Mammon

I am convinced that God does not desire to
pour out his wrath on the peoples of North
America, but wants his church as a significant
remnant on this continent to experience liberation from bondage to Mammon and enter into
lives of credible and costly discipleship. In
order to spell out some of the implications of
this liberation, we will consider what it may
mean to us as individuals, as congregations,

and even as nations, to obey God's command to
us today.

Liberation as It Applies to Us Individually

Although we can think globally, we can really
act only locally. The watchword has to be downward mobility. The per capita consumption in
the West measured against the limited resources
of spaceship earth and when placed into relation
with world poverty, is obviously too high. Our
lifestyles must be simplified, and our consumption scaled down. In line with the "Macedonian
example" which Paul related to the Corinthian
church (II Cor. 8-9), we must begin to share
goods in a way that cuts into our standard of
living, so that the voluntary self-impoverish-
ment of Jesus may be fleshed out among us, and
there may be a semblance of "equality" created.
It is simply a matter first of tenderheartedness: ·
how can we live affluently with the eyes of the
poor upon us? and secondly, a matter of justice:
what gives us the right to accept the privileged
position of the world's upper classes consuming
far beyond our fair share and as a result accen-
tuating the desperate plight of the poor? "Downward mobility" has nothing to do with asceticism,
which despises comfort, good food, and adequate
shelter. These things are good, and we wish they
were the lot of every man. Life cannot be fully
human without a satisfactory physical base beneath it. But an overabundance of these things
in a world where our excess is confronted by
extreme want is not good or right.

I believe that God is calling North American
Christians to a life which is simpler - simpler
in diet, in housing, in entertainment, and so
forth - a life that celebrates God's jubilee,
his good news for the poor and a righting of
economic wrongs. Let us accept for ourselves   ·
the spartan life which we have asked missionaries
to live in our stead in the past, and incorporate
into our evangelical spirituality dimensions of
practical mercy, simplicity, and justice. Jesus

promised that those who lose their lives in
costly discipleship will find them again. It
belongs to the paradox and irony of the gospel
that precisely this commitment to a simpler way
results in a full and a better life in the end.
Against the Madison Avenue lie, Jesus said
pointedly, "A man's life does not consist in the
abundance of his possessions." God is calling
us as individual believers to test the truth of
these words in our day. How else can a Christian
be said to carry the cross in a hungry world?

Liberation as It Applies to Us as Congregations

To be a Christian at all is to have been
joined by the Spirit to the body of Christ, a
fellowship in the context of which the tender
plant of our individual Christian freedom is to
be nurtured, challenged, and directed. It is
very difficult for an individual believer to be
radical in his obedience if his congregation or
fellowship circle remains indifferent and com-
placent. The anemic commitment of local congregations in North America to issues of human need
and social justice is most discouraging. Instead
of being seedbeds nurturing prophetic concerns,
they have become safety islands from which these
concerns are often excluded. And all this is
paralleled ironically by a considerable interest
in "church growth." Surely the mere numerical
growth of congregations, if it is resulting in
the proliferation of pseudo-disciples who can
hardly distinguish the cross from the flag, is
a very mixed blessing. The "church growth" most
urgently needed in North America is growth in
the knowledge of the biblical God, who loves
justice and mercy, and who calls us all without
exception to costly discipleship. We are most
definitely in favor of quantitative evangelization and are opposed to its being substituted
by or changed into the struggle for social justice. But what we must insist on is a radical-
izing of evangelism so that it is more than an
individualistic and spiritualistic exercise and
involves calling people to accept the full and

undiminished lordship of Jesus.

The New Testament congregations nurtured
people in radical discipleship. They shared
with each other so that economic needs were met,
and practiced spiritual gifts that led them to
feed and house those who were hungry and homeless. When the Spirit first fell, their economic thinking was so radicalized that they sold
their possessions, pooled their resources, and
moved in the direction of a social order in
which there was justice and equality. Since
that time there have been some sterling examples in the experience of the churches where
God's people have ventured out in faith, risked
their won comfortable security, and expended
themselves in Jesus' name on behalf of the
needy. Let us build up congregations that proclaim the jubilee of God's justice, that stand
for the ongoing servant presence of Jesus in
the world, that cross over the road and stand
by the needy neighbor in his plight. Until we
move in this direction, we are not really loving
God and the neighbor as Jesus commanded us.
Jedgment begins with the people of God. We are
being weighed in the balances. God is inspecting
the vineyard which he planted to see what fruit
is hielding. It is time for all of us in our
congregations to take stock, and bring our
priorities into line with the stated purposes
of God for the church.

Jesus has called his church to be a servant
people ministering to all the needs of mankind.
Much progress in social history has come about
through the impact of radical biblical ideas
upon the human spirit. Yet, sadly, as we have
become successful and established, we have come
to identify with the interests of the ruling
classes and the established order, producing
bourgeois Christianity, a church no longer willing to care for the needy and hear their cry.
Against such a church both God and man will
arise in protest and disgust. Let us repent
and return to our radical roots.

Liberation as It Applies to Our Nations, the United States and Canada

All Christians can agree that God's Word contains principles that are politically relevant, and need to be injected into present day discussions and decision making. I will list three of them: stewardship, neighborliness, and justice. First, since God has given the earth to all peoples as a sacred trust, it follows that no group has the right to exhaust the earth's limited resources in a lifestyle of unbridled consumption and as a result severely pollute the creation because of their insatiable greed. We must call for a global ethic based on the creational principle of stewardship. It is not enough to ask what will benefit our country. We must also ask what is just and right from a global perspective. Second, because God has made mankind of one stock, in personal relationship and mutual interdependence one with another, it follows that no group has a right to live in a wasteful and selfish way while huge numbers of their fellowmen lack even the basic elements of a decent standard of living. We have no right, for example, to feed huge quantities of our grain to cattle at the very time when millions perish for want of bread. People born into God's world have an inalienable right to eat, and it is a basic ethical obligation of ours to secure that right for them if we can. Third, in terms of justice, it is simply intolerable that six percent of the human race should have a corner on seventy percent of the world's real wealth. A "new international economic order" is essential as a matter of fairness. So long as the desire for profit motivates the world economic system, the needs of the poor cannot be met. Such a system serves only those who can command recources and enter into the market as purchasers. We have come to the point where, in the name of simple justice, human need must be put before profit, and resources must be shifted from wasteful, destructive projects into human development. Barbara Ward estimates that only one-half of the world's annual expenditures on armaments ($100 billion) would fund all the works of mercy and peace for an entire decade and result in significantly alleviating all of the major problems presently obstructing the prospect of a decent kind of life for the world's people. With such self-righteousness we look down on the minority of White settlers in Rhodesia, and we wonder what stops them from sharing the blessings of a well-endowed country with their Black majority. Why don't they move toward a social order which would be fairer and in every way wiser even from the viewpoint of simple survival, we ask. But we really need not wonder about it when we in North America are every bit as reluctant to give up our position of affluence on behalf of the hungry billions, and seem as intent as they are on global suicide rather than facing the awful prospect of justice. Nevertheless, it is no exaggeration to say that if we refuse to face up to global injustice today, tomorrow's world is likely to be horrible and violent beyond imagination.

The Bible offers politically relevant criteria that need to be injected into the processes of planning and governing. God is calling for political obedience. For the first time in history, the necessities of the situation and the obligations of the gospel practically coincide. Loving the neighbor has never before been so much a matter of political common sense. It is a time of God's testing. The handwriting is on the wall. The words of the prophets are on the subway walls. Let us arise and seek God's kingdom and his justice.

Conclusion

Evangelicals of late have been more inclined to defend the gospel than to do it. Before us there is a costly decision: whether to break with the false god Mammon and follow after Jesus, or to go back and turn aside because we have great possessions. Jesus said it was hard for the "haves" to enter the kingdom of God because of the demands the gospel makes upon them. False gods do not give up their captives without a struggle. We wrestle not against flesh and blood but against the fallen powers of darkness. Liberation will come only through the miracle working activity of the Spirit of God in our lives. But if that is what we want, and if we are willing to repent and really change at deep levels, then we can experience liberation. We are being weighed in the balances. Will we be faithful and wise stewards pursuing the will of the Lord, or faithless, disobedient servants who will in the end be punished and placed with the unbelievers?

WILL THERE BE A CHRISTIAN PROBLEM

By Theodore Plantinga

A possible title for this article ("The Jewish Problem as a Challenge for Christians") might seem to imply that the Jewish problem is not the Jews' problem but our problem. This is indeed the view of some writers who have dealt with this question. Louis Golding, in a little book entitled The Jewish Problem published just before the second World War, writes:

"The Jewish Problem is in essence a Gentile problem...I mean that the Jewish Problem has been a Gentile Problem from the very first decades in which it raised its baneful head, and will remain so until the Gentiles themselves have solved it. There is no contribution the Jews themselves can make toward a solution which is not sooner or later pronounced an aggravation." As we have seen, Jean-Paul Sartre holds a similar view, arguing that the Jew as Jew is a creation of the anti-Semite. If this is indeed the truth about the Jewish problem, a commitment on the part of non-Jews to halt anti-Semitic thinking, talk and behaviour should suffice to solve the Jewish problem."

Eminent Christians have been known to take similar attitudes. In a book entitled A Christian Looks at the Jewish Question (1938), the French Catholic philosopher Jacques Maritain quotes with approval a statement of Pope Pius XI, who had declared in September of 1938: "Anti-Semitism is unacceptable. Spiritually we are Semites." Maritain adds: "No stronger word has been spoken by a Christian against anti-Semitism..." The Pope, of course, is correct in declaring that anti-Semitism is unacceptable to Christians, for there is a definite spiritual kinship between Christians and Jews between Christianity and Judaism. Furthermore, as human beings Jews are entitled to the same rights and protections that the law affords any other citizens, and hence the restrictive measures that have been taken against Jews in many countries are wrong. Many of the Christians of occupied Europe during the second World War realized this, and therefore they resisted Nazi anti-Semitic politices; the King of Denmark even went so far so to wear a yellow star of David in public when this traditional Jewish emblem was made mandatory for all Jews.

Those Christians who insist that there is room for Jews to live as Jews in western Europe and North America today do so on the basis of an old notion of religious tolerance. A sharp distinction is drawn between the public sphere and the private sphere, and religious faith and practice are relegated to the latter. Christians have long lived with such a reduction of the meaning of their own faith, and many of them see not reason why the Jews cannot do the same. This way of thinking, of course, has it roots in certain views about the relation between revelation and reason, faith and culture, that arose during the Middle Ages. On this question there are striking parallels between Christian, Jewish and Islamic thinkers, for many of these thinkers freely borrowed ideas from thinkers of opposing faiths. Thus we find the same kinds of views that are expressed in Christian circles about the relation between religious faith and public life also being voiced is a private matter, we are told, then Jews in their public lives can be faithful, participating members of the communities in which they live, just as Christians have done for the last two centuries.

Most Jewish writers, however, realize that there is more to the matter. They realize that the Old Testament and the Talmud are concerned not only with ritual observances but also with questions of social justice and the everyday affairs of the human community. Therefore they admit that the Jewish tradition can and does

conflict with the political and social ideals
and values of some nations (e.g., Nazi Germany).
Milton Steinberg, a liberal American Jew and the
author of A Partisan Guide to the Jewish Problem
(1945), is well aware of the potential conflict.
Describing himself as a "survivalist" rather than
an assimilationist, Steinberg raises the question whether Judaism or being a Jew is compatible
with "Americanism" (a term that he does not
hesitate to use). His answer:

> Let is be recalled that I acknowledge only
> one political allegiance - to America; just
> as I profess only one religion - the Jewish.
> Here there is certainly no cause for conflict.
> Beyond that, I have two heritages - the
> American and the Hebraic. English is my
> language and that of my children. I was
> educated in the public schools of my commun-
> ity. The history of America is my history.
> But Hebrew is my tongue too, and Jewish his-
> tory my background also. Lincoln and Jeff-
> erson are my heroes together with Moses,
> Akiba and Maimonides. They all get along
> in my imagination most companionably. When
> I read Van Wyck Brooks on New England in its
> flowering and autumn it is in my own literary
> past that I am being instructed. I have
> studied Spiegel's Hebrew Reborn with the same
> sense of identification. I sing Negro
> spirituals, American ballads and Hasidic or
> Palestinian fold songs with equal ardor. On
> the Fourth of July I set off fireworks and
> attempt to transmit to my children an appre-
> ciation of the significance of the occasion.
> With equal earnestness I kindle Hanukkah
> lights and discuss with them the meaning of
> that festival. At no time am I conscious
> of strain between the two worlds. I move from
> one to the other with such naturalness that
> I am scarcely aware of the change in spiritual
> locale.

The process is immensely facilitated by
the essential sympathy in spirit between the

two traditions. Both are democratic. Both
emphasize the worth of the individual and
his wright to freedom. In both there is
passionate devotion to the ideal of social
mustice. And the vision of the more abundant
life is a secularized parallel of the ancient
Jewish dream of the Kingdom of God on earth.

This striking statement, like much of Jewish
thinking, runs closely parallel to the thinking
of some Christians. The prevalent Christian
dichotomy between "public" school education (for
training in the Canadian or American heritage)
and "religious" instruction in the church and
home (for training in the Christian heritage) is
based on just such thinking.

The difficulty with Steinberg's answer
to the Jewish problem, which amounts to a semi-
assimilationism, is that it has not worked out
in history. The balance between assimilation
and separation has not been and can never be
maintained for long. Some Jews who have attempted
it have eventually become totally assimilated and
virtually indistinguishable from their non-
Jewish neighbours. And those who have managed
to remain faithful to the Jewish religion have
earned the hostility of their nieghbours and have
thereby wound up living the life of separation.

Jewish public witness leads to hate

We have seen that writers like Golding and
Sartre look for the roots of **anti**-Semitism in
the non-Jew. But anti-Semitism can be better
understood on the basis of the Jewish religious
message. It appears that **wherever** a public
witness to the Jewish faith has been raised, it
has given rise to antagonism - and even hatred.
As long as the western world was dominated by
the Christian faith, the existence of the Jews
as Jewish believers was a public testimony against
that faith, and the inevitable result was hostility, distrust, suspicion, and antagonism. In
the eighteenth century the leadership of western

civilization was taken over by a new faith, Humanism, which has become ever more secularized and radicalized as time passed. The existence of the Jews as Jewish believers was also a public testimony against the truth of this faith, and again there was a hostile reaction. But with this new faith the rationale for anti-Semitism underwent a change, and with it the recommended solution to the Jewish problem. The anti-Semitism of the Christian era had reproached the Jews for crucifying Christ and rejecting the gospel, and it demanded the conversion of the Jews. But because the new Humanist faith was not entirely willing to admit that it was also a faith, the anti-Semitism of the Humanist era brought absurd, pseudo-scientific racial charges against the Jews. For the adherents of this essentially intolerant faith conversion was no longer an adequate solution; its more radical members demanded the elimination of the Jews from public life - by physical confinement, emigration, or extermination. Consequently, the anti-Semitism of the Humanist era has led to some of the most savage butchery that the world is ever likely to witness.

Some Jews, then, believe that their Jewish culture and beliefs are fully compatible with the religious worldview and beliefs of the dominantly Humanistic communities in which they live, but judging by the course of history during the last 100 years we must conclude otherwise. Public profession of Jewish belief is an offence to Humanism, just as Elijah's taunting of the priests of Baal was an offence to the worshippers of Baal (see I Kings 18). Thus race is not the most basic issue in the Jewish problem; the real issue is the stubborn refusal of certain Jews to worship the gods of our day and to publicly approve the prevailing way of life. As long as Jews continue to resist the dominant Humanist faith, it is likely that they will be maligned. What this all adds up to is that there is no easy solution to the Jewish problem, for the cost of the solution (i.e., complete assimilation

and acceptance of the Humanistic way of life)
is more than believing Jew would be and should
be willing to pay.

At ease in Zion?

But the Jews are not the only religious
community in North America whose principles and
confession of faith stand opposed to the dominant Humanist faith. There are also millions of
Christians in Canada and the United States. Do
they earn the enmity and hatred of the humanist
community by refusing to worship the Humanist
gods? Or is 'hatred' too strong a word to use
in this connection? Many Christians would insist that it is, and that Christians must think
only in terms of love. They would have us believe
that if the Christian lives his life in love and
obedience to God's will, he can expect only
love and acceptance from his non-Christian neighbours. But this is hardly what Jesus said to
his disciples when he spoke to them at length
before his crucifixion: "If the world hates
you, it hated me first, as you know well. If
you belonged to the world, the world would love
its own; but because you do not belong to the
world, because I have chosen you out of the
world, for that reason the world hates you"
(John 15:18-19). Is this our situation as
Christ's followers in North America in the twentieth century? And if not, is it because we are
not living in obedience to his commands?

'Hatred' is indeed a strong word, but we must
not be afraid to use it in describing the attitudes of the many false faiths to the true faith.
Liberal Protestants would have us believe that
the "essence" of Christianity (its ethical content) is virtually identical with the ethical
content of Humanism, and that the full blossoming
of both can only lead to a detente and full reconciliation between them. But this way of
thinking is far from the truth that Christ spoke,
for he emphasized that he is the only way to the
Father. If we take Christ at his word, we must

372

face up to the fact that antagonism - and even hatred - will result whenever Christians stand up honestly in the face of Humanism. As long as Christians stay within their churches, the Humanist community will probably be tolerant. But once the Christian faith is carried into public life, tolerance breaks down and is replaced by fury.

Will there be a Christian problem?

The title which I have chosen for this article is not "The Christian Problem" but "The Christian Problem?", for, unlike the Jews, the Christians in this part of the world simply do not constitute a recognized problem with a name of its own. Therefore we can only ask if there is - or perhaps should be - a Christian problem. At present the North American Humanist community simply does not recognize a Christian problem; Christians may be laughed at, but they are seldom taken seriously. No one would think of asking what is to be done about the Christians. But I am fully concinced that if Christians, as witness to the Way, the Truth and the Life, speak out about North American public life on the basis of a scriptural view of man and society and act according to their conviction, there will be a Christian problem. In this regard our Christian forefathers had more courage than we possess. The Christians in the time of the Roman emperor Nero refused to take part in the pagan religious rites of Rome. The Roman empire thus had a Christian problem, and many Christians lost their lives as witnesses to their faith. But here in North America we are content to believe that the demands which our faith lays upon us are perfectly compatible with "Americanism" and the democratic way of life. And as for the world hating us - that must be a reference to the communists in Russia, China and Vietnam!

As I have tried to stress, it is time

373

that the Christians of North America give
full expression to their faith - not only in
their churches but also in the public life of
this continent, both by speaking out on public
issues and by taking concrete action. If we as
Christians commit ourselves to such a program,
then the Jewish reaction to the Jewish problem
has some lessons and a challenge for us.

First, it is striking that many of the Jewish leaders, as well as their supporters, were
led to do something about their situation because of anti-Semitism and anti-Jewish actions.
Moses Hess and Theodor Herzl did not become
Zionists by attending synagogues or reading
books. Hess's thinking was changed by the Dam-
ascus blood libel of 1840, and Herzl became a
Zionist only when he experienced the depth of
anti-Semitic feeling as a witness to the Drey-
fus affair. Eastern Europe, the traditional
stronghold of Zionism, is also the area where
the Jews have suffered the most during the last
two centuries. And the murder of millions of
Jews during the second World War finally suc-
ceeded in making virtually every surviving Jew
a supporter of the idea of a Jewish state in
Palestine. Yet, by the time that this **broad**
support was finally achieved, the battle for
Israel had in principle been decided.

Action plus results lead to growth

If there is a real parallel between Zionism
and what some radical Christians in North America
are trying to achieve, the following lesson can
be drawn. Christians will, in general, be convinced of the necessity of Christian social,
cultural and political action only after they
have seen such action and its results. Christian
schools get broader support once they have shown
what they can achieve. Even such confrontations
as those between the Christian Labour Association
of Canada and the huge, secular labour unions are
useful, for they reveal an ugly side to our society which is apparently unknown to many unsuspect-

374

ing Christians. Hence the struggle for equality
and religious freedom under the law should continue in areas like labour, education and politics.
Many Christians fear conflict, but we must learn
to distinguish carefully between the conflict
that is carried out in courts, legislatures and
the press and the violence used by many revolutionary groups to attain their goals.

Don't postpone responsible action

Second, the story of the success of Zionism
suggests that it would be a mistake to postpone
action until all - or even most - Christians
are agreed on what must be done. If the Zionists
had waited for full support, there would be no
state of Israel today. They eventually got
broad support and should not expect to be able
to talk the majority of their fellow believers
into agreement.

By calling for action before the support of
the majority is gained, I am not opening the
door to irresponsible decisions. The Zionists
achieved their ultimate success only because
their support grew as the years went by. And
one of the main reasons for the increase in
their support was that Zionists had shown that
their proposals were responsible and feasible,
relative to the circumstances in which the Jews
found themselves. At the beginning many skeptics laughed at the idea of a Hebrew-speaking
Jewish nation and state in the barren land of
Palestine. It took decades of work to prove
that the skeptics were wrong, that it could be
done. Similarly, Christian action in the fields
of labour, education, politics, and communication media will gain the success envisioned at
the outset only if its proponents are able to
convince their skeptically inclined fellow believers that a Christian university, a Christian
political party, a Christian labour union, and
a Christian public press are indeed feasible.
If they are not able to prove this within a
reasonable period of time, the movement will fail

and become a mere footnote to Christian history. But if they wait for broad support before trying to prove their point, they will not even rate a footnote.

Third, it would be instructive to consider the role of the leaders of the worship institutions in the Zionist struggle and in the struggle of North American Christians committed to Christian action. It is noteworthy that we find very few rabbis in the ranks of the Zionists. The rabbis were more inclined to advocate the kind of semi-assimilationist position expressed by Milton Steinberg in the quotation above or the traditional view that the return to Zion will be accomplished only through divine intervention and the coming of the Messiah. Thus, the Association of Rabbis in Germany condemned Herzl's First Zionist Congress. Even rabbis in Palestine took a dim view of the **energetic** efforts of early Zionist colonists there to lay the foundations for a Jewish state.

There was a reason for this opposition on the part of the rabbis. When the Jews of the modern era accepted the reduced role which religious observance was to play in life according to the Humanist vision of society, the Jew's life as Jew came to be concentrated almost completely around the activities of the synagogue (a sharp contrast with Jewish life in the Old Testament). This naturally enhanced the power and prestige of the rabbis in the Jewish community. Many rabbis saw the growth of Zionism as a threat to the modus operandi that had slowly been worked out with the Gentile world, as well as a threat to their own leadership. Furthermore, some of them had accepted the Humanistic way of thinking about religion (i.e., the equation of religion with worship activities), and thus they could not see the Zionist enterprise had anything to do with the Jew as believer. Many of them therefore opposed Zionism for entirely honest reasons: they feared that it would distract the Jews from religious observance and eventually destroy the Jewish faith community.

Many of the Zionist leaders seemed to realize
that the rabbis could hardly be expected to be
whole-hearted supporters of Zionism, and hence
they did not make too much of the issue. They
generally ignored the attacks of the rabbis and
issued their appeals directly to the Jewish
people. Consequently, tensions between the
Zionist leaders and the Jewish clergy were
never strained to the breaking point, and as
time went by more and more of the rabbis went
over to the Zionist position.

The parallel with the Christian situation
is direct and obvious. Christians in the modern
world are forced to live with the same equation
of religion and worship activities, and they too
tend to concentrate their lives as believers
around institutions of worship. It should therefore come as no surprise that the leaders of
these institutions of worship tend to view Christian action in non-ecclesiastical areas as a
potential or actual threat to the health of the
church. It is true that movements for Christians
action have nonetheless been able to count clergymen and church leaders among their most faithful
supporters, but it is also true that the emergence of various non-ecclesiastical Christian
organizations in North America has had a disrupting effect on the lives of many churches
whose members have been involved. That the
clergy associated with such churches become sus-
picious and somewhat hostile is only to be expected. By virtue of their office, they bear a
tremendous responsibility to the institutional
church. Therefore they are rightfully fearful
of anything that might in any way undermine the
position of the church in the Christian community
or in society in general.

Little to be gained from stirring up clergy

Some clergy, of course, have accepted the
Humanistic vision of religion as a private,

optional matter involving only worship, and hence they will not become supporters of Christian action unless there is a major change in their thinking. But most Christian clergy in orthodox churches do confess that obedience to Christ involved the entirety of human life and thus cannot be locked up in any "private" sector of our lives. These Christians should be supporters of Christian action, and in time most of them probably will be - as long as it is demonstrated that what is proposed is both feasible and responsible, given the present situation of Christians in North America. Meanwhile, their seemingly excessive concern for the welfare of the church should not become an occasion for quarreling among Christians. There is little to be gained from confrontations that pit Christians involved in Christian action over against members of the clergy.

A final question that must be raised is whether we should follow the example of the Jewish Zionists to the point of becoming "Christian Zionists." This idea has arisen in a number of minds, and is already being discussed in guarded terms. What the ultimate answer to this question might be will depend heavily on events in North America over the next decade or two. If North American democracy lives up to its proud boasts and grants its citizens the full range of civil and religious freedoms and rights, there will be no need for Christians to consider "Zionism." But if Christians are to be denied a place to stand, they may eventually decide - as many Christians before them have decided - to move on, either to a more hospitable country or, perhaps, to a homeland of their own. It would be highly ironic if the descendants of the Pilgrims (i.e. the "wasp" establishment) were to force the Christians living in their midst to go elsewhere in search of religious liberty, but such irony is the fabric of history.

Prayer without action?

The Zionist movement has lessons for us, then, and it also poses a challenge. Through hard work, determination and a great deal of suffering, the Zionists of the twentieth century have succeeded far beyond the dreams of many of their founders. Triumph has been stained by tragedy, but the great Zionist aim of a Jewish state in Palestine has been realized. Are the Christians of North America willing to work as hard as the Zionists to make North America a good place to raise a child in the fear of the Lord? Or will they restrict themselves to prayer, in the hope that there will be another generation of Christians to do what must be done? Will prayer without action be any more effective than faith without works?

ABOUT THE EDITORS

Dr. Theodore R. Malloch is a political
theorist who received his Ph.D. from the
University of Toronto and his M.Litt.
degree from the University of Aberdeen,
Scotland. He is currently teaching in
the Political Science Department at
Gordon College, Wenham, MA.

Dr. William A. Harper is a student
of comparative politics and American
politics. He took his Ph.D. at Tufts
University with a dissertation on British election campaigning. He is currently chairman of the Political Science
Department at Gordon College, Wenham, MA.